THE PEACEFUL
REVOLUTION

MANIFESTO FOR A NEW GLOBAL CONSENSUS

LAURENCE J. BRAHM

Discovery Publisher

©2015, Discovery Publisher

This book was previously published as
"The Anti-Globalization Breakfast Club" by John Wiley & Sons.

Author : Laurence Brahm

616 Corporate Way
Valley Cottage, New York, 10989
www.discoverypublisher.com
edition@discoverypublisher.com
facebook.com/discoverypublisher
twitter.com/discoverypb

New York • Paris • Dublin • Tokyo • Hong Kong

We refuse to take part in the G7 merely to drink coffee and we have to have a more important role in discussions.

—Guido Mantega, Brazilian Finance Minister
Meeting of G20 finance ministers,
Sao Paulo, November 7, 2008

It must be made crystal clear that the domination of any country's economy by foreign capital investment, the deterioration in terms of trade, the control of one country's markets by another, discriminatory relations and the use of force as an instrument of persuasion, are dangers to world trade and world peace... This conference should condemn any application or instigation of economic measures by one state to infringe the sovereign freedom of another state and to obtain from it advantages of any kind whatsoever, or to bring about the collapse of its economy. In order to achieve the foregoing, the principle of self-determination embodied in the United Nations Charter must be fully implemented The conference should reaffirm the right of states to dispose of their own resources, to adopt the form of political and economic organization that suits them best, and to choose their own avenues of development and specialization in economic activity, without incurring reprisals of any kind whatsoever.

—Che Guevara,
United Nations Conference on Trade and Development,

Geneva, March 25,1964

THE PEACEFUL
RƎVOLUTION

MANIFESTO FOR A NEW GLOBAL CONSENSUS

LAURENCE J. BRAHM

This book is dedicated to my two sons,
Laurence *Xiaolonjj* and Robert *Xiaolin*.

Our generation, through our short-sightedness and greed,
has ruined their planet. I am sorry that their generation
will have to clean up our mess. But I am certain
that they will do things better.

CONTENTS

ACKNOWLEDGMENTS

I wish to begin by thanking Adriano Lucchese, founder of Discovery Publisher for discovering my writings and encouraging me to publish this book on new media. His vision of using the latest mobile and web technologies to create a new media platform is inspiring. I believe that publishers such as Discovery Publisher will revolutionize information and publishing. It is time to overthrow the monopoly of mainstream publishers, their agents, and the fossilized institutions that they stand for.

Special thanks are due to my editor, Robyn Flemming, whose intensely detailed work on this manuscript saved it and made it publishable. We have a karmic connection, as she has been editor on a number of my past works and can read my mind between the spelling errors and omissions.

I am greatly indebted to the editorial team of Paul Mooney and Thomas Hon Wing Polin, who joined me in the later stages of this manuscript and who worked tirelessly with me to polish, focus and refine the text. Without their dedication and help, this book would not have been published. I am indebted to you. In addition, Allen Cheng, Asia Bureau Chief of Institutional Investor, and Zoher Abdoolcarim, Editor of *Time Magazine Asia*, gave tremendous moral support to me when the going got rough during the writing and editing of the book.

I am exceptionally grateful to Lim Mah Hui, whom I met in 1979 as a green student at Duke University, when I first began studying Chinese and Third World politics. I didn't realize at the time that he was a Malaysian political dissident chilling in American academia after a stint as a political prisoner. Lim Mah Hui guided my studies then, and has been my anti-globalization guru ever since. In fact, in the summer of 2007, he visited my home in Lhasa, and made me sit down, focus and start writing this book. Without his encouragement, I may never have embarked upon it.

Endless support came from Johnston Li, who has pulled together hosts of relations and arranged my visits to the royal family in Bhutan. Tibet's Princess Yabshi Pan Rinzinwangmo has given much ongoing moral support and encouragement.

I also wish to express endless thanks to His Eminence Beru Khyentse Rinpoche for his omniscient guidance, and His Holiness the seventeenth Gyalwa Karmapa Ogyen Trinley Dorje for his bountiful blessings.

In Kathmandu, special thanks to Leela Mani Paudyal, now Nepal's secretary of the Ministry of Information and Communication whose close friendship brought me back to the beauty of Nepal and all that this wonderful nation has to offer. I am indebted to him for helping me understand so much about this culturally and spiritually rich land.

In Colombo, Nihal Rodrigo, former Sri Lankan ambassador to China, opened doors for me to this mesmerizing land of tranquility and farsighted NGO thinking.

In Dhaka, Ashfaqur Rahman, former ambassador of Bangladesh to China, exposed me to this culturally rich and marvelously multifaceted country.

I am grateful to my personal assistants Corrine Alphen Cordero, who in 2007-2008 handled all the administrative and communication matters related to this book, and Cathy Fransisca, who joined me in the summer of 2008 organizing everything and keeping me in one piece and on track during my waking hours.

I am indebted to Penpala at *House of Shambhala* in Lhasa. Penpala administers Shambhala's field operations and ensures that my ideas for medical, educational and micro-equity projects are realized on the front line. This is far from an easy task, and I express my heartfelt gratitude. Special thanks to Tibetan Buddhist monk Riche, who organizes my life in Lhasa; he keeps the shrines stocked with burning incense and yak butter candles.

Thank you to Blue Moon, a Hindu nun, for foreseeing the road I should take, and to Zouge Rinpoche for his guidance and calming influence.

I am indebted to you all.

Laurence J. Brahm
Lhasa, Tibet

INTRODUCTION

GLOBAL MELTDOWN
THE WASHINGTON CONSENSUS GOES BUST

How can there be laughter, how can there be pleasure, when the whole world is burning? When you are in deep darkness, will you not ask for a lamp?

—The Buddha

Washington Fundamentalism Dies an Unceremonious Death

On October 23, 2008, Alan Greenspan, former chairman of the United States Federal Reserve, was hauled before Congress to testify on the causes underlying the largest financial crisis since the Great Depression of the 1930s. "I made the mistake in presuming that the self-interest of organizations, specifically banks and others, was such that they were best capable of protecting their own shareholders," explained the ex-central banker.

Questioned by Henry Waxman, chairman of the House of Representatives oversight committee, Greenspan admitted he had "found a flaw" in his thinking. "It had been going for 40 years with considerable evidence it was working very well," Greenspan told Congress. "The whole intellectual edifice, however, collapsed in the summer of last year."

Unfortunately for Greenspan, his country and much of the world, that "flaw" in the assumptions which had guided the Fed for nearly a half-century was a gaping one. It also underlies the premises of the Washington Consensus thinking that created, in Greenspan's words, a "period of euphoria"—and in turn the arrogant application of self-congratulatory theory—which lasted over two decades. Nobody ever thought it would end in ruin.

Waxman, for his part, lambasted what he called "the prevailing attitude in Washington... that the market always knows best." It was a conviction that had guided the World Bank, the International Monetary Fund and the financial institutions purveying global development for the better part of 20 years. In autumn 2008, amid a global financial meltdown, that attitude, and the assumptions underlying it, was proven wrong. Five days after Greenspan's admission, Stephen Roach, chairman of Morgan Stanley Asia, observed in the *Financial Times:* "Driven by its ideological convictions, the

Fed flew blind on the derivatives front... This trust in ideology over objective metrics was a fatal mistake. Like all crises, this one is a wake-up call."[1]

The problem lay in the ideological fundamentalism of neo-liberal economics that has pervaded Washington since Bretton Woods, the conference held in 1944 by the soon-to-be-victorious powers of World War II to reshape the global financial system. Its core view was that market fundamentals would always be corrected and perfected by the "invisible hand." In other words, human impulse driven by material greed would right the markets. These premises underlay the "shock therapy" treatment applied by aid agencies and international donor and lending institutions in socialist economies under transition during the early 1990s and during the Asian financial crisis of 1997-98. Most beneficiaries of such aid and advice collapsed. With a global market apocalypse developing in the autumn of 2008, the fundamentalist, ideologically based theories of the Washington Consensus were finally discarded. At least by most countries.

Anatomy of a Breakdown

It was a stunning, almost unbelievable sequence of events which had brought things to a head. In the wake of a year-long sub-prime mortgage crisis in the U.S., on September 15, investment bank Lehman Brothers collapsed. American regulators announced their refusal to rescue the 158-year-old Wall Street institution. That same day a leading rival, Merrill Lynch, announced it was selling itself to the Bank of America to help cover massive losses in sub-prime-related investments. Stock markets plunged around the world.

U.S. regulators subsequently decided to save mega-insurance corporation AIG, after concluding that a collapse of the insurer, which had US$1.05 trillion in assets and 116,000 employees worldwide, might unhinge financial markets worldwide. The U.S. Congress two weeks later announced a US$700-billion bailout package, including US$200 billion to inject liquidity into the nation's banks, and a US$500-billion rescue of mortgage companies Freddie Mac and Fannie Mae. By October, a worldwide financial crisis had erupted, threatening a prolonged global depression as serious as anything since the 1930s.

The collapse of markets and financial institutions sounded the death knell of an era. Since World War II, a set of assumptions about human nature has underpinned all economic theories and global financial institutions that manage our markets. The hardline, sometimes called neo-liberal, belief is that human greed—the invisible hand of Adam Smith's theory of capitalism—will always bring about equilibrium. The events of autumn 2008 proved that this is not the case. At the very least, the neo-liberal view of economics is incomplete.

Human psychology is not governed solely by concern over how much money we can make and how much we can conspicuously consume. There is a multiplicity of factors behind human motivation and emotion, ranging from a sense of identity and community to assessments of quality vs. quantity of life. These are factors that fly in the face of the psychology of "one consumer melting pot" for the world. Compassion for the suffering of others can override self-centered greed. The quality of our living environment can be more important than how many branded products we can consume.

These are all trade-offs. In the end, the events of 2008 are not the death knell of capitalism and do not herald an era of socialism. Such debates simply miss the point. But these events have jolted people's assumptions and a readjustment will begin to take place, probably seeking a balance between extremes. Our global financial, economic and even political systems must change to reflect this realignment.

The clearest indicator that a tectonic shift is under way occurred on November 4, 2008, when Barack Obama, born of a Kenyan immigrant father, was elected America's first black president. It symbolized an outright rejection by the American people of the nearly decade-long neo-conservative agenda of the George W. Bush administration, which sought to impose on the world through either economic sanctions or military force a range of systems—economic, political, financial and social. In trying to construct a global empire with Washington D.C. as its epicenter, the Bush administration simply did not understand that the rest of the world did not want to buy in.

Our assumptions have been wrong. People worldwide have had enough of the Washington Consensus, with its combined neo-liberal economics and neo-conservative politics and most Americans were tired of the growing antipathy towards their country that these policies fueled. Reflecting a sweeping worldwide desire for change, Americans went to the polls on November 4 and voted for Obama—who enjoyed a landslide victory.

The challenge for President Obama is not in issuing more federal bonds to buy more time by passing on debt, or adjusting interest rates on home loans. These are technical measures that band-aid the wound but do not cure the underlying illness. The hard question is how to tell Americans that their way of life is no longer sustainable given the accelerating pace of global warming, the costs of the American lifestyle, which is being passed on to the developing world, and endemic poverty in the developing world.

The US$700-billion bailout package, which ultimately will be financed by China and other rising developing nations, will only remedy, and not solve, the core problem, which is an unsustainable financial order whose underlying assumptions are based on material greed. It is time to bring another set of values to the table.

Will a New President Adopt Fresh Approaches?

It is possible that this process will begin' in the era of Barack Obama. The global financial shock of 2008 was the final wake-up call. In many respects, across both financial and industrial sectors, executives have begun re-thinking the premises of their business models. They are placing new emphasis on corporate responsibility, environmental and labor concerns, and the very question of what constitutes shareholder value—the traded price of stock, or what the company actually gives back to society.

Consider the words of Lee Scott, Wal-Mart's chief executive. Recently, he told a meeting of 1,000 Chinese suppliers in Beijing: "I firmly believe that a company that cheats on overtime and on the age of its labor, that dumps its scraps and its chemicals in our rivers, that does not pay its taxes or honor its contracts, will ultimately cheat on the quality of its products." What a surprise. This is the same Wal-Mart reviled globally by consumer activists for mistreating its employees domestically, driving down wages internationally, and ruining the landscape of communities with its faceless mega-stores. So maybe something is changing—like basic assumptions and, with them, social values.

Scott himself declared to employees: "Some may wonder, even inside Wal-Mart, with all that is going on in the global economy, should being a socially and environmentally responsible company still be a priority? You're darn right sustainability should be a priority."[2]

Overhauling the Global Order

In October 2008, U.S. President George W. Bush announced an attempt to retool the global financial order in the form of a Bretton Woods-style summit to be held in mid-November. One item for discussion would be the creation of a global central bank. While this sounded reassuring to some in Washington as well as in some European capitals, it was not exactly what people in the rest of the globe had in mind. The initiative seemed like yet another Washington-centric "solution"—and lacked practicality. The world was tired of being dictated to by the U.S. on everything from economic and financial policy to the political governance process and which social values to believe in. Enough voodoo economics. What was needed was a shift away from America-centered approaches and real solutions to global problems.

In early November 2008, at a meeting of finance ministers and central bank governors from the G20 nations, Brazilian President Luiz Inacio Lula da Silva called for an overhaul of the global financial system, which had "collapsed like a house of cards" during the credit crisis. Emerging powers, he said, must have a greater say in key decisions affecting the planet. Addressing finance officials and central bank chiefs from around the world, Lula slammed the "dogmatic faith in non-intervention in markets" that has long been espoused by the United States and other countries. "We need new, more inclusive governance and Brazil is ready to face up to its responsibilities," said the burly former union leader. "It is time for a pact among governments to build a new financial architecture for the world."

The finance luminaries were meeting in Brazil's economic hub of Sao Paulo to grapple with ways to tackle the global financial crisis. The "BRIC" nations of Brazil, Russia, India and China for the first time forged a joint position that called for reform of institutions like the International Monetary Fund. The overhaul was intended to reflect the growing importance of developing economies.

The G20 group, which includes emerging and advanced economies, should take over from the rich-country G7 grouping as the main forum for discussing global finance, Brazil said. Lula had long criticized the dominance of the U.S. and other developed economies in the way decisions on global finance were taken. Many hoped that progress at the G20 gathering and a separate meeting of the Bank of International Settlements could be taken to a G20 heads-of-state summit in Washington in mid-November. One obstacle, however, could be George Bush, who was adamantly against major global financial reform. Prior to the meeting, French President Nicolas Sarkozy told European leaders in Brussels: "The time when we had a single currency [the dollar], one line to be followed, that era is over. It came to an end on September 18 when responsibility was taken, without our opinion being asked, with the failure of a major banking institution and the consequences that followed."

David Rothkopf, a senior economic official during the Clinton administration summarized the mood in a commentary in London's *Daily Telegraph.* "One of the reasons that the IMF has fallen onto such hard times," he argued, "is that it was seen as forcing the developing world to accept an orthodox recipe for capitalism that was politically difficult to swallow. This view—'the Washington Consensus'—was a tough sell even before Washington made itself anathema to the world with Mr. Bush's foreign policy. It became harder still when America threw many of its basic precepts out the window in its response to the recent financial crisis." Rothkopf suggested "replacing the World Bank and the IMF and creating new institutions such as a Global Monetary Authority: a central bank for the planet. It would also mean establishing a new set of international financial-market standards and strengthening the co-ordination between government regulators and central bankers."[3]

In Asia, however, big changes were already under way. Fearing a replay of the Asian financial crisis, which had paralyzed the region a decade earlier, alternative consensual responses were quickly drawn up. China, Japan and South Korea established a joint currency-stabilization fund for the region. The three countries put up 80% of the US$80-billion fund, with the remainder coming from Southeast Asian nations. This was a regional solution that could be applied to a global problem. The regional consensus and local approaches constituted an organic response.

Duvvuri Subbaro, governor of India's central bank, called for greater regional monetary coordination across Asia. "I think [greater coordination] would be helpful, especially in times of crisis like this," he said. "Although there is no institutional arrangement spanning Asia, there are some informal arrangements."[4] The locally coordinated consensual response to the global meltdown was regenerating the financial system, to some extent re-engineering it. The initiative could be the prelude to a new era of localization rather than globalization, and of multilateralism instead of unilateralism.

Jeffrey Sachs, director of the Earth Institute at Columbia University and special economic advisor to the United Nations secretary general, warned in a commentary in the *Financial Times:* "Before our political leaders get too fancy remaking capitalism next month at the Bretton Woods II summit in Washington, they should attend to urgent business... what they have not done yet is to coordinate macroeconomic policies to stop a steep global downturn. This is an urgent agenda."[5]

In his analysis, Sachs went on to outline a global roadmap of things to be done quickly:

[The] International Monetary Fund should extend low-conditionality loans to all countries that request it, starting with Pakistan... China, Japan and South Korea should undertake a coordinated macro-economic expansion... this would mean a boost for infrastructure but also loans to developing nations in Asia and Africa... Development financing can be a powerful macroeconomic stabilizer. China, Japan and South Korea should work with other regional central banks to bolster expansionary policies backed by government-to-government loans... the Middle East, flush with cash, should fund investment projects in emerging markets and low-income countries... the U.S. and Europe should expand export credits for low- and middle-income developing countries, not only to meet their unfulfilled aid promises but also as a counter-cyclical stimulus. It would be a tragedy for big infrastructure companies to suffer when the developing world is crying out for infrastructure investment.

A few days after his article appeared, Sachs invited me to join him for breakfast at the home of Khalid Malik, the U.N.'s ambassador to China. We talked about the current financial crisis and a range of ideas, from the "millennium villages" that the Earth Institute and Sachs pioneered to alleviate poverty in Africa, to finding the right balance between top-down infrastructure projects and grassroots initiatives.

"You need basic infrastructure," Sachs emphasized. "You cannot imagine how important electricity and clean water are. But most places do not have the money to invest in this. And health care is the basic priority." As more coffee was poured, we both agreed on a host of issues.

It is not a question of top-down infrastructure spending versus grassroots NGO initiatives. Actually, both are needed. It is not a question of being "anti-globalization" or "pro-globalization." The real challenge is to find pragmatic solutions to the problems that are making people's lives miserable. In the end, theory means nothing. Only concrete solutions that alleviate human misery and stop environmental desecration matter. And to be a fundamentalist on theory is just stupid.

I mentioned to Sachs that I was finishing a book on all the points we were discussing. He asked me its name. I told him. "*The Peaceful Revolution*. That is a good name for a book on this subject," he laughed. "Sure, aren't we it?"

Endnotes

1 "Add 'financial stability' to the Fed's mandate," Stephen Roach, *Financial Times,* October 28, 2008, p. 11.
2 "An ethics lesson from an unlikely quarter," Michael Skapinker, *Financial Times,* October 28, 2008, p. 11.
3 "Barack Obama's dilemma: Rich nations must learn to share power," David Rothkopf, *Daily Telegraph,* November 13, 2008.
4 "India call for united action over credit crisis," James Lamont, *Financial Times,* October 27, 2008, p. 1.

5 "The best recipe for avoiding a global recession," Jeffry Sachs, *Financial Times,* October 28, 2008, p. 11.

1

WHAT'S WRONG WITH THE WASHINGTON CONSENSUS?
IT FORCES ALIEN, IRRELEVANT MODELS ON DEVELOPING SOCIETIES

Peace is threatened by unjust economic, social and political order, absence of democracy environmental degradation and absence of human rights.

Poverty is the absence of all human rights. The frustrations, hostility and anger generated by abject poverty cannot sustain peace in any society. For building stable peace we must find ways to provide opportunities for people to live decent lives... I support globalization and believe it can bring more benefits to the poor than any alternative. But it must be the right kind of globalization. To me, globalization is like a hundred-lane highway criss-crossing the world. If it is a hundred-lane highway its lanes will be taken over by the giant trucks from powerful economies. Bangladeshi rickshaws will be thrown off the highway. In order to have a win-win globalization we must have traffic rules, traffic police and traffic authority for this global highway. The rule of "strongest takes it all" must be replaced by rules that ensure that the poorest have a place and piece of the action, without being elbowed out by the strong. Globalization must not become financial imperialism.

—Professor Muhammad Yunus[1]

A Movement Born of Discontent

This is not a book about anti-globalization. Rather, it is a journey in search of solutions—or maybe just alternatives—to the dark side of globalization.

We don't hear about this dark side of globalization in our mainstream media, because we have been conditioned to believe in a certain set of paradigms and we dismiss what we don't want to hear. I am a product of that environment—both professionally, as a commercial lawyer and investment advisor, and socially, having experienced the lifestyle afforded by the elitist corporate world. This book is about my choosing to leave that world behind in search of a different one.

The search is told through my own personal story and voices of discontent of the people I have met along the way. They are the voice of the voiceless—those marginalized and impoverished. Their view is collectively summarized in the conclusion "Manifesto for a Peaceful Revolution."

This Manifesto is really about a quest for an alternative—if not better, then at least more relevant—set of economic developmental paradigms and accompanying values. New economic-political paradigms cannot be achieved without re-engineering our own social values. It is necessary for our world to move from its current era of violence driven by greed, shortsightedness and frustration, into a new era of peace, respect for the environment and human dignity.

Should a nation's or an individual's success be measured in quantitative material terms, or in terms of social-spiritual happiness? Today, we measure success by how much gross domestic product a nation racks up, or how many luxury goods an individual acquires before they die. Should a company's worth be measured by its so-called shareholders' value, or by its positive impact on global society and its efforts to protect our environment for the next generation? Isn't it about time we redefine net worth and shareholders' value as absolute terms? Some may laugh at these questions, but others have realized that if we don't start asking them now, other generations may not be able to live on this planet and our own civilization will become extinct.

So, this book is not so much about anti-globalization as a movement, as it is about a search for new values in order to redefine the movement.

Let us begin by asking: What is the anti-globalization movement? Why is it called "anti-globalization"?

The problem is that the terms "globalization" and "anti-globalization" are being used out of context. This is convenient political and media lingo. But if we coolly think through what is really happening in our world right now, these labels mean nothing. Moreover, they are being used incorrectly in order to create confusion about what is happening all around us.

The so-called anti-globalization movement has expressed its anger in massive grassroots protests at World Trade Organization (WTO), G8 and World Bank-International Monetary Fund (IMF) meetings in Seattle, Genoa and Prague respectively. These protests have become violent and radical because the normal outlets for expressing concerns and ideas are not being provided at these venues. In fact, these forums have often had to be aborted, having been made dysfunctional by the street protests that are offering a new face of democracy and that are seeking to discredit these mega-lith institutions. To some extent, the global financial meltdown of autumn 2008 has already discredited these institutions. The voices of the street, once viewed as radical, in light of this global depression suddenly appear rational. So, perhaps we need to redefine what we mean by "democratic participation" as well.

Why aren't the views of these protestors being articulated clearly in the media, instead of being dismissed as radical and disruptive of a financial order that reeks more of monopoly and narrow, elitist self-interest? The voices of the new global justice movement, labeled "anti-globalization," are denied mainstream media exposure by heavy-handed editors who are effectively censoring dissenting ideas before they can even be expressed. That is why people go to the street.

Defining the Washington Consensus

Throughout this book I refer frequently to the "Washington Consensus." What is it? Joseph Stiglitz, former World Bank chief economist and Nobel Prize winner in Economics and another de facto leader of the anti-globalization movement, offers a clear explanation of the Washington Consensus theory in his book Globalization and Its Discontents. We will use his definition:

> Behind the free market ideology there is a model, often attributed to Adam Smith, which argues that market forces—the profit motive— drive the economy to efficient outcomes as if by an invisible hand. One of the great achievements of modern economics is to show the sense in which and the conditions under which, Smith's conclusion is correct. It turns out that these conditions are highly restrictive.
>
> Indeed, most recent advances in economic theory—ironically occurring precisely during the period of most relentless pursuit of the Washington Consensus policies—have shown that whenever information is imperfect and markets incomplete, which is to say always and especially in developing countries, then the invisible hand works most imperfectly...
>
> The Washington Consensus policies, however, were based on a simplistic model of the market economy, the competitive equilibrium model, in which Adam Smith's invisible hand works and works perfectly. Because in this model there is no need for government—that is, free, unfettered, "liberal" markets work per- fectly—the Washington Consensus policies are sometimes referred to as "neo-liberal," based on "market fundamentalism," a resusci- tation of the laissez-faire policies that were popular in some circles in the 19th century. In the aftermath of the Great Depression and the recognition of other failings of the market system, from massive inequality to unlivable cities marred by pollution and decay, these

free market policies have been widely rejected in the more advanced industrial countries, though within these countries there remains an active debate about the appropriate balance between government and markets...

The theory says that an efficient market economy requires that all of the assumptions be satisfied. In some cases, reforms in one area, without accompanying reforms in others, may actually make matters worse. This is the issue of sequencing. Ideology ignores these matters; it says simply move as quickly to a market economy as you can. But economic theory and history show how disastrous it can be to ignore sequencing.

The mistakes in trade, capital market liberalization and privatization described earlier represent sequencing errors on a grand scale. The smaller-scale sequencing mistakes are even less noticed in the Western press. They constitute the day-to-day tragedies of IMF policies that affect the already desperately poor in the developing world.[2]

The concept of a "Washington Consensus" was introduced in 1989 by John Williamson, an economist with the Institute for International Economics, an international economics think-tank in Washington, D.C. He originally used the term to refer to a set of 10 economic policy prescriptions that he felt constituted a reform package for developing countries. These themes were shared among Washington-based institutions, including the IMF, World Bank and the U.S. Treasury Department, which at the time believed such prescriptions could help Latin America recover from the economic crises of the 1980s.

Williamson later rejected the way the term began to be used as a reference to a more neo-liberal agenda that advocated market fundamentalism and which was imposed on developing countries by these Washington-based organizations.

But today, the two ideas are merged in people's minds.

People in the developing world largely consider these agendas unfair. NGOs and social and environmental action groups that oppose these agendas are often collectively labeled the "anti-globalization movement."

No one has their finger more firmly on the pulse of the anti-globalization movement than one of its de facto leaders, Arundhati Roy, activist and acclaimed author of *The God of Small Things*. In the kitchen of her New Delhi apartment, Roy described to me the structure of a global system that is fostering discontent.

"For the first time in history, a single empire with an arsenal of weapons that could obliterate the world in an afternoon has complete, unipolar, economic and military hegemony. It uses different weapons to break open different markets. There isn't a country on God's earth that isn't caught in the cross-hairs of the American cruise missile and the IMF checkbook. Argentina is the model if you want to be the poster boy of neo-liberal capitalism; Iraq, if you're the black sheep.

"Poor countries that are of geopolitically strategic value to the [American] Empire, or have a 'market' of any size, or infrastructure that can be privatized, or natural resources of value—oil, gold, diamonds, cobalt, coal—must do as they're told or become military targets. Those with the greatest reserves of natural wealth are most at risk. Unless they surrender their resources willingly to the corporate machine, civil unrest will be fomented or war will be waged.

"In the new era, apartheid as formal policy is antiquated and unnecessary. International instruments of trade and finance oversee a complex system of multilateral trade laws and financial agreements that keep the poor in their Bantustans anyway. Its whole purpose is to institutionalize inequality. Why else would it be that the U.S. taxes a garment made by a Bangladeshi manufacturer 20 times more than a garment made in Britain? Why else would it be that countries that grow cocoa beans, like the Ivory Coast and Ghana, are taxed out of the market if they try to turn it into chocolate? Why else would it be that countries that grow 90% of the world's cocoa beans produce only 5% of the world's chocolate? Why else would it be that rich countries that spend over a billion dollars a day on subsidies to farmers demand that poor countries such as India withdraw all agricultural subsidies, including subsidized electricity? Why else would it be that after having been plundered by colonizing regimes for more than half a century, former colonies are steeped in debt to those same regimes and repay them some US$382 billion a year?"

Roy further described both the frustrations and the spiritedness of those people in the streets who are fighting for their ideals and a strong sense of global justice and who have been labeled as the "anti-globalization movement." "We need to redefine the meaning of politics. The 'NGO-ization' of civil-society initiatives is taking us in exactly the opposite direction. It's depoliticizing us, making us dependent on aid and handouts. We need to re-imagine the meaning of civil disobedience. Fearlessly, but non-violently, we must disable the working parts of this machine that is consuming us. We are running out of time. Even as we speak, the circle of violence is closing in. Either way, change will come. It could be bloody, or it could be beautiful. It depends on us."

Defining Globalization

Dr. Walden Bello, executive director of the Bangkok-based government organization (NGO) Focus on the Global South and professor of sociology and public administration at the University of the Philippines, is acknowledged as another of the de facto leaders of the anti-globalization movement. In his commentary titled "The Stalemate in the WTO and the Crisis of the Globalist Project," he offers a definition of globalization and describes its rise and fall:

> Globalization is the accelerated integration of capital, production and markets globally driven by the logic of corporate profitability. It is a process accompanied by the coming to dominance of the ideology of neo-liberalism, centered on liberating the market" by institutionalizing privatization, deregulation and trade liberalization... bringing about the "coherence" of the policies of the WTO, IMF and the World Bank to create the framework of international economic governance that would assure global prosperity...
>
> In just five years, however, the globalist project, whether in its "hard" Thatcher-Reagan version or its "soft" Blair-Soros version (globalization with "safety nets"), was in very serious trouble. There were three key moments to this crisis:
>
> First was the Asian financial crisis of 1997. This revealed that one of the tenets of globalization, the liberalization of capital account, could be profoundly destabilizing. It was [a main factor in the collapse of the] East Asian economics, with 22 million people in Indonesia and one million in Thailand falling below the poverty line in just a few months. The Asian financial crisis was the Stalingrad of the IMF, the prime global agent of liberalized capital flows, bringing about a review of its record in Africa and Latin America, which showed that the program of structural adjustment that it had promoted alongside the World Bank had failed almost universally, institutionalizing instead stagnation, greater poverty and greater inequality.
>
> The second moment of the crisis was the collapse of the third Ministerial of the WTO in December 1999. This was due to the fusion of three volatile elements into a deadly explosion: the revolt of developing countries at the Seattle Convention Center, the massive mobilization of 50,000 people in the streets and unresolved trade conflicts between the E.U. and the U.S., particularly in agriculture.
>
> The third moment was the collapse of the stock market at the end of the Clinton boom in March 2001. This was essentially the

onset of a crisis in overproduction, the main manifestation of which was massive overcapacity... The stagnation of the real economy led to capital being shifted to the financial sector, resulting in the dizzying rise in share values. But since profitability in the financial sector cannot deviate too far from profitability of the real economy, a collapse of stock shares was inevitable and occurred in March 2001...

The crisis of globalization, neo-liberalism and overproduction provides the context for understanding the economic policies of the Bush administration, notably its unilateralist thrust... The Bush administration has supplanted the globalist political economy of the Clinton period with a unilateralist, nationalist political economy that intends to shore up the global dominance of the U.S. corporate elite economically and that parallels the aggressive military policy that is meant to ensure the military supremacy of the United States.[3]

But all that fell apart with the global financial meltdown in the autumn of 2008.

Understanding the Anti-Globalization Movement

We must ask ourselves the question: Is globalization the spreading of technology and medical research, or is it the spreading of Washington's fixed ideals concerning how the world should operate? Are the screaming protestors who swarm every World Bank, IMF, WTO and G8 meeting or World Economic Forum condemning the Internet and mobile technology, or are they against a system that attempts to use these tools to forward its political ideology and self-serving economic agenda? As legitimate media outlets don't provide a window for this growing voice of dissent, it has no choice but to take to the streets and radicalize in order to be heard.

If we apply cause-and-effect logic, the marginalized become radicalized because they have been marginalized. It is easy to discredit these protestors by labeling them "anti-globalization" in the mainstream media. Who would honestly want to be "anti" such beneficial things as technology and science?

So, labeling the movement "anti-globalization," is an easy way to dismiss it without understanding it. It's the lazy way out of trying to understand the needs of the developing world being voiced in the streets. Consequently, most people don't know what this worldwide, increasingly popular, grassroots movement actually represents. The point is that these protestors are not against the globalization of technology, trade, commerce, education and health research breakthroughs. If the closing of income gaps could become part of the globalization process—if we were talking about globalization of environmental protection—I am certain they would come out on the streets *in support* of globalization.

Indian economist and activist Lawrence Surendra explained to me his views on the use of the label "anti-globalization" during a tea break at the Gross National Happiness Conference held in Bangkok in November 2007.

"My point is that these protests are basically co-opted by the establishment and the mainstream media, especially TV, which plays a major role in directing, managing and co-opting public discourse in the world. These protests take attention away from the more serious struggles of society to redirect, if not transform, what globalization is. The word 'globalization' ultimately hides many things. We have an obligation to search for new language and new words in our search for humanity."

The diverse NGOs and grassroots organizations collectively labeled as the "anti-globalization movement" are against the globalization of Washington Consensus political-social ideology and market fundamentalism—that is, the belief that Washington's path is the only valid path for our world to follow. The Washington Consensus approach of "Washington knows best," telling other nations how to run themselves, should be popularly discredited. It has left a trail of destroyed economies, ruined nations and marginalized peoples. The rise of international terrorism is, to a great extent, rooted in such marginalized frustration. The merger of diverse interests that is called the "anti-globalization movement" is another, less violent—more often peaceful—expression of this frustration.

Reza Aslan, born in Iran, is arguably the leading scholar in the United States on current Islamic issues. He teaches at the University of Santa Barbara, in California. His book *No god But God* has been a revelation to many people who wish to understand the current dynamics between the Islamic world and the West. Aslan and I regularly exchange views on the globalization question. In one of our discussions, he noted: "By labeling it 'anti-globalization,' you are beginning with the idea of globalization as a constant, so what does not fit into your idea or philosophic concept of what globalization is becomes *anti*-globalization."

He explained how the polarization of ideas suits political convenience. "The sole purpose of being at odds with one another is to easily categorize or define the other, in a clash of civilizations. What is the 'West'—everything that is not Islam?"

Aslan points out that when U.S. President George Bush was asked by the *New York Times* in August 2006, "Who is 'the enemy' in the war on terror?" he replied: "The best way to describe their ideology is to relate to you the fact that they think the opposite of the way we think. Who is the enemy? They believe the opposite of what you believe."

Thus, Aslan believes, "Globalization confrontation is not confrontation with technology, but confrontation between starting points of values. Such polarization of ideas gives rise to marginalization, which in turn incubates frustration and ultimately can give rise to terrorism. Al Qaeda is not modern in Western criticism. But their thinking is as modern as it can get, because they call for a global caliphate using modern high technology. But because they reject the West, they are seen to be rejecting modernization. They are not saying 'go back to an agrarian society.' Al Qaeda is saying, 'Our transnational vision of a globalized Muslim world led by a single Caliph is a simply indigenous conception of modernization, starting with the same idea of a modern world but ending in a different place.' It is by no means a clash of values or ideologies. It is a different starting point."

The Backlash

Washington's blinkered political elite thought naively that free-market shock therapy in the 1980s, combined with the widespread adoption of digitized technology in the 1990s, would break through foreign economic, political and social barriers and become a conduit to promote American values throughout the world. But the cycle has come full circle.

In a front-page story in July 2007, the *Financial Times* of London reported that a "popular backlash against globalization and the leaders of the world's largest companies is sweeping all rich countries..." The FT/ Harris poll, which interviewed 1,000 people online, said those polled in Britain, France, the U.S. and Spain were about three times more likely to view globalization as "having a negative rather than a positive effect on their countries..." The *Financial Times* said that the "depth of anti-globalization feeling" shown in the poll will "dismay policy-makers and corporate executives..." According to the *Financial Times* story:

> Even though defining globalization defies many experts, the people in rich countries think dark thoughts when they hear the term. In no country polled did people believe globalization was having a positive effect on their countries; they thought it was having a negative effect... Since most economists believe globalization has been a boost to the economic performance of rich countries as well as poor, these results are worrying. Part of the concern about globalization is almost certainly the public's feeling that the gap between rich and

poor in their countries was getting larger.[4]

Ironically, in both developing and developed countries, those with a conscience are increasingly resisting these values. They were present at the protests in Seattle, Prague, Cancun and Hong Kong. They use the same technology the Washington Consensus is espousing as the forebear of globalization—the Internet and mobile phones—to mobilize resistance against the onslaught. This group of diverse interests bound by a common cause has become known as the "anti-globalization movement."

However, the protestors are not against globalization per se if it were manifested as peaceful global cooperation among governments in order to curb global warming, extend health care, wipe out AIDS or close the gap between rich and poor. Instead, it appears to mean one or two nations ramming their own economic and political systems and forms of ethics down everyone else's throats.

So, "anti-globalization" is a misnomer. The use of this epithet by the Washington Consensus to describe a number of broadly based international action groups is an easy way to discredit what may be rapidly becoming a truly worldwide people's democratic movement. Walden Bello prefers to call it a "global civil society." Others call it a global justice movement. Regardless of the terminology, as the movement grows and transcends national borders, it presents a new face of democracy.

Transnational coalitions have emerged linking NGOs that share social and economic concerns. But are they being sidelined by a system that claims to be democratic? Maybe that is why they have no choice but to take their grievances to the streets.

This growing movement incorporates different interest groups with their own agendas but similar concerns. Moreover, the interests within this broad coalition are excluded from participating in the policy decision-making that affects the communities they represent. By being tagged as "anti," the movement is denied the legitimacy its growing power warrants.

Walden Bello observed of the collapse of the fifth WTO Ministerial held in Cancun, Mexico, in 2003:

Non-government organizations have assisted developing country governments in the political and technical aspects of negotiations. They have mobilized international public opinion against the retrograde stands of rich country governments, as in the drug patents and public health issue. They have emerged as strong coalitions... With people's movements marching in the city center and NGOs demonstrating hourly inside and outside the convention hall from the opening session on, Cancun became a microcosm of the power of global dynamics of states and civil society... warned everyone at the convention center that they could no longer take the plight of the world's small farmers for granted... Truly, the collapse of the Cancun ministerial was another confirmation of the *New York Times'* observation that global civil society is the world's second superpower.[5]

The truth is, people want to control their own future. They don't want it to be determined by a distant power, or to be driven by an ideology that has no relation to their own ethnicity or geographic identity. They want to administer their own global future through localization, not globalization. Mail-order-subscription solutions from Washington are not what the developing world needs; indeed, they are implemented against the wishes of most developing countries. Global ideals need to be examined in regard to their suitability' in terms of local conditions and customs, and alternative ideas and solutions found. Forums must be encouraged to foster new approaches and ideas, and to prevent them from being marginalized and in turn radicalized.

Helena Norberg Hodge, an NGO activist and author of the book *Ancient Futures,* has spent years working in Tibetan communities in Ladakh. She spoke of the spirit of localization as a counter to globalization at the 2007 Conference on Gross National Happiness:

We must transform globalization. I have been working at the grassroots level, talking to economists and leaders. We need to shift from globalization to localization. This does not mean thinking locally, but shortening the distance between productivity and consumer and the use of resources. Investors, pension funds, specialized funds don't know what is happening to the environment and communities where they invest. In the European tradition, humans are separate from nature and we are separate from an interconnected way of life. Media and education systems seductively tell children if they are connected to their culture and even skin color, then they are backward and should become part of the mass consumer culture and then children hate each other. But meanwhile in the U.S. and U.K. there is an epidemic of depression, personal debt and obesity. I argue that these things are all connected and linked to CO_2 emissions.[6]

Searching for a New Consensus

This book describes my journey, beginning with my experiences in China and then my subsequent travels through other countries, particularly in South Asia, in search of commonalities of vision that could lead to other paths for development. I found that China's development experience—which departed from the World Bank and IMF approaches—offers an alternative model in its own right, albeit with its own sets of problems and post-transformation repercussions. But China isn't presenting itself as a model. The model can be found in its practical experience. It may—or may not—be applied in differing degrees to other developing or transitional economies. Each country must find its own individual path. Assuming and assuring one's own ethnic and cultural identity against the onslaught of a global mass market is part of this process and is essentially what is meant here by "localization."

I began to see the Himalayan mountain range as a symbol—a bridge, not a barrier, between East and South Asia. I have sought, by drawing upon local grassroots knowledge from this region, to develop in the "Himalayan Consensus" a new set of practical and meaningful paradigms. Drawing on the indigenous philosophies of the region, the Himalayan Consensus calls for a balanced combination of infrastructure investment and grassroots NGO-type initiatives. It seeks to address healthcare needs, as well as environmental protection in the context of sustainable development that ensures the protection and evolution of indigenous cultures and ethnic groups, rather than their extinction.

It is my hope that these can collectively serve as an alternative to Washington's recipe for melting-pot, fast-food economics, which has become nauseating to many throughout the developing world who are suffering from its effects.

I believe there are no black-and-white answers when it comes to development. Testing and experimentation are necessary. There are no cookie-cutter solutions. Academics in the United States are looking at the world's problems from the safe and comfortable distance of their university or think-tank institutions. Their research is often government-funded and guided by a specific political and ideological agenda. The results of the research usually reflect those agendas.

What is needed are practical solutions to problems on the ground that affect people's lives, not theories that justify conditions imposed by such Washington Consensus lending institutions as the World Bank and the IMF. "Soft lending" to developing countries by such bodies often comes with conditions attached that support Western political-economic ideological fundamentalism, which can lead to financial dependency and, in turn, poverty. In many developing countries, *this* is what the people are revolting against, but the media are silent on the issue.

The media and G8 politicians are locked into the Bretton Woods/ Atlantic Treaty framework for seeing the world and cannot—or will not— envision viable alternatives. But unless we empower people to undertake their own sustainable economic growth and independent cultural development, the world will never be economically efficient and politically stable. It is time to call a halt to the melting-pot process. The future of humanity lies in our continued ethnic diversity. And this will depend on culturally sustainable development.

What is ethnic diversity? Every society has the fundamental right to pursue its own ethnic traditions, lifestyle, culture and beliefs. Preservation of the environment is integral to the sustenance of many traditional lifestyles. Environmental desecration assaults ethnic diversity, whereas the preservation of ethnic diversity can help protect the environment.

The melting-pot ideology, with its commercialized "mainstream" value system, damages ethnic diversity, which should he considered a universal human right. Many of the world's social and security problems are reactions against this politically driven attempt to eliminate ethnic diversity through the unilateral and global propagation and rigid application of neo-conservative values. This erodes diverse ethnic identities, which are in many ways what define us as humanity.

What is culturally sustainable development? Cultural eradication isn't a prerequisite for modernization. Raising living standards doesn't mean replacing one culture with another. Culture can evolve with economic development and, in turn, provide the social fabric to ensure economic stability.

The Washington Consensus formulas for development fail because they force economic and financial models upon societies whose different cultures and conditions render those models inappropriate. Capital accumulation, conspicuous consumption and the erosion of indigenous cultural values don't assure personal happiness. Economic development should improve the quality of life, not undermine it.

It is for these reasons that so many individuals, grassroots organizations and NGOs are calling for new paradigms as an alternative to the Washington Consensus policies. These groups are forming a transnational movement that is becoming increasingly visible and vocal. With more cohesion, organization and political focus, it could become a global movement for the new era. These disparate voices echo a similar theme. As they gain critical mass, they will increasingly be heard. And what they have to say will shake the very foundations of the post-Bretton Woods political and economic systems and media-promoted values we have been conditioned to believe today.

Endnotes

1 "We Can Put Poverty into Museums", Nobel Lecture presented at Nobel Peace Prize Ceremony, Oslo, December 10, 2006.

2 Joseph Stiglitz, *Globalization and Its Discontents* (New York: WAV. Norton & Company, 2002).

3 Revised version of a presentation at the Hemispheric and Global Assembly against the FTAA [Free Trade of the Americas] and the WTO, Mexico City, May 12-13, 2003. A brief version was also delivered at the Transnational Institute Fellows Meeting, Amsterdam, May 16, 2003 and at the Jakarta International Peace Conference, May 18-21, 2003.

4 Chris Giles, "Poll reveals backlash in wealthy countries against globalization," *Financial Times,* July 23, 2007, p. 1.

5 Walden Bello, "Implications of Cancun," *ZNet,* September 23, 2003.

6 Helena Norbcrg Hodge, Gross National Happiness Conference, Bangkok, November 22-28, 2007.

2

THE WORLD NEEDS AN ALTERNATIVE
CONFESSIONS OF A FORMER
COMMERCIAL LAWYER

Thus the young independent nation sees itself obliged to use the economic channels created by the colonial regime. It can, obviously, export to other countries and other currency areas, but the basis of its exports is not fundamentally modified. The colonial regime has carved out certain channels and they must be maintained or catastrophe will threaten. Perhaps it is necessary to begin everything all over again: to change the nature of the country's exports, and not simply their destination, to re-examine the soil and mineral resources, the rivers, and—why not?—the sun's productivity... .If conditions of work are not modified, centuries will be needed to humanize this world, which has been forced down to animal level by imperial powers.

—Frantz Fanon, *The Wretched of the Earth*

Becoming a China Hand

I went to China for the first time in 1981, inspired by what I believed to be the iconoclastic, altruistic idealism of Mao Zedong. But by the time I arrived in Beijing, the country had already entered the era of Deng Xiaoping. Everyone had stopped talking about revolution; instead, they talked about money. Cadres were dumping Mao jackets for business suits. Following the shifting mood of China's soon-to-become "new rich" proletariat masses, I made the switch too.

I became a "China trade" lawyer. For nearly two decades I advised multinational corporations seeking entry into China's emerging and tumultuously transforming market. I was a kind of hired-hand negotiator, like a gunman in an old western movie. My job was to blast through the locked doors and get foreign multinationals inside, secure a foothold in the market, and then help them monopolize the market and raise prices.

After the students' uprising in 1989, China faced difficulties in attracting new investors. I went to Laos, Vietnam and Cambodia where, under the auspices of the Asian Development Bank (ADB), I became an advisor to the central banks of those countries. At that time, there was a need for a lawyer with experience in socialist-state foreign exchange and financial policy. My China experience fitted the bill.

Fighting the Washington Consensus in Laos

In those days, consultants from the World Bank and the IMF were preaching a kind of "shock therapy." It was the fashionable thing. The Soviet Union was collapsing. Everyone presumed that was a good thing, and that communism would be replaced by a golden era of America-centric globalization. In other words, democracy would be espoused as a priority over economic development—even in countries where development levels were so low as not to allow for basic education that would give people the means to understand what they were voting for. This despite the region's vastly different cultures, ethnic compositions and religious practices, not to mention the tumultuous political forces—pre-colonialism, colonialism, revolution and post-revolutionary socialist transitions—that had shaken the very foundations of these societies.

Coming from China, which had spent much of the past 100 years being convulsed by these forces, and injected with a dose of Deng's pragmatism, I thought that this IMF and World Bank theory being spouted by academic aid specialists was all theoretical bunk. The realities of economic reform for a socialist economy in a communist state touched all aspects of life. The socialist system couldn't be unraveled easily without considering the implications across the board, in every aspect of economic life—from education, employment, health care and retirement, to social intercourse and human aspirations and beliefs. Because, of course, the state monopoly in these socialist societies had provided *everything,* and people had become accustomed to such a system.

My university days had been spent in the gothic fantasyland of North Carolina's Duke University. One day, in an international relations class, a guest lecturer from the U.S. State Department ended his address by stating categorically that all the possible political, economic and social scenarios for a developing nation could be determined through the computer analysis of data such as population, per-capita income, inflation and so on. Everyone in the lecture hall sat in silence, seemingly stunned by the wonders of modem computer technology. But for me, it didn't make any practical sense. So I raised my hand. I think I was the only one with a question. "How do you put Islam in the computer?" I asked.

These same questions would arise 10 years later. In the central banks of Laos, Cambodia and Vietnam, there was a mood of uncertainty. For all of the theories proselytized by the World Bank and the IMF, the former Soviet Union had become a mess. Even a child could see this clearly. But China, despite its many problems, seemed to be going somewhere.

So, I ran a kind of monetary-policy shuttle diplomacy, flying back and forth between peninsular Southeast Asia and Beijing via Hong Kong, learning about the policies and regulations then under consideration by the People's Bank of China—China's central bank—and offering them for consideration by the central banks of Laos, Vietnam and Cambodia. I advocated a gradualist reform, with step-by-step observation of changing conditions. But that wasn't what the World Bank and the IMF wanted, and their representatives chewed me out.

In Laos, the World Bank had a program for so-called legal reform. They advocated bringing New York corporate law to the Lao people. But Laos was a small country. The idea of private enterprise was just nascent. The kip, the currency, was devalued to the point that a few dollars would buy you bags of the stuff. I asked to visit the Lao government's corporate registration department. It was a room containing a single desk, at which a clerk was asleep, and two metal cabinets with a couple of files stuffed inside—presumably, the sum total of corporate registrations.

When it came time to draft a corporate law, I put the whole thing down in just five pages and recommended that the government adopt supplementary legislation as the need arose. The Lao Council of Ministers liked the idea and adopted my draft Enterprise Decree, on the understanding that more laws could be drafted later as needed. The World Bank was irate and condemned me as a communist sympathizer.

Over the next year, the Lao government, which appreciated that I had the best interests of their country at heart, asked me to draft nearly a dozen pieces of legislation covering everything from credit cooperatives to constitutional reform.

One night, at around midnight, I received a visitor at the guesthouse on the banks of the Mekong River, where I was staying. Kham Leong was personal advisor to Premier and President Kaysone Phomvihane, who had led members of the communist, nationalist Pathet Lao organization from their jungle hideouts to take control of the capital, Vientiane, in 1975. Kham Leong was accompanied on his errand by General Thong Pang.

"We in Laos are poor," said Kham Leong. "All these lawyers want to change this line and that line. What use? So many changes! We in Laos need laws, lots of them. So, tomorrow, when you meet the Minister of Justice, you just tell him: 'Pass laws! Stop talking and just pass them!'" It was as accurate an assessment of the country's predicament as I'd heard.

Over the course of 1990-91, I drafted the Enterprise Decree, Central Banking Law, Commercial Banking Decree, Foreign Exchange Regulatory Decree, Insurance Decree, Arbitration Decree and Credit Cooperative Decree, and I was invited to work on amendments to the national constitution. Each of these documents was concise, clearly worded and addressed practical problems faced by the Lao government and people at the time. Nothing was intended to last forever, as the government, economy and political system were clearly all in transition. My role was to help with the transition.

For the Arbitration Decree, I studied how traditional Lao village chiefs arbitrate family disputes and basically wrote it up as legislation. As I prepared to write the Credit Cooperation Decree, I visited monasteries and watched how the monks gave rice to farmers in return for a percentage of their yearly harvest. My approach was a grassroots one—growing the grass slowly by nurturing the roots first; it was quite different from the approach taken by the World Bank and the IMF, which was the equivalent of mowing down people and their culture with a gasoline-powered lawn mower. It didn't occur to me that I was committing developmental theory heresy and was now on the black list of the Washington Consensus mandarins.

Coping with the Currency Crisis in Vietnam

I was invited to visit Vietnam in 1991, during the dong currency devaluation crisis, by the country's central bank officials, who had heard about my work in Laos. The World Bank, the IMF and the ADB had sent many "missions" to Vietnam to evaluate, then more missions to re-evaluate, then many more missions to re-evaluate the evaluations of the crisis. But they did nothing to fix the crisis, which continued to worsen.

"Can they stop spending so much money on evaluating our crisis and *do* something?" the personal secretary of the central bank governor pleaded, before asking me what China was doing about inflation and currency devaluation. I flew to Beijing and returned to Hanoi a week later with photocopies of China's foreign-currency legislation and drafts of new decrees in progress. Soon after, Vietnam adopted a series of measures, ranging from cutting money supply to supporting the price of key consumable commodities, which the World Bank and the IMF had insisted be thrown open to the market. The dong stabilized, then appreciated.

When Vietnam's first foreign-exchange market (loosely based on China's foreign exchange-swap-centers but adjusted to local conditions) was opened in Ho Chi Minh City, I was invited to give the keynote speech. (Years later, when I was having dinner in Beijing with old friends from China's central bank and the foreign-exchange bureau, they recalled visiting Vietnam and Laos and being pleasantly surprised to find that some of those countries' laws were based on Chinese legislation and had been applied successfully.)

Of course, this approach goes against that espoused by the Washington Consensus. During the Asian financial crisis of 1997-98, the IMF insisted that Indonesia's President Suharto lift price controls on key commodities such as edible oils while also depreciating the currency. The result was mass revolution and collapse of the government. Further cyclical poverty resulted, providing a welcoming base for Al Qaeda among the angry, impoverished, and frustrated Indonesians. The Bali bombings followed quick on the heels of September 11. For all the Washington Consensus's brilliant Ivy League economists and political analysts, any person living in a South or Southeast Asian slum can put the pieces together and figure out what is wrong, and what will go wrong if the policies of the Washington Consensus are adopted.

In Vietnam I continued to work with the State Bank of Vietnam on credit and securitization issues. I would often visit rural banks, where I learned that families would pledge pigs as collateral for loans. Of course, the value of the pig could appreciate, or it could become diseased and die, placing the bank at risk. But this was the reality that Vietnamese banks and farmers both faced; the theories being proposed from outside of that reality by the likes of the World Bank bore no relation to life as it was actually lived.

The Vietnamese dreamed of having a stock market but didn't know how to achieve this goal with only state-owned enterprises. I suggested that they begin by restructuring those enterprises. I was invited to restructure the first, Legamex. Then the World Bank turned up again.

The International Finance Corporation (IFC)—the investment wing of the World Bank—flew their executives into Hanoi, demanding that the State Bank of Vietnam work only with them on stock-market listing rules. The IFC's draft proposal, which its representatives claimed to be "classified," was immediately passed on to me by Vietnam State Bank officials for a second opinion. The document was a word-for-word copy of the New York Stock Exchange Listing Rules, with "Vietnam" substituted for "New York." It bore no relation to circumstances in Vietnam. When I tried to suggest to the IFC that they take a softer approach and consider instead simpler, more straightforward legislation that might be more suited to Vietnam's practical realities—a planned economy dominated by state-owned enterprises not yet reformed—they, too, called me a communist sympathizer. I was beginning to get used to the label.

The Vietnamese asked me what to do. I suggested that we work on restructuring a couple of enterprises to begin with, so that we could have something to list, before we talked about doing anything else. And so, despite the fury of the IFC, the State Bank of Vietnam moved another step closer to fulfilling its dream of setting up its own stock market. In a way, the IFC had met its own Dien Bien Phu in Hanoi.

Return to Beijing

In 1992, I was asked to re-open the Beijing office of a Hong Kong law firm for which I had worked. The office had been closed since the 1989 Tiananmen crackdown. One afternoon, I was contacted by several old Beijing friends whom I hadn't seen during the years I spent in Laos and Vietnam. They were working for an organization called the State Commission for Reform of Economic Systems, the premier's key think-tank for guiding and coordinating economic reform. My friends told me that Deng Xiaoping was about to take a trip to the south, and that he would then use the term "market economy" in relation to China for the first time. Moreover, they said, Deng advocated something he called "crossing the river by feeling for stones one at a time." This was the antithesis of the "shock therapy" being advocated by the Washington Consensus.

Everything changed from that moment. China entered an era of accelerated hyper-growth, investment rushed in, and reforms began across the board.

One evening, a Chinese lawyer friend who worked for the Legal Office of the State Council showed up at my Beijing home to tell me that he was leaving his post. "To go where?" I asked. A new organization was being formed—called the Industrial Production Office of the State Council—under the supervision of then Vice Premier Zhu Rongji, who had just arrived from Shanghai where he had served as its reform-minded mayor.

I was confused. Why was my friend, a lawyer, joining a production office? Soon the office changed its name to the State Economy and Trade Commission and transformed itself into a mega-organization along the lines of Japan's Ministry of Industry and Trade, supervising and coordinating all the industrial ministries, diminishing their capabilities, and wiping out their planning functions, one step at a time. It was a clear example of how Zhu Rongji used the tools of state planning to manage the emergence of China's market economy. State planning functions were dissolving as the market kicked in. It wasn't shock therapy, as advocated by the Washington Consensus, but it was therapy nonetheless. There was a palpable buzz in Beijing during the Zhu years.

Many of my old Chinese friends and former classmates were in the inner circle of reformists. One close friend, Li Jiange, was at that time Premier Zhu's key monetary policy advisor and chief secretary. I was frequently asked for my opinions on everything from legal reform to monetary policy. I recall having dinner one evening with some Taiwanese businessmen when the secretary of Deng Pufang (son of Deng Xiaoping) tracked me down and insisted urgently that I leave my dinner companions and join a planning session ahead of then President Jiang Zemin's first formal state visit to the United States. They wanted me to play shadow spin-doctor. I had no choice but to offer my apologies and leave my confused guests wondering about what might have called me away. The meeting didn't finish until almost dawn.

It was an exciting time to be in the thick of China's massive economic reforms and social re-engineering. Upon becoming State Council premier in 1998, Zhu Rongji dismantled all of the state's planning functions and launched a full market economy. However, the entire process was driven by a unique combination of market and planning tools—a program called "macro-control," which Li Jiange and I referred to as "managed marketization." Premier Zhu used the tools of planning to create a market where one had not existed before. He broke from the World Bank and IMF policies and ignored the Washington Consensus, seeking his own approach to China's economic reform based on local conditions and local obstacles.

During 1997 and 1998, I was invited to lead a team—comprising state officials, and American and Eastern European specialists—on state-owned enterprise (SOE) reform. The program, sponsored by the ADB, was the only time a multilateral lending body was permitted to participate in China's SOE reform process. Four heavy-industry enterprises in Anhui province were selected.

Everyone within the inner circles of policy planning was aware of the irony that Anhui was where the first agricultural reforms had begun in the late 1970s. They had been led by the then provincial party secretary Wan Li, who later rose to become probably the second-most-powerful figure in China after Deng himself. In 1992, Wan Li received me in the Great Hall of the People to discuss the imploding regional reforms nationwide.

Huge questions facing China's society were inextricably tied to the enterprise-reform process. These enterprises were created in Mao's time to offer comprehensive social packages—from education and entertainment, to hospitalization and retirement. A worker could be born, live and die in an SOE without ever leaving it or giving thought to the rest of the world. But the enterprises were commercially inefficient when challenged by the new market economy.

But all this was lost on DAI (Development Alternatives Inc.), the consulting firm that had tendered for the project. All they thought was required of them was to train enterprise cadres in market thinking. But this wasn't what was on the cadres' minds. For them, restructuring of enterprises required that entire social functions be re-engineered. It was a question of basic human survival in a society undergoing sweeping, confusing transformation. I recall watching the DAI representative run a kindergarten-type class on the benefits of capitalism for bored enterprise cadres who had entirely different paradigms in mind. It was a kind of self-pleasuring, pedantic proselytizing that was quite irrelevant to the lives of the Chinese. One of the Eastern European consultants discreetly filled me in. DAI was the consulting wing of the U.S. Agency for International Development (USAID), which was the developmental funding wing of another alphabet soup Washington Consensus organization—the Central Intelligence Agency (CIA). DAI consultants in many cases were former CIA officers.

In 1997, one afternoon at home in Beijing, I received a telephone call from an old friend. Badral had been Mongolia's ambassador to Laos during my years spent working there; he was now foreign policy advisor to Mongolia's prime minister. Badral explained that Mongolia was about to adopt a Company Law and, despite advice from the World Bank, the IMF and DAI, the prime minister wanted an independent opinion. A week later I was on a plane to Ulan Bator.

Mongolia, for all its vastness, had a population of less than three million, more than half of whom were nomads subsisting on a non-monetary economy. When a draft of the Company Law for Mongolia—which reflected the Washington Consensus approach—was sent to my hotel, I recognized the document immediately. It was a copy of the New York Corporate Registration Law, with one change: "New York" had been replaced by "Mongolia."

Again, I used the technique that had served me well in Laos: I asked to be taken to the corporate registration office. Once again, I found a tiny room with a clerk at his desk and a cabinet with some files of a few companies that had been registered. For Mongolia to put in place the procedures for registration recommended by the proposed law would have required an entire bureaucracy filled with legal minds on a par with the best New York corporate lawyers. The document bore no relation to reality. Such a bureaucracy couldn't yet exist—nor should it.

In a mostly nomadic society, families whose only real assets are sheep and horses should be able to register their own tiny family-based animal-husbandry enterprises. I suggested in a meeting with the prime minister that Mongolia's Company Law be redrafted and condensed down to no more than three pages, with a one-page attachment form for registering a limited-liability enterprise with minimal capital, or assets that could include animals.

The Mongolian government officials complained that whenever a formerly state-owned department store was privatized using the "shock therapy" approach routinely advocated by their Western advisors (which included distributing shares to the employees), the staff had no idea how to go about running the operation commercially, having previously depended on the state for the supply, pricing and distribution of all the store's products.

I met with officials who were desperate in their opposition to the World Bank's and IMF's insistence that the national state-owned cashmere company be privatized, as the state depended on this single business for most of its revenues. This shattered the traditional economic structure. Today Ulan Bator has Macao-run casinos, children living in underground sewers and prostitution is on the rise. This wasn't the case before the privatization. Wouldn't it have been better if a more gradual approach had been taken to strengthen the capacity of the cashmere industry and allow the economic structure to evolve, rather than shock it? *So,* American-style globalization may just mean Las Vegas-ization. Guess who was furious and called me a communist sympathizer for having an independent opinion?

The Washington Consensus Loses Touch with Reality

Following my visit to Mongolia, the Asian Development Bank invited me to serve as an independent evaluator of their China financial assistance projects. I would be required to assess the progress of their programs for banking and financial reform in China. Thinking that this was a very liberal approach for such a Washington Consensus-oriented institution to take, I accepted the challenge.

On visiting a number of Chinese banks with the ADB's project officer, I was surprised to find that the staff at the banks were hostile toward the ADB. Previous ADB consulting projects to China's state-owned banks had almost all been irrelevant to the needs of the country's transforming banking system. Accountants had been sent to the State Development Bank—China's banking policy arm—to lecture on retail banking. Accountants with no knowledge of banking whatsoever had been sent to China Everbright Bank, which needed help with its credit evaluation systems. In short, the entire package of ADB banking technical assistance to China's state-owned banks had been a disaster, a complete misuse of funds without any logical matching of the bank's individual needs with the consulting services provided. It seems that, when formulating the project, ADB officers didn't even take the time to determine which Chinese banks had the portfolio for policy, commercial or retail services.

When I drew the ADB officers' attention to the oversights and outright mismanagement that had characterized their reform program to date, they refused to allow me to raise my concerns in my report. Instead, they demanded that I write that all the projects had been a great success, even when this flew in the face of the facts.

I refused to bend.

They then demanded that I attend a meeting in Manila, where the ADB has its headquarters. To my surprise, when I arrived in the Philippine capital, I was assigned a computer, given copies of the annual reports of each of the relevant Chinese banks, and told to use the figures from the financial reports to show that the ADB's projects had been successful. Of course, all the annual reports showed that results tor the current year had exceeded those of the previous year. The ADB wanted me to present this as evidence of the success of their program, even when their assistance had been either irrelevant or disastrous for the banks concerned.

While in Manila I was invited by U.S. Embassy officials, who had heard I was in town. During a lunch, I was told that the Philippine economy was much stronger than China's and that this was due to its faithful adherence to the policies of the World Bank, the IMF and the ADB. China was the weaker of the two economics, my hosts explained, because it had refused to accede to Western policies and instead had chosen to take its own misguided approach to reform. Of course, the U.S. government had the most influential scat on the ADB board of directors. I couldn't believe how blinkered their thinking was. I had first visited Manila in 1982. Aside from some new shopping malls, it seemed that nothing had changed. Manila was still surrounded by satellite slums. It looked just like any city in Latin America that had followed World Bank and IMF policies; the poverty screamed in your face. At Smoky Mountain, a massive garbage heap that had been created under the Ferdinand Marcos administration, people lived out their entire lives subsisting on refuse. Marcos was long gone by 1997, but the impoverished population of Smoky Mountain was still growing.

I decided I'd had enough of this Washington Consensus abracadabra economics.

The Middle Kingdom Offers a Middle Road

In 1998, my attention was refocused to Beijing where Zhu Rongji had just been appointed premier of the State Council. He adopted a policy program of currency stability, low inflation and high growth. This was the opposite of what the Washington Consensus was calling for: currency devaluation, which would create inflation and in turn stifle growth. While Washington Consensus economists recommended shock privatization, Zhu adopted a comprehensive program of SOE reform, the complexity of which would have taxed the best of the minds among the Washington Consensus. To ensure the enterprises could operate efficiently, Zhu had to separate out and commercialize their health-care, retirement and education functions.

Moreover, the top-down planning functions of each industrial line ministry were coupled with quotas on transportation. The means of supply and distribution had to be handed over to the market, and the retail industry needed to be liberalized. Zhu had created the State Economy and Trade Commission to carry out this function, effectively an incubator of market economics during the transition from socialism. He demoted the industrial line ministries, converting them into bureau-level departments under his new mega-ministerial body. These planning ministries would later all be converted once again to mere "chambers of commerce" for the sector under their portfolio.

Zhu wanted to incubate a market economy within the nurturing nest of state socialist security. In this way, he could prevent China going the way of the unfortunate state-owned department store in Mongolia. Besides, he didn't want China to be just another wrecked micro-example of Washington Consensus naiveté.

While many foreign investors and financiers applauded Zhu Rongji's reforms, I viewed what he was trying to accomplish as something bigger than just the internal re-engineering of China's economic and financial system. By adopting a program that combined planning with market forces— using the tools of planned economics to drive the transformation from a socialist to a market economy—Zhu had effectively pioneered an alternative approach to economic development that could successfully lead a socialist economy toward capitalism without any of the political shocks or conditions associated with "shock therapy" and the Washington Consensus.

Zhu's experiment and the China experience had paved a middle road. Years later, an ambassador to China from a Latin American country commented to me during a Beijing cocktail party, "Washington insists that one must be capitalist and a democracy; if not, one is socialist and not a democracy. This thing of China's, they are neither capitalist nor socialist, while they are both capitalist and socialist. There is no black and white. It is all mixed. So, what happens if this experiment works? The foundations of Washington Consensus thought will be uprooted!"

I suggested in a commentary published in the international press that Zhu Rongji should be nominated for the Nobel Prize for Economics. I then tried to lobby this through several Scandinavian embassies in Beijing. While the Danish ambassador to China was extremely positive, feedback from the others was negative. "No Chinese can be given the Nobel Prize for Economics," we were told by the Norwegian Embassy. "It would not be politically correct!"

I began to wonder about political correctness and its relation to Zhu's pragmatic approach. I then wrote a book, *Zhu Rongji: The Transformation of Modern China* (also published by Discovery Publisher). It was not a biography of Zhu, but rather the story of China's financial and economic reforms during the 1990s when Zhu served first as vice premier and then as premier. His office made available to me records of many of the policy decisions that had been taken.

During a discussion on economic policy one morning in the Great Hall of the People, I asked Premier Zhu what he thought about after midnight, when deliberating on and having to decide on a policy that could go either way. What did he think about at that crucial moment?

The Premier's answer surprised me. "Everyone knows that within economics there has to be a social psychology effect, which is also called the effect on a mass of sheep," he said. "If people lose faith in your decision-making, even correct decisions will be difficult to implement. Therefore, China's current decision-making level completely weighs up all sides, analyzes and compares, and after making a policy decision, the entire party, the entire population, must support its implementation. If we are afraid that such policy has a weakness, in later days revisions and further completion can be carried out. This point has given me the deepest impression. If people are skeptical about your policy, even if it is correct, it will be difficult to implement and will be useless in producing any effect."

I understood this to mean that, regardless of how good your economic theory is, if you cannot get the people to buy into it and react the way you need them to, then the theory and its subsequent policy are useless. I came to realize that knowledge of local conditions and of human psychology is more important in stimulating and guiding a nation's economy than any classroom theorem. Moreover, cookie-cutter models based on isolated assumptions don't work, and can often make the situation much worse.

Dr. Supachai Panitchpakdi, former director-general of the WTO, later commented to me on the pragmatism of Zhu Rongji's approach to economic reform, which combined state planning, market forces and local considerations. "There is actually no mystique behind this recipe for success," said Supachai. "After all, Zhu's thinking is done principally on the basis of rational economic logic. Allied to this, though, are the additional ingredients of pragmatism and a deep understanding of Chinese conditions and of a culture that requires no clinical advice from established institutions that should be engaged in more humble studies of the conceptual framework that informs Zhu Rongji's considerable successes."

My book on Zhu Rongji was published in March 2002. My publisher wanted to launch it at the World Economic Forum meeting in Beijing. However, the Forum refused to include the book launch in its program, since my views didn't fit with their globalization dogma. They listed instead various other after-dinner programs. Nevertheless, we held an after-dinner champagne and wine reception in the lobby of the Grand Hyatt Beijing, where the conference was being held, to which we invited journalists and business leaders.

I decided to add a soft touch of anti-globalization guerrilla warfare. During the Forum dinner, my friend Flora Cheong-leen, an eclectic Hong Kong fashion designer, presented a show of her "Tibetan-fusion" designs. Following the show she brought her Chinese models along to our reception.

"Do you need them to cut a ribbon or something?" Flora asked.

"No," I replied. "I just want each model to hold a glass of champagne and chat with the business executives who will join us tonight."

Needless to say, there was a bull run of businessmen joining our book launch reception following the official banquet. Attendance at the other post-dinner programs was so poor, even the organizers themselves joined in our party—presumably out of an interest in Zhu's financial reforms. Or perhaps the gurus of globalization had little interest in alternative economics but appreciated the company of beautiful models?

I was asked to make a speech about my book that night. It was a very short one. "I would like to thank my publisher, John Wiley, for their support. Now, after writing about Premier Zhu's economic and financial reforms, I have nothing left to write about China. This is my last book on China. For those who have been with me in Beijing, thank you for all of your support over these years. Now I'm leaving."

The next day I closed my legal consulting firm, referring my clients to friends who were lawyers or consultants. I began making plans to go to Tibet. I wanted to produce and direct a documentary called *Searching for Shangri-la*. It would be based around a single question: Where is Shangri-la?

I had no inkling at the time that, after searching for Shangri-la, I would move there.

目

3

GRASSROOTS APPROACHES THAT SOLVE REAL PROBLEMS
FOUNDING AN NGO IN THE HIMALAYAS

The mass of men lead lives of quiet desperation. What is called resignation is confirmed desperation... A stereotyped but unconscious despair is concealed even under what are called the games and amusements of mankind... No way of thinking or doing, however ancient, can be trusted without proof. What everybody echoes or in silence passes by as true today may turn out to be falsehood tomorrow, mere smoke of opinion, which some had trusted for a cloud that would sprinkle fertilizing rain on their fields.

—Henry David Thoreau, *Walden*

Searching for Shambhala

In the course of making my documentary film that posed the question, "Where is Shangri-la?", I learned that the name is a misspelling of "Shambhala." This core Tibetan Buddhist concept describes a more equitable world where the gaps between rich and poor are diminished, different ethnic groups respect each other, the environment is protected and the world is at peace. So, my journey to Shambhala began by searching for Shangri-la.

My travels took me from the Tibet Autonomous Region across Qinghai and Yunnan provinces—an area known to Tibetans as "historical Tibet." Along the way, I met monks, nuns, artists and environmental activists who were undertaking, at a grassroots level, to preserve and sustain the cultural heritage and improve the livelihood of their own people through small-scale but effective efforts in the areas of health care and education.
Several people abruptly changed my thinking.

Tibetan artist An Sang took me to visit a factory dedicated to making Tibetan handicrafts and to reviving Tibetan paper and incense making. The factory, established by a former monk, employed only people with disabilities. These workers supported not only themselves by reviving these traditional Tibetan crafts, but also a school and orphanage for a hundred or so orphans.

Famed Bai ethnic dancer Yang Liping established a school for the children of Yunnan's minority hill tribes in order to preserve traditional dances and songs that are in danger of being lost from the culture's oral tradition as a result of the rapid pace of development. She choreographed a performance called "Yunnan Impressions," which has helped to keep her people's culture alive while providing her now nationally famous dance troupe with a means of earning a living. Yang Liping has devoted her own resources to documenting and preserving her people's ethnic diversity and her contribution to cultural sustainability is now recognized by the national government.

A monk named Jigme Jensen established a cheese factory in a region frequented by nomadic herders, from whom he could purchase yak milk without disrupting their traditional lifestyle. He then manufactured for export exotic yak-milk cheeses, the income from which he invested in building schools for the children of the nomads in the highlands. By taking education to the children in this way, they were spared the necessity of being resettled in the townships, which is the official Chinese policy.

Dolma Chugi, a graduate of the University of Massachusetts at Amherst, turned down offers of highly paid employment with an investment bank in the United States on completing her studies. She chose instead to return to Tibet, where she was determined to use her education to improve the lives of her fellow Tibetans. She now works for a meager salary with an NGO dedicated to providing eye care. Every year she takes teams of doctors into the tough Tibetan outback, where she organizes and coordinates eye-care camps for the treatment of hundreds of nomads and rural poor with vision problems or diseases of the eye who couldn't otherwise access or afford such treatment.

Nyima Tsering, the abbot of Jokhang Monastery, Tibet's most sacred pilgrimage site, talked with me at great length during my first visit to Lhasa and has continued to do so since I made my home in the ancient capital. He envisioned a new global order based on human compassion, rather than aggression and with governments taking a long-term view of how we can protect future generations and the environment, instead of serving as the puppets of egotistical chief executives whose globalization agendas stem solely from their own appetite for material wealth and power.

These people changed me. I began to turn away from the world of multinational corporations, CEOs and the trappings of power, wealth and privilege that had been my comfort zone as a corporate lawyer for the past decade or so. I stopped wearing suits and silk ties and dug out my old jeans and T-shirts. I threw out my cufflinks and switched my Omega timepiece for an altimeter-compass watch. Instead of being glued to stock reports and attending investment banker conferences, I meditated and began to raise Siberian huskies.

Changing Values

I wrote a series of books based on my notes from my sojourns through Tibet: *Searching for Shangri-la, Conversations with Sacred Mountains, Shambhala Sutra* and *New Age Sutra.* Some people thought I had lost my mind. Others saw in my writings a vision of something different. I stopped caring what people thought. Reflecting back on my travels through the Tibetan outback, several things became clear to me.

China had broken from the World Bank and IMF models in forging its own independent path toward a market economy. But that model was unique to China's particular circumstances and probably could not—should not—be duplicated elsewhere. But it wasn't just China that was different. *Every* country is unique, with its own most appropriate path to follow. There should be no one "model" for economic, political or social development. Washington Consensus economists tend to be fanatical in their adherence to models such as "privatization," "liberalization of currency and trade" and, of course, "democracy." While these models may suit one country at a certain point in time, they may have little practical value to offer other nations. Furthermore, whether or not they are appropriate, models should be of little importance. We should discard theory-based fundamentalism—theory is irrelevant if it doesn't work. Let's focus on solving concrete problems.

I realized that the role of government should be to alleviate poverty, close income gaps, protect our environment to ensure the survival of generations to come, and give people hope for a better future. The form that a government takes, or the political model it adopts, is less relevant than what it accomplishes. Attempting to apply theoretical models to cultures and ethnic groups for whom they have no relevance, just in order to prove a point, is without value and may be counterproductive. In a way, the Washington Consensus's devotion to free-market theory and democracy is as deluded as the Soviet Union's communist imperatives of another era, which had insisted that the only acceptable model was a centrally planned, top-down one. Both are equally misguided in trying to impose on others what they believe works for them, whether or not the conditions and circumstances make such a model relevant.

I was reminded, also, that ethnic diversity is essential. In fact, the more diverse our global ethnicity, the better it will be for the human species. Why should everyone merge into a single melting pot? Of course, if everyone thinks alike, multinational corporations will find it easier to globalize their marketing and bring costs down against profits. But is this a good thing for the survival and development of the human race? I don't want to become another consumer zombie and I hope that I may be able to help others from falling into that trap. We human beings are more than statistics. Moreover, *quantity* of life, as expressed through conspicuous consumption of branded goods, doesn't necessarily mean *quality* of life. Small can be beautiful and work done at the grassroots level can change lives for the better.

I learned that sustainable economic foundations are essential to each individual culture's survival and evolution. Idealism as a notion or goal in itself isn't enough. We need to adopt pragmatic approaches and techniques in order to realize our ideals. If the economic rug is pulled, the remnants of cultures will be relegated to museums in the form of artifacts and costumes. But establishing functioning and sustainable businesses can assure that cultures can preserve their individual identity while continuing to evolve. The objective is to establish bulwarks so that the individuality of each ethnic and cultural group isn't absorbed within the globalization of the American-style melting pot.

Furthermore, each cultural and ethnic group is the best arbiter of what is best for itself. Peoples have the right to determine their own future. Imposing external economic or political models based on totally different experiences is potentially harmful, rather than helpful. However, providing the tools that empower—or re-empower—a people can contribute to their development. Attempts by a dominant culture to force models or conditions of development upon other cultures will only deter, and possibly reverse, their progress, in the end bringing disaster.

I was inspired by the examples I found of monks, nuns, artists and NGOs working on the ground, whose micro-efforts were changing the lives of individuals for the better. In fact, what I saw in Tibet changed my life. After writing up my notes for the four Tibetan books, I left Beijing. Taking my two huskies with me, I moved to the top of the world.

Re-discovering the Power of Local Heritage

These ideas would later become a feature of how I chose to live my life. When I moved to Lhasa in 2005, I began to focus not on how much money my business could make, but on how much I needed to raise each year for work I was undertaking in health care, education, micro-financing and ethnic heritage-preservation projects. To the chagrin of those working with me, business almost became secondary to this work and only interested me as far as it was necessary to make money to finance the humanitarian and social development programs that I was creating each day.

Today, I live in Lhasa, Tibet, within the historic quarter of the city, in a 200-year-old house made of the traditional materials of stone, adobe and wood, tucked away in a narrow, nondescript alleyway. Just a five-minute walk from my door is Jokhang Monastery, Tibet's most sacred pilgrimage site. It is for Buddhists what Mecca is for Muslims, the center of spiritual energy, an anchor for Tibetan Buddhist culture. Inside, yak-butter candles burn dimly, creating a natural radiant glow that illuminates the *Jowa* image of Sakyamuni, the first Buddha. Hundreds of Tibetans lie prostrate at the door outside.

In the incense-fragrant inner sanctum, a Chinese guide demonstrates his cultural insensitivity to a group of Chinese tourists following his yellow flag. "Do you see that Buddha, the one everyone is bowing before? It is antique, made of real gold. I said REAL gold! Can you imagine how much it is worth? Can you see all the jewels encrusted in it? They are real, too, not fake! Imagine how much all of this is worth!"

Such insensitive tourism has plagued China, ruining some of the most magnificent, pristine natural environments and eroding delicate ancient cultures. But the problem is a worldwide one. Many of America's natural wonders and indigenous cultures have faced similar obliteration through the globalization of crass commercialism. Even formerly unique holiday destinations in Asia haven't been immune, causing travelers to seek alternatives to these places as well.

On the other hand, sensitive cultural travel—often called heritage tourism or eco-tourism—can serve to preserve, sustain and evolve local ethnicity. Such an alternative destination travel approach can provide both fulfilling vacation experiences and exchanges of values between cultures. Whether for jetsetters or backpackers, the search for this experience in its many forms is increasingly becoming a trend in Asia.

Moreover, I recognized the need to support ethnic diversity through culturally sustainable development. Sensitively developed tourism can provide the economic platform assuring such sustainability. Tourism does not have to be defined only by Disney. Rather than mimic, it should serve as an economic basis to protect and allow culture to evolve in its own right. The spectrum is enormous—localized products such as coffee, honey, tea, textiles, fashion, music and even media—can all be considered branches of culturally sustainable tourism. It is not just about hotel rooms and restaurants. It all begins with a recognition of the intrinsic power and beauty of local culture, dusting off the corrosion of globalization and getting back to basics. Protecting traditional local architecture is a first step.

My own experience of protecting heritage architecture began in 1995. Infuriated by the massive destruction of ancient sections of Beijing in the name of development, I began my own program of restoring historic buildings. I started by restoring the courtyard house that is still my studio and home in Beijing. Then came other heritage courtyard restorations that became the Red Capital Club (1999) and Residence (2001) concept in the city. The concept evolved from my desire to preserve Beijing's architecturally unique courtyard houses. In the run-up to hosting the 2008 Olympics, the municipal government embarked on a concentrated policy of cultural self-destruction by bulldozing many of the buildings that had once defined the rich heritage of the ancient capital.

The authorities felt the need to showcase modernity, which for them meant destroying Beijing's own thousand-year heritage and smothering everything with cement, steel and blue glass, in the American "Highway One" style. This policy of emulating everything American has seen Beijing (as well as China's other mega-cities) fall prey to America's problems of destruction of the natural environment, water pollution and toxic air, which in the coming years may create an environmental and humanitarian disaster for the capital along the lines of that experienced during the SARS crisis of 2003.

We sought in our own small way to go against this tide and to attempt to preserve neighborhoods through grassroots efforts, such as acquiring old courtyard houses and bringing craftsmen out of retirement and putting them to work restoring the buildings. Through these efforts, combined with extensive lobbying of the municipal government, which had no comprehension of what we were trying to achieve, we managed to preserve an entire neighborhood in what little remained of Beijing's old city. It is one of only several authentic historic neighborhoods remaining in China's capital today. These days, the city's architecture increasingly resembles a bad mock-up of Las Vegas, complete with cement hotels filled with prostitution, gambling and crack dealing.

We then extended the concept to a natural mountain reserve along the Great Wall outside Beijing. The area had originally been slated for flooding and development by local authorities seeking to create a poor imitation of a Disney-style water park, which would have guaranteed the total destruction of one of Beijing's last environmentally sound rural areas. Using the preservation model of architectural space being kept to a minimum in relation to nature, we created a barely visible, traditionally designed village that was tucked into the mountainside. The construction had the comfort of modern amenities, but was built using ancient wood and bricks that we salvaged from sites where the city government was knocking down the capital's heritage structures.

Staffed by ethnic Tibetans working under our own affirmative action program, Red Capital Ranch at the Great Wall (an intentionally cheeky name) is Beijing's first, and probably only, eco-tourism lodge. As a result of this project, large tracts of open natural mountain landscape and vulnerable areas of the Great Wall have been protected from the locally insensitive, abrasive approaches to tourism development that have already ruined many parts of the city.

Founding an NGO for Culturally Sustainable Development

In 2003, the governor of Tibet, Xiangba Pingcuo, heard about my work filming documentaries in ethnic minority regions of western China and invited me to share my experiences with him. I used the opportunity to lobby the Lhasa municipality to preserve the city's historic quarter as a first step toward developing culturally sensitive destination travel. Knowing that actions speak louder than words, in 2005 I moved to Lhasa, where I purchased two heritage buildings that I restored the following year. The buildings, revamped as the House of Shambhala boutique heritage hotel, sparked the revival of an entire neighborhood and set an example of what can be done with sensitive care and attention to local culture and heritage.

Only Tibetan craftsmen and women were engaged in the restoration process, assuring the authenticity of the preservation. All the lanterns, furnishings, pillowcases, bedspreads and ceramic dinnerware used in the hotel were made by families living in the city's old quarter, which made the project an integrated community effort focused on cultural preservation and sustainability.

Through restoring and opening the House of Shambhala in Lhasa we established a micro-model of sustainable cultural preservation. Since we became the first licensed "family inn" in Lhasa's old quarter, the government has permitted many local Tibetan families to open tiny guesthouses in their homes. This has enabled Tibetans to continue to live in the old city, carrying on their traditional lifestyle, but with sensitive tourism as a sustainable economic factor. This differs from many cities in China, where the local people have been forced out and their traditional homes replaced by oriental Disney "Main Street U.S.A."-type tourist facades.

Using House of Shambhala as our flagship, we founded an NGO—Shambhala Foundation—with the aim of applying elsewhere our model of supporting both ethnic diversity and culturally sustainable development. The model calls for restoring heritage buildings and reviving ancient neighborhoods in a manner that assures their sustainability and, where possible, preserving large swaths of land by creating an eco-tourism lodge as a keystone.

Like language, architecture is a foundation for ethnicity and culture. It represents a dialogue between an ethnic- or culture-based group and its own environment. An old house was meant to be a place where people live, eat and enjoy familiarity together. So, converting old houses into unique heritage hotels and restaurants staffed and managed by local people both assures their sustainability and accommodates changing economic paradigms.

Taking Action

Our heritage restoration hotel became a base for community outreach for ethnic diversity and culturally sustainable development. In turn, Shambhala adopted three action initiatives.

The first is our micro-equity program, inspired by Professor Muhammad Yunus (see Chapter 8). Micro-equity differs from micro-credit in that we invest instead of lend, becoming ourselves stakeholders in the business, which must be connected to cultural preservation through the evolution of a sustainable commercial social enterprise. The emphasis is upon empowering marginalized women and people with disabilities by helping to instill in them a sense of pride, identity and accomplishment.

Along with boutiques in the Shambhala restorations, which serve as outlets for products made by sustainable cottage industries, we launched a series of micro-equity enterprises. These include the following:

- "Tibetan Turquoise Revival." Most Tibetan-style jewelry sold to visitors in Lhasa is imported from Nepal or India. We are trying to empower marginalized Tibetan women to design and craft their own jewelry.

- "Save the Tibetan Tiger." This communal initiative has revived the craft of tiger-rug making, which once helped save the Himalayan tiger from being decimated by the British Raj's bounty hunters. Most tiger rugs sold in Lhasa are synthetic and are made in Beijing or Shanghai; we use natural wool and dyes and have revived the craft among village women.

- "Tibet Children's Initiative." Disabled individuals are producing children's puppets and dolls.

- "Mala Bead Breakfast Club." Former begging nuns are designing, stringing and blessing high-fashion prayer beads.

- "Tibetan Textile Revival." This initiative empowers Tibetans with disabilities, who design and sew fashion and lifestyle products—from handbags to pillowcases—using local fabrics.

Without sustainable economic foundations, ethnic cultures cannot survive and evolve. Instead, they will be relegated to museums, where mass corporate tourism, run by national or multinational operators, takes over. This is the kind of globalization of insensitive commercialism that we wish to avoid—and even perhaps to reverse—through the efforts of the Shambhala Foundation.

Our second action initiative involves medical outreach. Our focus is to bring medical clinic facilities to monasteries by training monks and nuns as paramedics or doctors of traditional Tibetan medicine. Where monasteries were partly destroyed during the Cultural Revolution, our aim is to restore the buildings and install medical clinic facilities. This initiative will provide a sustainable income to the monastery, which traditionally serves a community function, both as psychological support and provider of traditional Tibetan medicine. For skeptical Chinese authorities, we can point to the monastery as a community center and provider of community services, not just religious ones.

Our flagship clinic at Tashigang Monastery (built with support from the Embassy of Ireland in Beijing) is located in a village about an hour outside Lhasa. Here monks are being trained as medics and traditional Tibetan medicine reaches out to local village communities, offering treatment and medicine at prices a third lower than those at government clinics, which are often located in city centers difficult for rural villagers to visit. Moreover, monks are now subsidizing rural health care by producing high-end herbal spa oils and medicinal incense. While spa-goers pamper or indulge themselves, they are also participating in our broader social and community-outreach program.

Using the clinic as a base, we launched a mobile medical clinic using outfitted four-wheel-drives as ambulances. Official Chinese policy is to settle nomads into concrete apartments in new-fabricated townships. Denied their traditional lifestyle, without work, depression sets in, they become alcoholic, similar to the situation Native Americans faced when settled on reservations a century ago. One excuse the government uses in forcing this settlement is that nomads living at high altitudes cannot get medical treatment. We believe in taking medical treatment to them. As long as they retain their traditional lifestyle, the environment in which they live will be protected. Moreover, they will be psychologically better off".

The Tashigang clinic model has since been reproduced at Damkar Monastery in Yushu, a remote ethnic Tibetan prefecture of Qinghai province, where monks and nuns provide traditional Tibetan medicinal treatment (also supported by Ireland). In addition, Shambhala launched a program to combat blindness on the Himalayan plateau called "Let the People See." This project is in conjunction with SEVA, an NGO that focuses exclusively on preventing unnecessary blindness through cataract operations. With the support of the Luxembourg Embassy in Beijing, a full clinic dedicated to the prevention and cure of blindness was established at Damkar Monastery and run by Tibetan doctors supported by a team of monks and nuns. Shambhala has also launched a campaign to raise funds for cataract operations conducted by SEVA. It amazed me how small amounts of money could transform lives. A cataract operation in a Chinese hospital might cost RMB4,000 (US$585). For most Tibetans such a cost is prohibitive. (In villages near Tashigang the annual per-capita income is only RMB2,000). However, with volunteer doctors an operation can be done for as little as RMB400 (half for the intra-ocular lens and the other half for medicine). So for approximately US$58, a blind person can see. I thought about how much money I had wasted on Starbucks coffees and began campaigning to raise funds for eye operations.

Our third action initiative involves bringing progressive education to disadvantaged children. From our NGO base at House of Shambhala, we have established a rural school providing free education to more than 100 impoverished children, with plans to expand as future capacity permits. The teachers are trained by Montessori International in Beijing. We are also introducing a Montessori curriculum alongside traditional Tibetan and required Chinese. Montessori Beijing founder Caroline Chen became an endless resource of materials and programs, sending foreign teachers to train in Tibet and welcoming Tibetan teachers to train in Montessori Beijing. While registered as a "pre-school," we have children up to 14 years of age who have never previously attended school. As many of the children may have only this opportunity to get a basic education with which to sustain their future, we offer an accelerated art program taught by Tibetan modern artists who volunteer their time by serving as role models.

It is our intention to develop similar programs across Tibet in the coming years, based on integrating concepts of locally integrated heritage restoration or eco-tourism. The programs will offer exploration of the local culture and nature as part of the experience and the opportunity to outreach through connected education and medical schemes serving villages and nomads in the region.

These efforts, as simple as they are, have already sparked a following of compassionate individuals who wish to use their resources and skills to enhance the lives of others. Increasingly, we have guests who wish not only to visit our projects, in addition to Tibet's historic and religious sites, but also to volunteer their time and energy to help, either as professionals—such as doctors and teachers giving first-hand training—or by raising funds to support and expand such outreach efforts. Many are now coming to Lhasa as volunteers during their vacation time in order to help others through our various programs.

More and more travelers are rethinking the notion of what makes a good vacation. Following the 2004 tsunami in Southeast and South Asia, many people volunteered their time to help with the rescue efforts and with rebuilding villages. A good many are finding that time spent helping others is more satisfactory than playing golf, say, which wastes precious resources such as water.

Creating New Models

Shambhala Foundation action initiatives support alternative approaches to development. Our programs in Tibet serve as collective models of what can be achieved in diverse ethnic regions, both within China and in other countries facing the dilemmas of cultural identity during economic transition. Unlike the World Bank and IMF economists, we don't claim to have the answers. But we do have a lot of questions. By seeking answers to questions, we have found sets of experiences that we are willing to exchange with others. They, with their own experiences of local conditions and cultural circumstances, can in turn teach us.

Small increments of growth are often more effective than large-scale economic growth models based on theories and derived in isolation from local realities. We believe in solving concrete problems, at the grassroots level, by working with actual people and the real-life conditions they must face. Therefore, we are uninterested in textbook formulas. We have found that a little effort, combined with resources focused in the right place, can dramatically change lives for the better. So, this is where we are putting our energy and resources.

Moreover, the building blocks for sustainable development lie in the cultures of the people concerned. They have the right to determine the direction of their own economic development and cultural identity. We condemn the attachment of political conditionality to aid or technical assistance, as required by the World Bank and the IMF. I have realized during my journey that representative political institutions should be developed on the foundations of the indigenous people's own culture and local value systems. If not, then such political institutions themselves cannot be sustainable.

Through the work of our NGO, I have come in contact with a widening circle of NGOs and individuals who are taking action with their own hands and changing people's lives for the better. It doesn't matter how small each effort is; I saw that, when positive energy and attitude are at the forefront of action, the power of many micro-efforts can accumulate.

Having come from the institutional blue-chip corporate world of multinational expansionism, I know that many people feel trapped by a lifestyle that is materially very comfortable but spiritually impoverished. I realized that some of these people might also want to break out from the value constraints imposed upon them by their social conditioning. It became clear to me that the efforts of these frontline NGOs and individuals could inspire others as they had inspired me. If stories of their daily fight to better the lives of others and the environment could be told to more people, they too could show the way.

Forging a Himalayan Consensus

A Zen riddle says: "If a tree falls in the forest and nobody is there to hear it, does it make a sound?" I realized that it was time to give these efforts a voice. Moreover, offering a voice could bring together individual strengths in a collective force. I began to seek out the pieces of a puzzle that might form the mosaic of this new wave.

I was invited by Professor Muhammad Yunus to visit Bangladesh in order to see and experience at first hand his pioneering micro-credit program, which is aimed at alleviating poverty in that country. While Henry Kissinger—a symbol himself of the Washington world view—once declared Bangladesh a "basket case," Yunus was proving him wrong, while also providing the world with a new model that could shatter the former monopoly of banking services by the rich, who see the poor as unworthy in a capitalist caste society.

I shared with Professor Yunus the vision of the U.N. representative to China, Khalid Malik, which is to revive commerce and culture along the ancient Silk Road as a way to re-empower the much-maligned South and Central Asian states. This plan would recognize those states' Islamic heritage as a powerful and beautiful tradition to be extended into the future—and not as the source of terror depicted in the crusading Western media. And I learned much from Islamic scholar and author Reza Aslan about how Islam, like Buddhism, offers a community and cultural identity, which aspect is so often dismissed by the advocates of Western-style globalization.

I sought to understand the anti-globalization movement in the context of the WTO negotiations and the protests blocking those sessions. Walden Bello, of Focus on the Global South, offered me on-the-ground insights into issues linking the various NGOs and ethnic groups who were struggling to protect their own communities and lifestyles against the unilateral economic and political onslaught. I realized that the anti-globalization movement is now a seamless, borderless, democratic, force for social justice, the nemesis of multinational corporate culture and political lobbying.

I visited the royal family in Bhutan and spent time with political leaders and social advocates there who were promoting the concept of "Gross National Happiness" (GNH) in place of Gross National Product, as a measurement of a country's economic and political success. The concept is now revolutionizing the very notion of what qualifies as "wealth." I recognized that this simple but revolutionary idea, born in the tiny Thunder Dragon kingdom of the Himalayas, had the potential to shake up all our global economic assumptions. The monks in Bhutan taught me something that none of the economic theorists in university could: assume nothing!

I participated as an economic advisor in the struggle by Nepal's Maoists—40% of those under arms are marginalized women—to forge an equitable non-caste society, close income gaps and eliminate the cyclical poverty created by World Bank, IMF and USAID programs. Their guerrilla leader, Prachanda, envisioned the Himalayan mountain range, with all its NGO and grassroots democratic models for localized development, serving as a new source of global values for economic development. In effect, he saw the Himalayas becoming the "Waterloo" of the Washington Consensus.

I also discovered the vision of Sri Lanka's Buddhist opposition party leader, Athuraliya Rathana, who is calling for a post-Bretton Woods system built on the foundations of Buddhist compassion, rather than Adam Smith's greedy "invisible hand," and for a global uprising against that system through pacifist disobedience. He also pointed out the direction in which I should go next.

Fired by my encounters with such people who had a new vision for this region of the world, I began a new journey, reaching out as an NGO activist to other groups. It seemed that these efforts were all emerging along the Himalayan mountain range, so rather than acting as a barrier between East and South Asia, the mountains formed a kind of bridge. Some NGO representatives I spoke with from Thailand, Cambodia and Laos suggested the Himalayan Consensus vision encompasses those regions as well, linked by Buddhism and the Mekong River, whose source lies in the glacial realms of Tibet.

Using Lhasa as my base, I began traveling from the Himalayas to Nepal, India, Pakistan, Bangladesh and further south to Sri Lanka, seeking a consensus of new ideas and new values drawn from the traditions of the region. Sources of inspiration were the grassroots efforts to alleviate poverty and close income gaps and the values of people whose environment hadn't yet been destroyed. Such people seek the technology and health-care sciences that are on offer in a greater global village, but don't accept the globalization of Americanization as the only standard by which to live their lives.

I asked myself a question: What do the political leaders on both sides of the Himalayan mountain chain have in common? China's President Hu Jintao, Nepal's Maoist leader Prachanda, Sri Lankan Buddhist opposition party chief and monk Athuraliya Rathana, Bangladesh's Nobel Prize-winner Muhammad Yunus and Bhutan's King Jigme Singye Wangchuck are all calling for innovative and local solutions to global problems in the form of a new regional consensus. In sharp contrast to Washington Consensus approaches to development, economics, politics and global values, the new geographic nomination—the "Himalayan Consensus"—is being gradually discussed and accepted from Colombo to Islamabad, from Lhasa to Beijing, embracing three pillars of new-era idealism.

First, China's economic experience has overturned assumptions once taken for granted in IMF and World Bank economic development theory. So, throw out the theory. Each country's experiences will differ based on local conditions. For instance, while China's emphasis is on GNP growth, Bhutan is calling for growth to be measured in GNH. Each is suited to the unique circumstances prevailing in those countries in terms of their population density, the gaps between rural and urban incomes and so on. Each according to its own circumstances, with no one model for all. Instead, different countries could share their disparate experiences concerning development, with positive results achieved through an emphasis on grassroots, microfinance and combined market and planning approaches. There should be an end to the blind application of Washington Consensus economic-module fundamentalism, which bears no relation to local realities.

Second, since World War II, the United States has essentially set the tone of global values, embracing "cookie-cutter" democracy and conspicuous consumption, dished up with a heavy dose of Judeo-Christian morality. The Himalayan Consensus prefers to draw its value paradigm from the indigenous ethical values of Buddhism, Hinduism and Islam, all of which have similar aspirations for equality among humanity, closing the gaps between rich and poor, the universal right to medical treatment and respect for the environment as the basis of humanity's own sustainable development, including finding peaceful solutions to global conflicts.

I asked Reza Aslan, the top American Islam scholar, whether the vision of a Himalayan Consensus might offer an alternative to the black-and-white views preached by the Washington Consensus. "A Himalayan Consensus can draw positive commonalities among different cultures," he said. "It was not some Hindu in the Himalayas who came up with the clash of civilizations. It was a Westerner who created the clash of civilizations to highlight the advantages of one over the other. This is not scholarship."

I also ran the idea past Ian Baker, *National Geographic* explorer and the author of a number of books on Buddhism in the Himalayan region. "Engaged social interaction without violence is a Buddhist, Taoist, Hindu and also Islamic vision," he explained at his home in Kathmandu. "The Himalayan Consensus approach should mean positive social action," he replied. "Don't spend time looking for a perfect world. That's just escaping. Go create it!"

The third pillar, based on the two described above and explained to me by Baker, is that every country should have the right to develop its own political system, independent of any other country. That system should incorporate the nation's own unique ethnic, religious and social groups as it sees fit. Evolution, rather than reform, should be the name of the game. Indigenous models of participatory government should be created based on the foundations of each country's local cultural, tribal, historic, political and economic models, as appropriate. While such ideas may be anathema to Washington, the reality is that forcing a particular model of government on nations that have no relevant historical, social or cultural commonality with the country transferring its system will only lead to ineffective government, political instability and social-humanitarian disasters.

Baker, who has lived for many years in Kathmandu, suggested: "Close the gaps between meditation and social transformation. The essence of Buddhism—purifying oneself—goes beyond self-help to helping others." Baker would soon join me as a director of the newly established Shambhala Foundation.

Walden Bello also pondered the emergence of a Himalayan Consensus. "My book *De-Globalization* reflects the same views as you," he said. "We don't need Jurassic institutions and the one-model-fits-all approach is the second big mistake in terms of prescribing economic models. The first was the centralized socialist model. We should learn from the failures of both neo-liberals and socialists and have a model of sustainable development that goes along the lines of the Himalayan Consensus, which says that what developing countries need is space to develop and to be able to put together the development models that respond to the values of *their* societies. At the same time, we cannot say that there are no universal values. The way people construct their societies, their principles of sustainable development, may be different, but there are universal values—equity, community solidarity, justice and democracy. It's just that the particular institutional configuration that puts these principles together is diverse. And diversity should be respected."

Bello went on to note that this appeal for diversity should not be "perverted by authoritarian governments for their own ends. So, I would say that when the Burmese junta says it is anti-West, I would put little credence in the junta because it is using diversity as a mechanism to suppress its own people. The Chinese government doesn't respect diversity per se, but rather refashions ethnic groups in the interests of Beijing. I support this manifesto for a Himalayan Consensus, as it makes diversity a very important principle. I would supplement it to say we have common values and objectives as human beings and the key challenge is to have a creative relationship between universality and diversity."

Ian Baker had similar thoughts. "The Shambhala vision is based on questioning. It cannot be separated from the world as a whole. This differs from the Christian view of a 'Garden of Eden,' which is a world within a cage. The Shambhala vision is of a world without limitations. Paradise includes all things and everything is included; it's not a dual world. In the politics of opposition you cannot win, because you are always opposed to something."

Baker gave an example: "In Nepal, politics means freedom and working for the common good. Democracy as a system went against what people wanted, which was to work together collectively. Democracy, with its emphasis on duality, has its own deep flaws. It perpetuates ways of thinking that can never lead to an enlightened view in all-embracing, holistic societies.

"It all comes down to politics. Buddha renounced politics to go sit under a tree. Now it's time for Buddha to get back into politics, not sit under a tree. Because the trees are all being cut down."

4

THE PEACEFUL REVOLUTION
EMERGENCE OF A GLOBAL JUSTICE MOVEMENT

But, to speak practically and as a citizen, unlike those who call themselves no-government men, I ask for, not at once no government, but at once a better government. Let every man make known what kind of government would command his respect and that will be one step toward obtaining it.

—Ralph Waldo Emerson

Toward Global Mass Protest

As I sat down to coffee with Arundhati Roy in her New Delhi apartment in January 2008, I thought to myself, the concept of the "The Peaceful Revolution" begins with conversations like this, where new ideas dawn at the breakfast table over roast coffee beans from Guatemala, Kenya or Vietnam.

Prophet-like, Roy expounded on the impending collapse of the free market 10 months before its historic September 2008 crash.

"The free market (which is actually far from free) needs the state and needs it badly," Roy pointed out. "As the disparity between the rich and poor grows, in poor countries the state has its work cut out for it. Corporations on the prowl for 'sweetheart deals' that yield enormous profits cannot push through those deals and administer those projects in developing countries without the active connivance of the state machinery. Today, corporate globalization needs an international confederation of loyal, corrupt, preferably authoritarian, governments in poorer countries to push through unpopular reforms and quell the mutinies. It's called 'creating a good investment climate.'"

"When we vote in these elections, we will be voting to choose which political party we would like to invest the coercive, repressive powers of the state in. Right now in India, we have to negotiate the dangerous cross-currents of neo-liberal capitalism and communal neo-fascism. While the word 'capitalism' hasn't completely lost its sheen yet, using the word 'fascism' often causes offence. So we must ask ourselves, are we using the word loosely? Are we exaggerating our situation? Does what we experience on a daily basis qualify as fascism?"

"But as long as our 'markets' are open, as long as corporations such as Enron, Bechtel, Halliburton and Arthur Andersen are given a free hand to take over our infrastructure and take away our jobs, our 'democratically elected' leaders can fearlessly blur the lines between democracy, majoritarianism and fascism."

It is ironic that in this age of high technology and instant information exchange, we are witnessing the rise of an unprecedented unilateralism in what should be a multilateral world following the collapse of international communism, with institutions such as the World Bank, the IMF, the WTO and aid agencies such as USAID, facilitating this new world order. The tripartite arrangement between U.S. multinational industrial corporations, the military and the government in Washington crystallizes this order, which is acceded to by the G7 nations, whose foreign policies are subservient to Washington's.

Many adopting this view see the White House as seeking to create a unilateral world order. Trade policy, of course, serves as part of the formula, with the WTO a tool for achieving this end. Given this current environment, developing countries are prepared for the possibility and are taking measures to brace themselves for the impact. For this reason, developing countries and NGOs are calling for "fair," as opposed to "free," trade to enter the WTO agenda.

Call to Close the Gap

In 2005, France's trade minister, Christine Lagarde, noted: "Trade alone will not lift developing countries out of poverty. Access to health care is also important." She added that the agenda of the Doha Development Round of trade talks "should serve as an opportunity to deliver a legal framework allowing poor countries without manufacturing capacities access to affordable pharmaceuticals."

The gap in health between rich and poor countries and between rich and poor people within countries is "unfair, unjust and unavoidable," stated a report commissioned by the World Health Organization (WHO) released on August 28, 2008. WHO's Commission on the Social Determinants of Health declared that social injustice was "killing people on a grand scale." It blamed a "toxic combination of bad policies, economics and politics," and called for a reduction of health inequalities as "an ethical imperative."

Sir Michael Marmot, chairman of the 19-member commission and professor of public health at University College London, explained:

> We do have the knowledge which, if applied today, could really make a difference to inequities in health between and within countries. Differences in health between groups that are avoidable and could be avoided by social action are quite simply unfair. The commission found within all countries, even the richest, health worsens progressively down the social hierarchy. For instance, a boy born in Calton, a poor suburb of Glasgow in Scotland, has a life expectancy of 54 years—less than a child born in India. But a boy born a few miles away in Lenzie will live to 82. To tackle this inequity, the commission called tor measures to improve living conditions and create safer workplaces, better housing and access to healthcare. Moreover, face head-on unequal distribution of power money and resources within a generation.[1]

Some nations have resources as a result of their geography, demography or location, while others are deprived of them. There are inequities in education and health-care provision, favorable climate, efficient transport links and various other conditions. The historical evolution of nationhood is also a factor. Who was colonized? Who colonized? Unresolved problems and the economic structures set up during the colonial era have been carried over into our time and perpetuated in a somewhat different form by the Bretton Woods system. For this reason, every WTO ministerial meeting— from Seattle to Cancun and Hong Kong—has seen popular mass protests outside the convention centers hosting the event, while delegates from the developing countries challenge the G7 bloc within.

Every WTO ministerial meeting is dominated by talk about promoting "free" trade as a panacea for solving the world's problems. Meanwhile, the streets are filled with the voices of international groups bent on economic and social action and calling for an equitable trading system. The discussions collapsed in Seattle and Cancun and ended in a stalemate in Hong Kong. Why? The answer is being voiced on the streets.

It all began at the end of 1999 when, as Walden Bello explains, "the global elite in Washington, Europe and Asia, congratulating themselves on having contained the Asian financial crisis, tried to launch a new round of trade negotiations under the WTO. We then witnessed a dramatic series of events that might, in fact, lead to that time when, as Karl Marx wrote in *The Communist Manifesto,* 'all that is solid melts into air.'"

On November 30 and December 1, 1999 the Third Ministerial of the WTO collapsed in Seattle when some 50,000 militant protestors outside the Seattle Convention Center combined forces with the delegates from developing nations who were opposed to the WTO proceedings taking place. As Bello recalls in his essay "2000: The Year of Global Protest against Globalization":

> Most of them were united by one thing: their opposition to the expansion of a system that promoted corporate-led globalization at the expense of social goals like justice, community, national sovereignty, cultural diversity and ecological sustainability... And the fallout from Seattle might have been less massive were it not for the brutal behavior of the Seattle police. The assaults on largely peaceful demonstrators by police in their Darth Vader-like uniforms in full view of television cameras made Seattle's mean streets the grand symbol of the crisis of globalization... With the Seattle collapse, however, realities that had been ignored or belittled were acknowledged even by the powers-that-be whose brazen confidence in their own creation had been shaken. For instance, that the supreme institution of globalization was, in fact, fundamentally undemocratic and its processes non-transparent was recognized even by representatives of some of its stoutest defenders pre-Seattle. The global elite's crisis of confidence was evident, for instance, in the words of Stephen Byers, the U.K. Secretary for Trade and Industry: "The WTO will not be able to continue in its present form. There has to be fundamental and radical change in order for it to meet the needs and aspirations of all 134 of its members."[2]

Anatomy of the Peaceful Revolution

From this point on, a series of massive protests by what would come to be labeled the "anti-globalization movement," but which many would prefer to call the "global justice movement," erupted across the world, demonstrating a new-found solidarity. Their milestones include:

- Two months later, when the IMF and World Bank met in Washington, D.C., some 30,000 protestors were met by a phalanx of 10,000 policemen, who arrested hundreds in front of the worldwide media. The following month, when the Asian Development Bank (described by Walden Bello as "a multilateral body notorious for funding gargantuan projects that disrupted communities and destabilized the environment") met in Chiang Mai, in northern Thailand, 2,000 poor Thai farmers protested against the meeting and demanded its closure.

- In September 2000, when the World Economic Forum held its meeting at the glittery Crown Casino in Melbourne, Australia, 5,000 protestors blocked entrances to the building, resulting in three days of street battles and forcing organizers to bring key delegates in and out by helicopter.

- Late that month, some 10,000 protestors from across Europe descended upon Prague, where they engaged in a confrontation with the World Bank and IMF, trapping delegates inside the building and paralyzing the meetings.

- In late July 2001, peaceful protestors at the WTO conference held in Genoa, Italy, were bludgeoned by police. The then British prime minister, Tony Blair, publicly insisted that the international media not broadcast the protestors' views, as if only the "democratically elected" politicians of the G7 had the right to speak on world issues. In mid-September 2003, the WTO Fifth Ministerial collapsed in Cancun, Mexico, after huge protests were held outside and Korean farmer Lee Kyung Hac committed suicide following the refusal by the U.S. and the E.U. to make any significant cuts to their high levels of agricultural subsidies while demanding that the developing nations reduce their tariffs.

- In December 2005, the WTO ministerial held in Hong Kong was paralyzed by protests led by Korean, Sri Lankan and Philippine action groups, that turned the waterfront Wanchai nightlife district into a battle zone.

The watershed Gancun ministerial witnessed an uprising by developing nations led by Brazil, India, China and South Africa—nations representing half of the world's population and two-thirds of its farmers. As a result, a new political configuration was formed, the Group of 21, which squared off against the neo-liberal/neo-conservative G7.

"After Cancun," said Bello, "the challenge for global civil society was to redouble its efforts to dismantle the structures of inequality and to push for alternative arrangements of global economic cooperation that would truly advance the interests of the poor, the marginalized and the dis-empowered."[3]

Arundhati Roy recalls: "For all these reasons, the derailing of trade agreements at Cancun was crucial for us. Though our governments try to take the credit, we know that it was the result of years of struggle by many millions of people in many, many countries. What Cancun taught us is that in order to inflict real damage and force radical change, it is vital for local resistance movements to make international alliances. From Cancun, we learned the importance of globalizing resistance."

The ongoing frustration with the WTO process is best summarized by Charlene Barshefsky, who was the U.S. trade representative during the 1999 Seattle summit. "The process," she said, "was a rather exclusionary one. All meetings were held between 20 and 30 key countries... And that meant 100 countries were never in the room... [T]his led to an extraordinary bad feeling that they were left out of the process and that the results... had been dictated to them by the 25 or 30 privileged countries in the room."[4]

It is apparent that there is a huge gap between the objectives and perceptions of those in the ministerial meetings and those of the protestors barricaded outside.

The World Social Forum

Every winter the G8's corporate and political elite meet at the World Economic Forum in Davos to develop a corporate agenda for the year ahead. "Can the anti-globalization movement challenge this?" I asked Walden Bello during one of our conversations.

"Yes," he replied. "Davos is an attempt by the global elite to get together and figure out what is happening throughout the world; to look forward and create scenarios. Challenges such as the anti-globalization movement serve as a sounding board for the global elite. In 2001, at the same time that Davos was being held, the World Social Forum met in Porte Alegro, Brazil. The World Social Forum, which is held every two years, has become a place where global movements can come together to exchange views and experiences and to affirm their solidarity and common purpose." "Given the seeming reaffirmation of globalization among the corporate elites and G8 leaders at the World Economic Forum each year, how can the global justice—or anti-globalization—movement affirm the rights of developing nations?" I asked.

"I think that institutions like the World Social Forum are very good forums for exchange and education and for getting more people into the global justice movement and expanding the moral sphere, as I call it," Bello replied. "However, at the same time as we work in an anti-hierarchical fashion, we still need a strategy that will enable us to support the creation of alternative institutions and to assist movements in different countries in the same fashion as the human rights movements. We must be able to coordinate our efforts, but in a decentralized fashion, so that we can intervene to support local, individual movements against corporate power and local repression."

My own observation is that the World Social Forum has lost its momentum as an advocacy platform. It has become a festival of Third World culture. It should re-generate its political activism. Specifically, it should be a convention or congress of NGOs from around the globe. Representatives of the globally discontented should be elected to present platforms collectively agreed and voted on at the World Social Forum and to lobby for them at the WTO, IMF, World Bank and G8 meetings. The World Social Forum should be a platform for democratizing these bodies that have been criticized for being elitist and excluding voices from the developing world. "Where will our movement's biggest challenge come from?" I asked.

Bello ventured: "From both the corporate elites in the United States and the authoritarian elites in China. They have been trying to write us off since the late 1990s, but they are becoming more concerned every year as our solidarity grows."

I asked: "Do you believe that the movement has been given fair and balanced representation in the mainstream Western media?"

Bello said: "We can expect nothing from the Rupert Murdoch-type mainstream media. However, the liberal media represent another viewpoint—the view that perhaps the global justice movement has a point, even if they then tend to put it down. But many people are turning to the Internet as an alternative source of news and analysis of events and this is leading to a decline in television audiences and newspaper circulations. In a way, by giving people more choice, the Internet is destroying the hegemony of the right wing and liberal media, which is a good thing."

I said: "Given the ability of our global justice movement to paralyze the World Bank, IMF, WTO and even G8 meetings through grassroots mass protests, do you see a parallel with the Communist International movement of a former era?".

"Our movement has transnational vision and spirit," explained Bello. "But the way the movement is organized is exactly the opposite of how the Communist International was organized. Our movement is opposed to power hierarchies and is very concerned to keep decision-making local. It is a movement that prefers participatory decision-making. It is anti-hierarchical and transnational, but also localized. There is no one recognized authority. Our vision is moral, rather than corporate, which is what gives our movement its legitimacy. Our instruments of moral vision and transnational, grassroots values will ultimately prove to be more powerful than the instruments of financial coercion used by the forces of globalization with which we are in conflict."

"Globalization is a failure and its institutions are in retreat," Bello prophesied less than a year before the massive collapse of global markets in the autumn of 2008. "Bretton Woods created the 'North,' which was a social policy state and the 'South,' which was a social development state, but within the structure of U.S. hegemony. But the liberalization of trade and finance from the 1980s on has promoted global capital at the expense of development and social welfare. Globalization has favored an international, deregulated system that serves corporate profitability. It has destroyed regulations that kept capital from circulating around the world and has destabilized or destroyed unions that previously constrained global capital's ability to exploit people. This has happened since the 1980s and that is what people are reacting against."

Endnotes

1 Frances Williams, "WHO calls for action to tackle social injustice," *Financial Times,* August 29, 2008, p 3.

2 Walden Bello, "2000: The Year of Global Protest against Globalization,"*Focus on Trade,* No. 58, January 2001 (Focus on the Global South (FOCUS), c/o CUSRI, Chulalongkorn University, Bangkok 10330 Thailand).

3 Walden Bello, "Implications of Cancun," *ZNet,* September 23, 2003. Quoted by Walden Bello in "Why Reform of the WTO is the Wrong Agenda," *Focus on the Global South,* www.focusweb.org.

4 Walden Bello, "Needed, A Moratorium on Trade Liberalization," April 4, 2001, Guerilla Information Network, Transnational Institute.

Ⅎ

5

TIME TO REVAMP THE WTO
JOINING THE PEACEFUL REVOLUTION

Ever since monopoly capital took over the world it has kept the greater part of humanity in poverty dividing all the profits among the most powerful nations. The higher standard of living in those nations is based on the misery of ours... but we must agree that real liberation or breaking away from the imperialist system is not achieved by the mere act of proclaiming independence or winning an armed victory in a revolution. Freedom is achieved when imperialist economic domination of a people is brought to an end...

There should not be any more talk about developing mutually beneficial trade based on prices rigged against underdeveloped countries by the law of value and the inequitable relations of international trade brought about by that law.

—Che Guevara[1]

The "Battle of Wanchai"

"Officer, believe me, the Shambhala Foundation will not be organizing any violent protests during the WTO ministerial," I explained at the headquarters of the Hong Kong Police, as two plain-clothes officers stared at me blankly. This was in November 2005, just weeks before the meeting was to be held. I was wearing a suit from my former life as a lawyer, with a neatly pressed white shirt and some borrowed cufflinks. My boots, army jacket and Tibetan prayer beads were at a friend's flat.

"Are you sure?" asked one officer. "We understand the Shambhala Foundation has already rented space at the Fringe Club and that you are holding some kind of organized meeting. Do you know there are rules in Hong Kong governing organized meetings of over a certain number of people?"

"It's not a meeting," I explained. "We are organizing a film festival."

"Film festival?"

"Yes, a film festival."

"Why?"

"Because too many people don't understand why so many people will be protesting against the WTO ministerial at the Wanchai waterfront. So we will be showing films discussing the issues and explaining why so many people will take to the streets to protest. I will also invite journalists, academics, businessmen and delegates from the trade negotiation teams of different governments to hold discussion forums between each film to raise awareness and, more importantly, increase people's understanding of what is taking place just a few blocks away."

"So, there will be no protest?"

"No protest."

What I didn't mention was that most of the films being shown are effectively excluded from mainstream Western media, many made by underground directors and by organizations such as Guerrilla Television. The films included *Ruckus in Prague, Fourth World War, Kilometer 0, The Corporation* and *Mickey Mouse Corporation,* among others. Between each film we had breakout sessions discussing why the protestors were on the streets. Local Nepalese and Indian high school students also performed some South Asian song-and-dance numbers between the sessions. Soon the "film festival"—which was intended as a cover for Shambhala-organized discussions of the issues raised by the protestors—turned into a block party.

As Nepalese and Pakistani youth danced, a harder message was brought to Hong Kong's streets by protestors during what the international media dubbed the "Battle of Wanchai." This occurred when Korean and international justice and solidarity movement members from as far afield as the Philippines and Sri Lanka joined forces to storm police barricades set up outside the waterfront Hong Kong Contention Center.

For these protestors, the issue wasn't the question of shared prosperity through free trade, but imbalances perpetuated through an unfair trading regime. Their underlying protests may not have been against using the WTO as a policy forum within which to negotiate constructive bilateral trade agreements, but rather against using the WTO as a platform from which to forge a unilateral, American policy-driven world order.

While the "Battle of Wanchai" was raging along Hong Kong's waterfront, at the Fringe Club in Central, Hong Kong's financial district, I delivered the Shambhala Foundation's "white paper" on the WTO. Some excerpts:

> As this WTO round commences, sadly, even before it has begun, there are signs that no concrete progress will be made. Because certain G8 countries know they will fail to push through their agendas, they have chosen to postpone G20 concerns. Issues will not disappear. At this session, they are just being avoided. [...]

The World Trade Organization should not be the United Nations of trade—a forum where poor nations can say what they wish, but rich countries continue to dictate policies. To avoid future impasses, this modus operandi has to change. Moreover, horse-trading tariff and subsidy formulas offer political but not economic solutions. If this point is unclear, ask the people and organizations protesting on the street. We need to listen to what they are saying. Their voices are real; this is global democracy at work. [...]

Two approaches need to be adopted. The first is for the WTO to return to the path of trying to achieve its original principles. If this can be done, it would be the best approach given existing foundations and resources of the organization. If not, the WTO would have to re-engineer itself and refocus its functions in order to be effective amid present realities. The powers that be are locked into an abstraction of academic formulas. [...]

GATT's original aim was to create a forum to facilitate free market access, particularly for developing nations, while avoiding the emergence of regional trade blocs, which might lead to protectionism. In recent years, however, the WTO has increasingly deviated from GATT principles. It has been transformed into a leverage tool for developed nations to practice protectionism in their own markets while instituting policies that have contributed to economic meltdown in many developing nations. [...]

The Bilateral and Regional Alternatives

At the time, China had just signed its first bilateral free-trade agreement (FTA) with Chile. The document—which covered market access, origins, safeguards and trade revenues—not only opened up both markets, it also positioned Chile to become Latin America's window to China. Furthermore, it leapfrogged ahead of China's previously negotiated FTA with Southeast Asia, which was set to come into effect in 2010, as the China-Chile agreement would take effect immediately upon being ratified by both countries' legislatures. Was experience once again creating a new model through action, rather than theory?

When China, the world's export powerhouse, signed its own bilateral FTA with Chile, it perhaps signaled the beginning of a new direction that could actively undermine, or offer a new alternative to, the WTO. At the very least, it was a sign that the time had come for a new approach to issues. Chile's FTA with China fascinated me, as I realized that the deal could pull the rug out from under the WTO ministerial meeting that was scheduled to be held in Hong Kong in December 2005, since it offered a concrete and practical alternative to the WTO framework.

Bilateral FTA arrangements and networks could be used to cushion the impact of sudden changes by G8 players, such as the United States, which often politicize trade. They could be of particular benefit to developing countries, which often don't share Washington's political positions, but are unable to withstand its trade leverage extortion.

I asked Mike Moore, a former WTO director-general and New Zealand prime minister, about his view of the bilateral trade agreement approach.

"If bilateral regional deals are compatible, then they should be used," he said. "Were I a trade minister, I would be doing them flat out! Many are not free-trade agreements, but preferential agreements. For example, in Korea, U.S. beef can get in, but not beef from Africa. Many have no binding dispute mechanisms and many create less—rather than more—trade."

"Then how is a binding dispute mechanism created?" I asked.

He replied: "That is the key to the WTO. It is the only international institution that has a binding dispute mechanism."

Moore defended this aspect of the organization. "The headlines are all wrong. When you see 'Boeing and Airbus Trade War Breaks Out!' what does it really mean? There is no trade war, because they are going to the WTO to use legal dispute means and systems to resolve their differences and that decision is binding."

"Is this the main function of the WTO?" I asked. "I can't see any other advantage the WTO offers over regional agreement solutions."

"Regional agreement mechanisms take too long and their remedies are imperfect," Moore said.

Clearly, one advantage of the WTO was that it brought all the parties to a single table. "But equally clearly, regional governments don't always have the resources to resolve disputes with the G8 big guns by means of the WTO mechanism," I said.

Moore sighed, then shook his head in exasperation at the constraints bureaucracies often place upon their own functions, which in turn damage the very causes they wish to support. "We set up a fund—although I had to do it outside the WTO, because some members didn't like it—for small countries and poor countries wishing to get legal advice and to take cases to the WTO. Like legal aid, there were those WTO members who didn't like it and said, 'Why should we pay for others to take this action against us?' Some ambassadors were very helpful. A wonderful woman from Colombia did most of the work and some small European countries helped to make it work. I was told I shouldn't be doing it, so I did it on my own time, not the company's time!"

Jusuf Wanandi, an Indonesian commentator, observed in *The Jakarta Post*. "The ASEAN countries ... will continuously reform, restructure and integrate their economics towards the creation of a single market and production base in 2020. China, for its part, is making the same effort and is doing that at a remarkably rapid pace." Organic regional integration through organizations such as ASEAN and the East Asia Summit could provide better foundations than the WTO for addressing concerns meaningfully in the future, especially as the WTO is increasingly perceived as working in the interests of the G8—the most industrialized nations—and against the core interests of poorer countries.

For another perspective, I asked anti-globalization movement leader Walden Bello what he thought about bilateral agreements replacing the WTO, whose ministerial meetings rarely rise above talking about doing.

"Bilateral and multilateral agreements must make a distinction between those that are based on free trade and those that the U.S. wants to push, together with European Union and partnership agreements," Bello said.

"Are there viable alternatives?" I asked.

"Those multilateral and bilateral agreements are for economic development of the different partners going beyond free trade," explained Bello. "For instance, the option favored by Venezuela and Bolivia is to have a development agreement, not just trade agreements. This is what people in the South are looking for."

"How does NAFTA differ from the Bolivian options offered by Chavez and Morales?" I asked.

"NAFTA's first priority is to serve corporate interests and the WTO," Bello replied. "The North American Free Trade Agreement helps solidify corporate rule globally. The way to go is through South-South accords that are mutual and complementary and you will see more and more of these emerging. The U.S.- and E.U.-initiated bilateral agreements are just as bad as the WTO."

The WTO: An Uneven Playing Field

In October 2005, two months prior to the WTO ministerial in Hong Kong, Pascal Lamy, the trade body's director-general, visited Hong Kong to meet with NGO activists. It was a public relations effort intended to dissuade

NGOs from protesting the WTO's imminent ministerial meeting. However, when Lamy told the activists, "The WTO's core business is not distributing welfare; it is creating wealth," whatever goodwill he had created by meeting with them was destroyed.

Such a statement by the WTO chief underscored the very concerns NGOs continue to raise about the WTO process and its possible outcomes. Lamy's broadside highlighted the widely differing agendas between the G8 and the G20. This dichotomy is now fundamental to the organization's future. Will the WTO pursue the original GATT values of free-trade paradigms for equitable development, or will it become a rich boys' trading club? On this question, the WTO is increasingly unable to offer a platform for a meeting of minds between the developed and underdeveloped worlds.

First, the WTO is *not* a business. It is not run for growth and profit. It is not intended to be used to accumulate wealth for anybody in particular. Part of the problem is that the organization has been misused by some narrow interests and a few dominant nations to benefit themselves. Instead, the WTO should be the biggest NGO of all, representing a broad scope of interests, including removing protectionism—from the struggling developing nations and from the developed nations alike. Instead, the WTO has been evolving in such a way as to now represent an entirely different set of interests and principles from its GATT origins. It should be an umbrella under which government trade representatives and NGOs sit together to work out the sustainability of the movement of goods and services for money and how it impacts people's lives.

Second, the WTO is *not* about creating wealth. It is allowing certain interests to continue to create wealth for themselves; that is, wealth that is being concentrated within the G8 at the expense of much of the rest of the world, which is assured cyclical poverty as a result. While the Western media are quick to comment on the growing gap between rich and poor within China, Lamy's self-stated mission as director-general of the WTO was to openly support a system where certain corporate interests and individuals within certain nations "create wealth" at the expense of impoverishing others. For some reason, no one in the Western media so much as raised an eyebrow at his statements.

The WTO's aims were based upon the original GATT principles of defining and establishing mechanisms to implement the norms and rules of international trade while also evolving the organization into the ultimate arbitrator of trade disputes. Its purpose was to create fair rules and an even playing field, even when some nations have more resources than others.

Apparently, Pascal Lamy thought differently. During his October 2005 visit to Hong Kong, he offered NGOs an apparent concession: the United

States might be persuaded to withdraw its agricultural subsidies; Europe and the G20 would then have to follow. Lamy's motivation was clearly to avert a Cancun-type breakdown in the talks; however, to some extent, he may have precipitated it.

Politics of Subsidies and Evolution of Protectionism

The U.S. spends US$20 billion and the European Union more than US$80 billion annually on agricultural subsidies for fewer than 100 million farmers. Meanwhile, 200 million farmers in China live on less than US$1 per day and some 2.5 billion farmers in other developing countries also live in poverty. China's concerns are shared by Brazil, India, Indonesia, Egypt and a host of developing and underdeveloped nations.

Mike Moore explained the situation to me. "Rich countries spend US$1 billion a day making food more expensive. If there is a subsidy to help poor people we can understand it, but a subsidy to help rich people doesn't make sense. These subsidies are direct transfers from the poor to the rich, but internationally. It is interesting that the agricultural subsidies of places like India go to rich farmers, not poor ones."

"If subsidies—whether in rich or poor countries—create irreparable economic distortions, should they be removed across the board?" I asked.

"The smaller countries need the rules, too, not just the big ones," Moore replied. "Look at fishing subsidies. We have the capacity to over-fish the world's fishing grounds by several hundred percent. So, rich countries put in place billions of dollars of energy subsidies in order to fish the grounds of the poor countries, and the poor fishermen can't compete. These odious subsidies in countries like China create a situation where the poor countries rent their fishing grounds out to rich countries and all that money goes to offshore bank accounts of politicians and bureaucrats. This is one area where green NGOs support the WTO agenda on fishing reform.

These issues create huge problems for government. Either you fish or you lease out the fishing rights, and that money goes directly to the governments or government agents."

In the global order, it is natural that the more powerful countries will try to dominate the weaker ones and to establish economic and political pacts as a way to sustain their dominance. But if the WTO's goal is to strengthen the democratic process among nations in the interests of promoting fair and reasonable international trade, it should ensure that fair trading principles are in place. Only that will allow market access on all sides between developed and developing nations—and strengthen the comparative advantages of each, thereby promoting economic development.

If the WTO really intends to work toward not just free, but equitable, trade, then it should force markets to open not only in developing nations, but also in developed nations, where protectionism is as severe. It should also make possible regional economic integration without allowing protectionist regional blocs to arise.

However, the WTO now encompasses a bundle of cumbersome agreements and economic and trade formulas created in the distorted-reality world of Western think-tanks that it seeks to impose on developing nations. As it becomes clear that one formula cannot fit all, new forums are being sought and nations are seeking a return to reality by looking for regional cooperation. Despite the WTO's intention to create an umbrella to cover all the world's trade, this vision appears less practical for many developing nations.

A more constructive approach than trying to hold together something that is falling apart is to re-engineer it altogether. It would be more appropriate if the WTO sought to establish new mechanisms to promote exports from those developing nations that seek access to the markets of developed nations where protectionism, often in hidden form, is still alive and very much resented by the rest of the world.

The big question that arises is whether the WTO is now too unwieldy an organization to be a suitable platform for resolving international trade disputes and creating a level playing field. Maybe we need to start looking at alternatives and to begin thinking outside of the G8-WTO box. If it is to survive, the WTO needs to evolve into something other than the wealthy nations' wealth-aggregating business that Pascal Lamy suggested it had become.

At the Hong Kong ministerial held two months later, Bo Xilai, then China's commerce minister, told delegates, "If the theme of development only sticks to slogans without any substantive content, the world will be disillusioned by the Doha Round [of trade talks]."

The WTO as an organization carries the baggage of G8 conditionality. While its theoretical agenda is to promote fair trade, it falls short of that goal and appears instead to represent unfair—or at least unbalanced—trading interests. The G8 modules narrow the WTO agenda by excluding the diverse realities that developing nations face. But sooner or later, these must be addressed if "fair trade" is to become the real objective.

Instead of being a champion for fair trade, the WTO has come to be seen as a forum for the G8 to extract trading conditions from lesser-developed nations. The rising volume of protests at ensuing ministerial sessions only underscores these perceptions.

Mike Moore has his own perspective on the evolution of protectionism. "The WTO was created from GATT, which was established at the same time as the IMF and the World Bank," he said. "This was a result of our parents having gone through the Great Depression. Governments panicked, put up barriers and things got worse. There is some instinctive reaction that the tariff is a way to get us out of bad situations."

"But are those mechanisms still relevant? And hasn't the credibility of globalization institutions been shattered since the Asian financial crisis of 1997-98?" I asked.

"In the past few years, even during the Asian financial crisis, governments haven't used those mechanisms," he replied. "We have central banks we didn't have before and a new understanding of trade flows that we didn't have before."

"What about the role of NGOs?" I asked.

Moore surprised me with his response. "NGOs are delivering services governments cannot provide."

I suggested to Moore that perhaps the WTO as an organization isn't being used correctly, as it is not possible to apply the "fast-food" economics espoused by Washington and institutions such as the World Bank and the IMF to every single nation's situation. I suggested the same to Walden Bello.

"There was no need for the WTO in the first place," said Bello. "It only came into being in 1995. Before that we had GATT, which was a fairly flexible system that allowed a number of countries to develop using trade policies and mechanisms of trade substitution. The U.S. pushed for establishment of the WTO under the guise of 'you need global rules to prevent anarchy.' Before 1995 there *was* no anarchy. The U.S. wished to have a set of rules that would enable it to penetrate the world economy and get global leverage. It would also create conditions that would enable it to legitimize its dumping and to monopolize technological innovation with trade-related intellectual property rights. Historically, there was no need for this type of coercive mechanism called the WTO, which is so patently a method for the U.S. and the E.U. to institutionalize their global hegemony. So, the opposite of no WTO isn't anarchy, but space for developing countries to develop."

Endnote

1 Afro-Asian Conference, Algiers, February 26, 1965.

Ǝ

6

REDEFINING CONTEMPORARY DEVELOPMENT
TRASH THE IDEOLOGY AND USE WHAT WORKS

The Third World ought not to be content to define itself in terms of the values which have preceded it. On the contrary, the underdeveloped countries ought to do their utmost to find their own particular values and methods and a style which shall be peculiar to them.

—Frantz Fanon, *The Wretched of the Earth*

China's Value Dilemma

During my years in Beijing, I had participated as an outside advisor in China's reform process and had long been an advocate of its fresh approach to capitalism ("state capitalism," as opposed to the IMF-World Bank's market capitalism). But I also had concerns about the direction in which China's economy and social structure were headed. By 2008, I saw overall deterioration expressed by corruption, crime, prostitution, gambling and alcoholism. It seemed that liquor had become China's new opium. So, while China's economic model had seen the country succeed in material terms, it had left a gaping spiritual void. Quantity of life had displaced quality of life.

The Chinese model of macro-control development had worked very successfully in merging the tools of state planning with the market mechanism. But now, having adopted a Western—almost American—value standard of conspicuous consumption as a measure of human worth, it had become a country where human values were being smothered by greed and where corruption was perpetuated by the desire to accumulate brand-name goods. How could China now serve as a future model to anyone else?

Part of the problem is that China's leadership still adheres strictly to a philosophy of dialectical materialism. This is one reason why it has been so easy for Western multinationals to convert the population to consumer-brand fanaticism. In turn, China has lost much of its own culture over the past decade. In this cultural free-fall state, its leaders are now groping for a way forward. Unfortunately, they have yet to look seriously to their own roots in trying to grow the tree to its next stage.

In 2005, I had the opportunity to serve as an intermediary between Beijing and the Dalai Lama in the hope of restarting a dialogue between the two sides. During a private meeting I had with the Tibetan spiritual leader in 2005, he expressed his view. "China seeks a new ideology," he noted. "Marxism succeeded and worked for two decades. Then it became confused. This is because class struggle fostered hatred. Our teaching is non-violence. Now, the market ideology of capitalism has failed to build a meaning-ful society. Cultural heritage is easily destroyed. The Chinese Communist Party feels now that people must have money and this will give the party credibility. It must learn from the U.S. and Europe that money alone does not fulfill human beings."

The Dalai Lama went on: "China is an ancient nation. Money is not sufficient. China is seeking a new spirituality. Tibetan Buddhism is our own culture. They [the party] find it easier to accept [Buddhism] rather than Western religions such as Christianity. With Buddhism in the spiritual field we can help with internal values, while the Chinese provide external values, and both will have mutual benefit. They will understand our centuries-old culture is rich. They will then respect Tibetan culture more and understand what we mean by our demand for meaningful autonomy."

In America, we have attempted to meld other cultures into one "plastic" culture that has little depth and stands for nothing at all. Ethnicity was uprooted through two centuries of genocide of Native Americans by Christian fundamentalists. Today, much of the society is materially rich but spiritually impoverished. China is repeating this pattern. Minority cultural groups in America turn to rap music as an expression of their ethnicity, in the search for roots that have long been severed. In China, their lyrics are censored.

Buddhism and Islam are the fastest growing religions in America. One might ask why. Arguably, both are philosophies more than religions, based on clear concepts of equality among all before nature, and the sense of community with a clear cultural identity—*ulma* in the case of Islam, and *sangha* in Buddhism. Will these communities also grow as fast in China?

How Sustainable is China's Economic Model?

During the Tang dynasty, the poet Du Fu commented on the social inequities of the time, penning a poem on the debauchery prevalent among corrupt officials and the wealthy:

"Within vermilion gates wine and meat rot, while on the street outside people starve to death."

Today, the finest seafood in the world and the most expensive imported wines are available in Beijing's five-star restaurants. Outside, luxury cars disgorge officials and entrepreneurs with their wives or mistresses, who vie for the title of "Most expensively dressed" or "Most recently returned from an expensive overseas trip" (probably paid for from state coffers as a government "inspection" or "study tour").

Meanwhile, at the end of 2007, official statistics put the number of impoverished people in rural China who simply do not have enough to eat at 23.65 million. In addition, 40.67 million low-income earners are searching for a way out of their desperate situation. Crime, drug use, prostitution and even human slavery rackets have now become pillar industries of the Chinese economy. If one were to raise the problem with Beijing officials dining in the posh Maison Boulud à Pékin, Beijing's first Michelin-rated restaurant, they would likely simply wave away these issues as problems of the *waidi ren,* "those rural outsiders." China's new class system now appears to be more about caste than class.

Many international economists have expressed concern about the widening income gap in China, and have questioned the sustainability of the country's economic model. With the gap between rural and urban incomes stretching beyond what anyone might have predicted only a decade ago, China's Gini coefficient has reached the internationally acknowledged warning limit of 0.4. This has set alarm bells ringing in Zhongnanhai, the central government headquarters in Beijing.

In August 2006, the Central Committee of the Communist Party of China (CPC) called a symposium of various interest groups, including the All-China Federation of Industry and Commerce, so-called democratic parties, and a host of non-communist social representatives. The purpose of summoning so many groups from across the board was to discuss how to cope with the issue of "reforming and standardizing income." From another perspective, it might have been seen as a massive lobbying effort to keep a social pact between the CPC and the rest of society, given that it is mostly government officials and the managers of state-owned enterprises who are spending lavishly on five-star lifestyles, while rural China struggles with survival. The fact that the meeting was held within the secure Zhongnanhai compound underscored the importance and sensitivity of current CPC concerns over the problem.

I have always succeeded in shocking Americans by saying that they and Western Europeans are the best practitioners of Marxism. Marx envisioned violent social revolution arising from class struggle due to the widening income gaps that arose during the Industrial Revolution. Developed Western economies avoid this inevitability by constructing a massive, multilayered middle class that keeps the rich from having to deal with an uprising from the poor, as so many interests are vested in between.

China's per-capita GDP ranges somewhere between US$1,000 and US$3,000, depending on the region. This figure symbolizes the success of two decades of reforms, which have raised incomes across the board. It also heralds an era of new problems also being experienced by other developing countries such as Indonesia. As long as income is stable without widening gaps, society remains naturally stable. As income gaps widen, social contradictions intensify and the probability of turbulent situations arising with short notice can increase sharply. There is no magic behind this formula. It is not Marxism per se. Rather, it is quite straightforward common sense.

It was these very concerns about income disparities that allowed Marxist ideals to filter into Peking University in the first half of the last century, where people such as Mao Zedong became inspired to overthrow the existing system with all of its inequities. Certainly, the increasing impoverishment of rural China was the fundamental basis of Mao's constituency.

China then had a government lacking in principles that catered to foreign economic interests, who basically controlled all exports, manufacturing and domestic consumer brand consumption. Obviously, the situation today could be said to be starting to resemble the past, and the wounds that existed in the old society could be re-opening. If Mao's ghost were listening in on the meeting held in August 2006 at Zhongnanhai, what suggestions might he have made?

"China has enjoyed three decades of high economic growth by whatever indicator, and without domestic violence," explained Huang Ping, director-general of the American Studies Institute at the Chinese Academy of Social Sciences (CASS). His argument glosses over the brutal crackdown against protests in 1989, and the fact that—despite the draconian police system—in recent years the number of violent demonstrations by farmers, factory workers, and dissatisfied urbanities has been running as high as 80,000 incidents a year, often involving as many as 0,000 rioters. Many of the protests have targeted government and police brutality, sometimes resulting in the burning of police cars and the destruction of government offices.

Huang Ping has an intimate knowledge of the Washington Consensus development models, it having been his job to research them. Moreover, he is considered the nation's leading specialist on social harmony. Unlike many other Chinese think-tank specialists, he dares to espouse new ideas that challenge head-on the past models that see GDP growth as a panacea.

"Despite all of our problems, 200 million people have emerged into a new middle class, while another 300 million have been lifted out of poverty," Huang noted. "What has happened is probably the world's largest-scale development miracle since Britain's Industrial Revolution." At the same time, Huang is aware of the problems that have accompanied that growth. "It has led to growing income gaps, social governance problems, and environmental desecration as the costs of such development and transformation." Whether these costs are an acceptable trade-off is currently the subject of intense debate among Chinese state officials and future planners.

China's super-development has occurred within a short period of time and on a stupendous scale. Nearly three decades of 9% growth led one billion people out of the poverty that resulted from the policy excesses of China's Great Leap Forward and Cultural Revolution. Such growth has also been achieved without China expanding its borders or engaging in wars against other nations, as has been the historic experience of many empires and superpowers, both past and present. However, the speed of growth has had its costs and repercussions. Policies now generally viewed as successful have given rise to entirely new sets of problems that are destabilizing and threatening to unravel the system. Topping the list are corruption, blind materialism, flagrant disregard of the environment, and the evisceration of Chinese traditional social values, the very fabric that has kept the society intact over two millennia. To a large extent, while China has rejected the hard-line models of the IMF and the World Bank, it has accepted—lock, stock and barrel—the materialist, consumption-driven values promoted by the advocates of American-style globalization.

Will this be China's century—or the era of its collapse? Or will it be the era when China becomes a global threat? Pessimists among certain Western think-tanks and academic institutions predict an imminent end to China's mega-growth cycle. These views may be extreme and represent protectionist fears expressed in wishful doomsday scenarios. Cold War thinking has resurfaced in theories and books. The optimists, usually business analysts who point to another decade of sustained hyper-growth, counter these views. China has always bent with the winds of change, they argue. So why should the future be any different? The truth and what transpires in the future may fall somewhere in between these two opposing views.

The "China threat" may not be in the form of military expansion or the flooding of world markets with cheap exports. It may instead take the form of environmental desecration, stimulating the acceleration of global warming; that would indeed menace all humanity. Or perhaps there will be a combination of all these factors in different degrees.

Another view emerging within some circles among Beijing think-tanks is that the pressure is on to find a practical road forward and not to get lost in the illusion that the past two decades of growth is sustainable. But can China's current leaders think outside of the box and formulate new agendas to cope with the future?

Much of the work of coming up with new development blueprints and ideological platforms is being thrown to the Beijing think-tanks. They are talking about these issues openly—even in the local press—which has never occurred before. Admittedly, even if a problem is not completely solvable, identifying and discussing it is a first step toward addressing it. At least it is better than smearing it over with dogma, as was done in the past.

Huang Ping noted that Beijing think-tanks are even going so far as to question "whether we have followed the Western model too closely without consciousness of its negative effects." Such think-tanks are challenging the consumption-driven, materialism-based model China has adopted and are instead calling for new paradigms of development. But will they find them?

Time for a Great Leap Sideways?

"Globalization is a misnomer," said Huang Ping. "All nations want globalization in technology trade. So, a better phrase would be 'global integration of technology and science.' But when this means the Americanization of the world, it runs counter not only to China's political and economic structure, but to its historic culture and sociological structure as well."

Huang noted that an "us-vs.-them, black-vs.-white" attitude was the main problem in Western thinking. In China, however, during the reform years of the 1990s, the curtain on ideology went down and a brief era of enormous flexibility prevailed, under Deng's notion that "It doesn't matter if a cat is white or black as long as it catches mice," or whatever works economically is good. During this brief window of open thinking an inherent flexibility in responding to changing conditions made it possible to fuse various approaches to economic development—capitalist and socialist, market and planning—which has led to the country's current economic boom and prosperity.

Now, despite this boom, China's development model is being tested. For Beijing's leaders during the 1990s, achieving a market economy was the overarching goal. For its current leadership, the hypermarket economy poses new burdens: the country does not have the energy to support its own growth, the environment has been degraded, and the social order has been frayed. As a consequence, Beijing's economic think-tanks are asking if a better model can be developed. Actually, the real problem probably lies in corruption and excesses of privilege imbued with the Communist Party, which has created an almost-surreal Orwellian-Dickensian system. Culture and ethical values—the mainstays of Chinese society for two millennia— were bulldozed as infrastructure and property projects went ahead.

The antithesis of this can be seen in pockets of community rebuilding efforts among ethnic minorities and the rural poor, involving more than the usual infrastructure and road development. Huang commented: "It involves trying to understand how people communicate and share values, cope with problems, and identify issues of security and solidarity." Places such as Lijiang and Zhongdian, in Yunnan province, are going against the national development trend. Rather than emphasizing infrastructure and the growth of GDP, their long-term interest is the preservation of culture and the environment.

A new national ideology is necessary in order to plan for the next 20 years. Globalization, and models associated with it, is neither a goal nor a panacea where ideologies are concerned. Neo-liberalism and neo-conservatism offer nothing of value to China or the developing world. At the same time, it isn't practical to go back to Marxism, which China has already shed. It is also unlikely that many other nations would embrace it. And Confucian thinking is one of the Chinese Communist Party's biggest problems: the party is more a classical Confucian bureaucracy than an egalitarian body.

The Himalayan Consensus: 84,000 Paths of Development

Imagine the challenge to our economic assumptions coming from the rooftop of the world. Nyima Tsering, the most senior monk in Lhasa's Jokhang Monastery, is one of the most forward-looking people I've ever met. From his contemplative position in one of Tibet's oldest monasteries, he is in tune with the changing pulse of the world and he's prepared to challenge established beliefs.

" 'Globalization' as a term has come to mean a singular way of applying things—economic, financial, social-behavioral and political—to the world in an attempt to make the world into one monolithic system," said Nyima Tsering. "How can this be achieved? Our world is about diversity among cultures, climates, people, their way of life, and beliefs. So how can everyone melt into one global culture, one economic and political system, one set of values?

"The terms 'globalization' and 'anti-globalization' are probably misnomers. Everyone can support the globalization of technology, pharmaceuticals, HIV cures, social programs, and disaster relief. But globalizing one financial-economic system, or one political ideology and its bipartisan mechanisms, doesn't make sense when imposed on peoples whose historical and cultural experiences are vastly different," he said.

"This so-called globalization approach of telling other people in other countries and cultures that 'my way is the best, and yours is not' just represents ignorance. Then when they want to follow their own path, these globalization types get angry. Why are they pushing their system on others to begin with?"

The Washington Consensus, comprising IMF and World Bank theorists, argues that if everyone buys into the one system—*their* system—it will solve all the world's ills. However, this approach actually has the opposite effect of antagonizing people when systems entirely inapplicable to their culture and lifestyle are imposed upon them.

Nyima Tsering gestured toward the adobe rooftop of the monastery. "Why are there so many different religions? How can you say only one system applies to all? In Buddhism, we accept the diversity of *all* sects—*all religions,* for that matter. Look at us. Are we all the same? Do we all have the same interests, tastes, desires, moods, education, culture or background? Of course not! So, why should we try to put everyone into one mold? It cannot be achieved, nor should it. Everyone's acceptance of ideas and motivations is different, so the methods we adopt to achieve the same goal can be different as well."

The point is that globalization, in itself, is not the goal, but perhaps just a tool—and maybe not the best one.

"So, then, what is the goal?" I asked.

The philosopher-monk reflected for a moment before replying: "Regardless of where people are in the world, they all want the same thing: happiness in life, which comes from less suffering. Only by reducing suffering can we have happiness. The role of any political or economic system, regardless of its form, is to give happiness to its people by reducing their suffering. One goal, that's it. You cannot take a single model and smash it on to the heads of others and expect them to accept it. In fact, the result of this approach will create even more of a mess. This approach is too simplistic. We need to think rationally."

"The advocates of globalization and the mainstream Western

media dismiss the anti-globalization movement as not offering any viable alternatives," I said. "But *are* there any?"

Nyima Tsering responded immediately: "In Buddhism we have 84,000 paths a practitioner can follow. Each is different. That means there can be all kinds of models for development, for economics or politics, or for living. Each suits different people's needs. No one model is correct for all. The only requirement is to use rational thinking, and care and compassion for others, in finding one's own way. You don't want to hurt others along the way in seeking your own path. This should be the precondition.

"It is unfortunate how social values are created through advertising and mass-media consumer trends. For many people, possessing a famous luxury brand becomes the very identification of their status, of their human worth. But actually, these things are often not even as good or enduring in quality as this rug we are now sitting on.

"With the current globalization of consumer-driven values, people think it is so important that they own famous luxury brands. Often, people will spend their life working to save money just to buy these things. They will live a life of frustration, spending, and even borrowing beyond their means to have these brand symbols to show others that they have achieved worth in the eyes of mainstream society. In fact, these brands are worthless, empty symbols, the result of advertising and promotion in an illusory mass media, which misleads people into following paths of ignorance and greed. So, they are wasting their lives on totally meaningless pursuits. Think of how many positive things could be accomplished if this same energy and effort were put into benefiting our world, rather than chasing illusions of so-called luxury."

In an ancient Tibetan monastery 3,600 meters above sea level, a single monk is challenging the accepted world financial order. What can be done to change it? Certainly, Dow Jones, Time Warner and Rupert Murdoch—the forces that control what we read and hear—would never advocate anything or anyone who might question these foundations, especially a meditating monk from Tibet who is proposing that the Washington Consensus be displaced by a new one.

"What we are talking about now is the need for a new economic system," said Nyima Tsering. "The 21st century has taught us that materialism alone is not enough. Spirituality can overcome materialism. We need an economic system that can combine wisdom and compassion with materialism. Then our world will become a real Shambhala."

Redefining Development

Sometimes an entire philosophy grows from a simple, humble idea. Carter Malik is an American woman who grew up in Nepal and has spent much of her life in Asia. Active in seeking community cohesiveness through cottage-industry programs, she understands the potentially powerful and positive impact of small-scale development. Today, she is one of the key driving forces encouraging sustainable development through a fusion of eco-tourism and artisan revival in Shangri-la. Malik lives in a restored ancient Tibetan home on a "street of the Tea Caravan Trail" that runs right through Shangri-la's old town, now under heritage protection.

"Shangri-la" is the name given to the Diqing Tibetan Autonomous Prefecture in Yunnan province. The local community of three million people integrates some 15 ethnic groups, including Tibetan, Lisu, Naxi, Mosu and Yi, living side-by-side. The county governor-cum-party secretary, a Tibetan named Qi Zhala, has become known for taking a unique approach to development. He is focusing on quality—rather than quantity—of life, and is taking the view that the natural beauty and ethnicity of this region are assets to be preserved, rather than liabilities to be obliterated tor the sake of development, as in some other parts of China. Eco-tourism is the all-encompassing development model of Diqing, which is one of the world's 200 most highly bio-diverse regions, filled with animal and plant species under threat of extinction. This is all the more reason to find a sustainable model of development based on preservation.

Learning of Carter Malik's work, and inspired by the visionary experiment being led by Qi Zhala, I visited Shangri-la. If "sustainable development based on preservation" sounds like something of an oxymoron, Carter Malik certainly believes in it and established the Yunnan Mountain Heritage Foundation (YMHF) to prove that it can work. Having lived in Nepal and Uzbekistan, Malik understands the intrinsic value of local cottage industry in developing economies. Cottage industry contributes a major part of GDP for India, Thailand and Nepal, and provides employment while pre-serving culture. Malik brought this experience to Shangri-la. The county's perceptive and forward-thinking leader, Qi, immediately welcomed her expertise.

Malik refers to herself not as a development expert—which she really is—but as just "a friend of Shangri-la." Her modest assessment of her role is in sharp contrast to the self-importance of visiting World Bank and IMF economists, whose theories and models typically have no relevance to life outside of their five-star hotel's conference room. In contrast, Malik rolls up her sleeves and becomes intimately involved in hands-on work, becoming an integral part of the community around her. "All I would like is to lend a hand in the process of bringing sustainable tourism development to this exquisite region," she explained.

Upon arriving in Shangri-la, Malik recognized immediately that several development factors could be built upon. "First, Diqing is a key stop on the 'Tea Caravan Trail,' with the movement and trade of *pu'er*—tea—as a central cultural theme." The ancient Tea Caravan Trail once linked rich tea-growing Yunnan with India, via the Tibetan plateau. Tea from China went by pony-back to India. Buddhist scriptures came to China when the ponies returned. "Fair trade" began here!

"Second are the multi-ethnic handicraft traditions of this region along the Trail," she said. Malik observed that in nearby Lijiang, a heritage-protected city of ancient Naxi architecture built around charming interconnecting canals, products from other parts of China and from other ethnic groups had displaced the local Naxi handicrafts. She didn't want this to happen in Diqing.

"The seemingly more pressing requirement was eco-tourism," she recalled, "and how to integrate handicrafts into a larger heritage package of preserving traditional lifestyles of which handicrafts is an important conduit." Malik realized that her role would be to bring expertise to Shangri-la to help preserve its traditions.

"Because a good part of the population lives in rural communities, we see handicrafts as an earning link between them and the tourist community," she explained. "So, we need products tourists can buy. They have handicrafts they use in their own culture, and these are often made to be developed into sustainable craft industries for tourists and international community lifestyles as well."

Following the establishment of the YMHF, Carter Malik arranged for a team of six social-work students from Hong Kong Polytechnic University to undertake research in Shangri-la and to compile an oral history of the women there. The results of the study offered a fascinating perspective on quality of life and happiness, and the need to balance these against rapid growth, which is often the only standard by which development is judged. Interestingly, the community of women in Shangri-la is tightly bonded, sharing the traditional jobs of harvesting barley in the fields, tending the herds of yak and undertaking traditional communal craftwork.

Traditionally, men of the area worked on the tea caravans. Today, they head to the towns to work as taxi drivers, truck drivers and construction workers, where they face the frustrations and cost pressures of urban life.

The women are more satisfied with their lives because of their sense of being part of a local community. Being farmers and yak breeders, they do not feel the need for more education. But should their children have more schooling opportunities? The advent of modern tourism brought this question to the fore as the villagers began making crafts for a changing economic environment. To produce items that tourists wanted, the women came to Malik in search of ideas and designs.

"To stimulate production and development, it is not necessary to be manufacturing handicrafts ourselves as a foundation, but rather to let local women really understand the beauty and value of what they make. For the tourist market, they really need to just stick to their traditional designs with appropriate modifications. They weave yak wool carpets, pillow covers, bedspreads and door covers. The Shangri-la Women's Centre [founded by Malik] is important as a first step in this process, but we must keep in perspective the greater eco-tourism issues."

Malik also spearheaded the "Workshop on Developing a National Park System in Shangri-la," held in January 2006. The initiative aimed to set a blueprint for eco-tourism and culturally sustainable development that could be used both in Shangri-la and as a model for other regions facing similar dilemmas of balancing external pressures for modernization and development against cultural heritage and environmental preservation. Participating were members of the Diqing Tourism Bureau, Diqing Forestry Department, professors and directors from Southwest Forestry University, Kunming University and Tsinghai University in Beijing, as well as representatives from the World Tourism Organization (UNWTO), a specialized agency of the United Nations, the International Centre for Integrated Mountain Development (ICIMOD), the International Union for Conservation of Nature and Natural Resources (ICUN), the World Wildlife Fund (WWF), the Nature Conservancy, and eco-tourism investors from abroad. The aim of the workshop was to draw up a practical strategy for future sustainable tourism growth in the region, which could be used as an example for other regions to consider, as well as to draw up a "best practices compendium of eco-tourism procedures for development."

Malik hopes that this initiative will be a catalyst for integrating larger natural areas under unified legislation and development standards, and that it will prevent "wildcat developers" from grabbing land, by protecting villagers' rights to their own land, discouraging them from selling it off to developers, and laying down the conditions for development.

True Development

Qi Zhala is ethnic Tibetan. Clearly, he doesn't look like a Communist Party cadre from China. Qi takes great pride in wearing a dark Tibetan robe with long sleeves. He chooses to meet me not in a stiff, formal government conference room, but on a simple wooden bench, on a nameless street along the Tea Caravan Trail, in the old section of Zhongdian, the former capital of Shangri-la county.

Qi Zhala knows who he is and is perfectly at ease in his hometown. While other cities in China are busy destroying their old precincts, obliterating their own heritage in the name of development, Qi has placed old Zhongdian under a heritage protection order. He has banned plastic bags, ordered that the ancient forests be protected, and banished industrial investors from the town. Moreover, he shuns the national trend of relying on GDP growth as the only measure of development.

The Shangri-la approach is in stark contrast to Beijing's. China's capital razed much of the old city for the Olympics, destroying virtually everything of heritage value except for places such as the Forbidden City. "We think differently," Qi Zhala says confidently, dismissing Beijing's development model. "The old should be preserved, with cultural protection as the central objective. Some cities tear down their old sections and replace them with steel-and-cement structures. We have chosen a separate path—to protect the old heritage, because history is continuity. Preserving our culture within is true heritage protection."

Qi Zhala points to Lhasa's Barkor Lijiang and Dali as well-preserved cities, and examples to be followed. But for the most part, cities in China have followed the capital's example, mimicking the architecture of Las Vegas, and adopting an American appearance of faceless gas stations, fast-food drive-ins and tomb-like shopping malls. China's national architecture today is all about cement structures covered with bathroom tiles and blue glass. The whole country seems fixated upon Freudian bathroom fixtures as decoration themes.

"We recognized the problem early and are determined to tear down the tiles and blue glass, creating a Tibetan look for the new city structures using original materials," said Qi Zhala. He personally ordered that all new buildings have facades of Tibetan stone and adobe, and wooden window frames. "It is not just face-masking the city," he insists, "but reviving the original Tibetan architectural style and heritage in the new city. As for the old city, it will not be touched." Greedy developers are warned to think twice.

"Shangri-la is a rare ecosystem zone," said Qi Zhala, "with an enormous diversity of environment, ecology and culture. So it needs to be protected. Protecting the environment, architecture and traditional culture, along with the supporting sectors, is an integrated effort. Forests, water and mountains need accelerated protection measures that also involve fighting pollution and garbage." Qi became a near-legend in Yunnan when he forbade the use of plastic bags in Zhongdian. Since then, he has regulated agricultural pesticides, applying strict requirements to protect soil sustainability and prevent adverse side-effects.

Where Beijing's city government, in the name of development, has obliterated its cultural heritage and turned the capital into an environmental debacle, Shangri-la's approach to development emphasizes protecting the indigenous culture. "We feel our environment is part of our human heritage," said Qi Zhala. "Too often in striving for development, we ignore the interrelationship between the two, and yet it is essential to our own human diversity and the sustainability of mankind."

Qi believes that by keeping traditional lifestyles intact, Tibetan values can be preserved. "Tibetans by nature will protect the environment, because that, in itself, is integral to their culture." As long as their culture and value system can be protected, they will protect their own environment. The reverse of this can be seen in those Han Chinese areas of the country that have bulldozed their heritage, losing in the process both their culture and their environment.

"When we talk about ecological protection, we must talk about our Tibetan culture," Qi Zhala said. "We Tibetans herd animals, which is a traditional occupation in conflict with industrial development. We do not need industrial development here in Zhongdian."

Qi's approach goes smack up against the heavy-handed and large-scale industrial approach toward growth favored by institutions such as the IMF and World Bank. Moreover, it runs counter to the Chinese hyper-GDP growth model promoted by the state planners-cum-capitalists in Beijing. However, using the "small is beautiful" approach, emphasizing traditional values in the context of gradual, sustainable economic growth, Qi Zhala offers an alternative.

"We have selected sectors to develop, such as traditional herding, agriculture and crafts. We do not want the kind of industrial development that will destroy our ecosystem," he explained, sitting on a rough-hewn log bench in the old cowboy town that is Zhenjiang's heritage. "People and nature should be in a close relationship. They should not be in conflict. Nature is not to be destroyed, or we will destroy ourselves."

How does he feel about his county being called "Shangri-la," I ask? Is it an official label for commercial tourism development purposes, or does the name have a deeper meaning?

"Shangri-la may only be an ideal from a philosophical perspective," he explained. "But a place where humanity and environment are in harmony, and where spirituality exceeds materialism, is an ideal that *can* be achieved.

"Real development involves the question of environmental and ethnic heritage protection. Recognizing and protecting what is really important represents true development. Actually, ecological protection is a sector unto itself. This sector fits our traditional lifestyle and our own region. We have chosen it."

How does he feel about all the development models imposed on underdeveloped nations? What about the pressure from Beijing to industrialize and urbanize? How does Qi balance the two?

"The total picture of development is not just high-rise buildings and smoke stacks," he said. "Sure, you can urbanize yourselves, but this doesn't necessarily mean you are developed. Development is not only large-scale industrialization. We have over 300,000 people here. We see development from a larger perspective.

"For us, protecting our mountains, forests and lifestyle is *true* development."

З

7

THE ENVIRONMENTAL PRIORITY
WE ARE RUINING THE EARTH FASTER THAN
THE GLOBAL ECONOMY IS GROWING

You are not a stranger in Umuofia. You know as well as I do that our forefathers ordained that before we plant any crops in the earth we should observe a week in which a man does not say a harsh word to his neighbor. We live in peace with our fellows to honor our great goddess of the earth without whose blessing our crops will not grow. You have committed a great evil. His staff came down again. The evil you have done can ruin the whole clan. The earth goddess whom you have insulted may refuse to give us her increase, and we shall all perish.

—Chinua Achebe, *Things Fall Apart*

Connecting the Dots

Following the opening of the rail link between Lhasa and Beijing in the summer of 2006, I met John Vincent Bellezza, a visiting scholar at the University of Virginia and a member of Oxford University's Bon Translation Project. He showed up at my home in Lhasa dressed like Indiana Jones, somewhat reminiscent of Himalaya explorers of another era. Bellezza has spent more than two decades researching Bon (pre-Buddhist) archaeological sites in Tibet, and has written five books on the subject. Having traveled to virtually every township in upper Tibet, he has seen more than any tourist could imagine.

An expert on Tibet's lost Xiang Xiong civilization (a vast empire that stretched across the Himalayas between 1000 BC and AD 700), Bellezza draws parallels between that civilization and our current one. "Climatic change made the environment colder and dryer, leading to the economic collapse of the means of production. The average tourist will be looking at a bunch of rocks and ruins, but there is an object lesson that can be learned here."

Sometimes we forget to take lessons from our past, he says. "Climatic change can lead to the demise of even very powerful civilizations, even those that seem very adapted to their environment or with strong military and technological capabilities, such as Xiang Xiong. Even though civilization is now undergoing globalization, it could potentially suffer the same fate. So we should take the lessons of Xiang Xiong seriously. We need to work quickly to ameliorate the negative impact that our societies are having in the modern world."

Is it realistic to think that China might take the lead in the global fight against environmental degradation when it is one of the main culprits, I asked?

"I think China can," said Bellezza. "It is a large country in terms of geography and population. It possesses many of the world's most important ecosystems, and at the same time it is developing rapidly. Thus, China is in an excellent position to affect the environmental quality of the planet in the decades to come through protection of its biodiversity and natural habitats, and through safeguarding its ethnic-minority cultures whose lifestyles are integral to environmental protection."

I asked Bellezza what role Tibet could play in this process.

"Tibet is important because it possesses four or five world-class ecosystems," he replied. "These natural environments are unique on the planet and include grasslands, deserts, jungles, and alpine forests. Tibet is extremely valuable as a planetary natural asset, because it possesses these vital natural resources."

The key steps are to protect both Tibet's delicate ecosystems and its cultural heritage.

"In order to protect the natural and cultural heritage of Tibet, China must once again look to its ancient traditions in both Taoism and Buddhism, where harmony with nature and society are supreme values."

Bellezza is suggesting that by protecting Tibet's heritage, China may find a path forward in creating its own ethos for the new era. Can it? How?

"Tibetan Buddhism, in particular, could prove to be of great value," said Bellezza. "It has a highly developed ethical system based on its sophisticated understanding of the nature of reality. In Tibetan Buddhism, all physical and biological aspects of the world are seen as being interconnected. Plants, animals and people constitute 'sentient beings' possessing intrinsic spiritual value."

This is a concept very alien to the hard-line political administrations in both Beijing and Washington.

"According to this view," said Bellezza, "even such an insignificant living creature as an ant or a worm has the same right to exist as a human being, because it is thought that since the beginning of time, these living beings have all undergone the process of cyclical evolution. This means that every being is dependent upon every other being."

This may seem like exotic mumbo-jumbo for cynics in Washington and Beijing, but scientifically it makes sense. All aspects of our global ecosystem are interrelated. The giant, historically unprecedented tidal waves that struck coasts of South and Southeast Asia during Christmas week in 2004 were connected to global warming. Earthquakes that devastated western China in spring and summer 2008 are as well. A seriously ill planet is undergoing retching convulsions. Ultimately this is connected to the size of the car we drive and how much fuel we use. This in turn is linked to our own personal consumption, driven by the values of what we believe makes life worth living. It is all interconnected.

China's Toxic Shock

The other side of the problem, far from Lhasa, can be seen in Beijing Riviera, one of the many artificial suburban communities in the suburbs of the Chinese capital. Reminiscent of a scene from a Norman Rockwell painting, the foreign ghetto seems incongruous—even "tacky"—in this rural suburban setting. By day, it looks as sanitized as a hospital ward; by night, it's as lit up as the Rockefeller Center at Christmas.

Beijing Riviera stands as an icon of globalization, of how global Americanization has supplanted the traditional values of Chinese society. The hoped-for fusion of those traditional values with modernization has been forgotten, submerged by the crass materialism that so offended Naomi Klein, author of *No Logo,* and which overtook China over the past dozen years.

Beijing's overdeveloped highway network is clogged by massive traffic jams, and the city chokes under a thick film of carbon-concentrated smog. But this is only the tip of Beijing's energy-wasteful and polluting bio-system, which, along with that of the United States, is threatening our very existence. Indian economist and activist Lawrence Surendra commented to me at the Gross National Happiness Congress in Bangkok in 2007, "In a recent talk on climate change, I spoke about the physical death of humanity due to climate change, but also about how, before that, our 'humanity' is dying and will continue to die before we actually perish as a species.

This I feel applies to both the visible, loud protestors against globalization and to those who direct it and benefit by it."

Ironically, "transportation isn't the largest emissions factor," explained Mark Dembitz, vice president of Carbon Capital in Beijing. "Most polluting carbon emissions actually come from inefficient insulation of buildings, rather than from automobiles and air transport." Certainly, Beijing will take the Olympic gold medal in excessive construction of inefficiently insulated and wastefully tit-up buildings. Large areas of cement and glass used in the construction of office and apartment complexes make them energy-inefficient and expensive to heat. Beijing, for all of its pre-OIympics fervor of construction, is a disaster zone in terms of insulation, and the city will pay for its shortsightedness in this respect in the future. The residents of Beijing will also pay a huge cost of an expected sharp rise in environmental pollution-related diseases, which may bring the city's overburdened and hopelessly corrupt medical system to its knees.

The numbers are revealing. China's GDP has been growing at a rate of 10% per annum for the past two decades, and its use of energy is continuing to skyrocket. But the country is naturally poor in energy resources, with the exception of coal, of which it has billions of tons. To keep up with the demand for electricity, the nation is now building one 500-megawatt coal-fired plant every two weeks. However, coal is one of the least efficient and dirtiest forms of energy and a major producer of carbon emissions. Coal burning has an efficiency rate of only 20-30%, with some 70% wasted without generating electricity. This rate of waste production will be disastrous for China's—and the world's—environment, if the situation doesn't change soon.

Carbon Capital is a pioneer in introducing non-polluting technology into China as part of a sophisticated system of international trading of carbon credits. Dembitz explained to me how such a credit project works: "We completely create the project for a polluting factory that has no incentive not to pollute. We say, 'Let us come in and give you a piece of technology to reduce pollution.' Then we will ask them to use it. We will teach them how to tip waste, install gas connections, and capture methane out of landfill pumps through a generator to create electricity."

Creating electricity from methane and earning carbon credits for reducing emissions helps on two fronts. Instead of methane escaping from the landfill, it is captured and used to generate power from a clean source. It is then sold back to the grid or used in creating carbon credits. The landfill process enjoys upgraded technology, and training is provided in how to "tip" waste in more efficient ways to maximize land use. The tipping policy also reduces the amount of smell, a common problem from sewage back-up in China's cities. Everyone wins.

Dembitz is attempting to build awareness in China of alternative, more efficient, energy sources and methods—such as powering lighting systems from solar sources, which have no carbon emissions. "Some developers are trying to be more careful about what they are building," he said. "But if you are taking energy from the grid created by coal, then an increase in demand will rack up the amount of coal-fired plants needed, along with subsequent pollution."

Unfortunately, this is what is happening in China today. Bureaucrats' emphasis on super-fast GDP growth is outweighing the need to ensure that such growth can be sustainable and without toxic or lethal side-effects. There are now tens of thousands of American-style kitsch communities and shopping malls spreading across China fueled on the carbon grid. The taste today is for big and bright, the energy inefficiency of which heralds an environmental disaster for China in the coming years. In 2008, as China hosted the Olympics, it surpassed the United States not only in athletic gold medals, but as the world's biggest emitter of greenhouse gases.

River Story

A Chinese folk song says poetically of the Yangtze: "A river's spring water flows east." Now, reflecting the changing times, a more popular version warns: "A river's poisoned water flows east." The Yangtze, China's "great dragon," is dangerously polluted, with 90% of the industrial enterprises along its banks releasing pollutants into its waters. Of all human wastewater dumped into the Yangtze, 30% isn't treated. And it all flows east, where most of the population is concentrated.

While environmental protection has become a slogan of the National People's Congress and Chinese People's Political Consultative Conference annual meetings, their promises have produced little concrete action. The State Council in 2006 promised to reduce energy consumption by 4% and the discharge of pollutants by 2% per annum during the eleventh five-year plan (2006-10). More than one year on, these goals have not yet begun to be met. This means that China will need to play catch-up—a poor start to what observers feel is a hopeless cause, given the country's gargantuan industrial needs and growing desire for luxury goods (15% growth in 2007 alone).

Although the plan calls for a reduction in pollution discharge, it also envisions massive industrial programs for eight cities along the Yangtze, the pollutants from which would be pumped into the river. Apparently, the convenience of transporting energy upstream and finished goods downstream, and of dumping waste in the river, has outweighed considerations of people's long-term future.

Such environmental damage also may cause the extinction of a nationally protected species, the white dolphin, which once inhabited the Yangtze delta but no longer exists in the area. In the 1990s, 150 dolphins lived in the region. In December 2006, a six-nation group of scientists spent

38 days in a search of 1,750 kilometers of the river. No white dolphins were seen. In Yichang, a city on the Yangtze in Hubei province, Chinese tourists are shown by the proud authorities a mechanical model of the Yangtze carp (now extinct as a result of pollution and over-development), which "swims" in a fish tank for gawking tourists to photograph. The authorities seem unaware of the irony.

China's material needs and waste of natural resources exceed what its environment can support. The statistics are shocking: 90% of the nation's rivers are heavily polluted; 75% of its lakes are toxic; one-third of all Chinese live and breathe heavily polluted air; and one-third of the land is under an acid rain belt. Drinking water is unsafe for consumption. Most urban sewage pipes are defunct and leak, causing wastewater to mix with the potable supply. Less than half of China's cities have water-treatment plants, and 60% of these are not being used. This is because most of the plants are fakes, having been built to meet official requirements that were never enforced due to corruption. Short-term thinking predominates over long-term planning, leading to corner cutting and cheating. The result is that there are no environmental standards in rural areas.

Even just an hour outside Beijing's center, the city is an environmental mess. In Huairou district, nearly all the potable water is toxic. Drinkable sources can be found only 100 or more meters beneath the surface—*if* the water table is beneath rock. This is within the environs of the nation's showcase capital. Beyond Beijing, the situation is much worse.

Waste is disposed of, often buried, without being treated. About 360 million rural people have no access to safe drinking water. The population is thus slowly being poisoned by polluted water, which is placing a huge burden on the health system as the number of cases of cancer and related diseases increases. State Environmental Protection Administration officials shake their heads when they hear the government slogan "Construct new socialist rural villages": the sentiment is meaningless when basic standards for human survival cannot be met.

On the Eve of Destruction

China's impending environmental self-destruction can be seen in the two opposing forces at play, says Pan Yue, deputy director of the State Environmental Protection Administration. "It is a struggle between the political achievement of some leaders and the people's very survival. On the surface, whether China's unqualified projects should cease or commence is a question of environmental protection. But, in reality, it is a question of the power struggle between the center and the regions."

Pan Yue has a lot of headaches. On average, a major case of environmental destruction lands on his desk every two days. Most cases involve regional environmental abuses, resulting from failed supervision—or deliberate neglect—by dysfunctional local governments. Pan's harsh criticism of the mainland's environmental failures makes him one of the few high-ranking officials who is questioning the same industrial model that is being praised in Western financial circles. Rather than seeing miracle growth as a guarantee of social stability, Pan sees red flags of impending humanitarian disaster.

The phenomenal GDP growth in China over the past decade has been driven largely by fixed-capital investment, which has caused irreversible environmental destruction while squandering resources. While Beijing may set environmental standards, all corrupt local governments effectively ride roughshod over the rules. Regional governments, which often have vested interests in ignoring abuses, fund local branches of SEPA and so have no real inclination to listen to Pan.

Through his criticism, Pan is questioning the very structure of the economy and administration. Ironically, and as an indication of China's lack of real priority for environmental protection, while Pan Yue might be a full ranking minister in terms of benefits, he has been denied any seat on the powerful CPC Central Committee, where real power is vested.

While investment forums held in five-star hotels belch out statistics proclaiming China as the world's future market for luxury consumer goods, the prospects are anything but glittery. Unfortunately, the central government cannot control the provinces, which in turn cannot rein in city administrations that fear township leaders, and so on. The government apparatus that enabled China to manage its mega-growth program 15 years ago has now broken down, leaving the country a free-for-all for those who seek to get rich quickly at any human or environmental cost.

The mainland economy grew over 11% in 2007, ahead of government targets. The high-growth formula has assured jobs and, in turn, economic and political stability. The highly over-rewed industrial engine driven by fixed-asset investment and the export of cheap goods could therefore be viewed as healthy for China and the world. However, uncontrolled growth signals a deeper problem—an economy, and governmental system that the central authorities cannot control or even manage effectively.

Regional industrial fixed-asset-driven projects have swept the nation, using the 2008 Olympic Games and the need for "beautification" as a rationale for spending. This frenetic pace sucks in cement, steel and aluminum, which spurs factory output to soar above GDP. Coal is in high demand, despite attempts to ban illegal operations or to control dangerous mining practices that kill more than 7,000 coal miners each year. But, as the rural workforce moves into industrial zones in the mainland cities, the demand for coal will rise further to fuel urban energy needs.

While the carbon-dioxide emissions per capita remain small, China's total emissions over the next 25 years are estimated to be double those of all the industrial nations in the world combined. In the past, China's leaders assured the world that by making its citizens rich, stability, security and a modicum of human rights would be ensured. Clearly, no one has considered the new equation.

In 2008, China led the world in greenhouse-gas emissions, surpassing even gas-guzzling America. It will also become the biggest cause of ozone deterioration in the world. China's shortsighted ethos of worshiping money may be detrimental to the existence of the planet. While, according to Walden Bello of Focus on the Global South, "China is a member of the South, at this point it is at the crossroads. As China develops relations with the South, which are not exploitative in the European sense of the term, it is beginning to follow another model of development, which it took from the World Bank. That model turns its back on issues of global warming out of self-interest, promoting energy consumption for capital-intensive development."

Bello's point is that China is throwing aid money at infrastructure in Africa, but its real aim is not development. The purpose, he asserts, is to gain control over the resources of Africa, to fuel its life-threatening polluted hyper-growth.

"But can China stand with the South on issues of global warming if it is becoming economically and diplomatically dependent upon the North for its export markets?" I asked.

"China is at the crossroads and can represent the South, or it can follow the United States and Europe. The issue of global warming is of concern to so many countries that want to have a stake in where China goes. The main concern of many people in the South is the ecologically very destructive consumption in the North."

"China could take a lead in environmental issues, but instead it seems to be following," I said.

"We are also worried about China's direction. We can no longer accept a situation where China and India, just because they are developing countries, are not subject to mandatory limits on their greenhouse gases," Bello replied. "But China and India should have development limits, and a new Kyoto accord should have even tighter standards for the North and integrate China and India into a mandatory regime."

China is a signatory to the Kyoto Protocol, while the United States, until 2008 the world's largest emitter of greenhouse gases, refuses to sign. The Protocol, signed in 1997 by most countries, identifies six greenhouse gases as the major source of global warming, amongst them carbon dioxide and methane.

In 1990, benchmarks were established under Protocol standards requiring certain reductions. On average, these require a 5.6% reduction per country, while individual variations apply to each. China falls into Annex 2, designating it a developing country. This designation exempts it from meeting a 2012 target, by which time most of the signatories must have reduced their emissions.

The Kyoto Protocol divides the world into two spheres, "developed" and "developing" countries, and applies different standards to each. "It wouldn't be fair to ask Uganda to spend a lot of money reducing greenhouse gases when that money is needed for development," said Mark Dembitz of Carbon Capital. "This same standard cannot be applied to the United States, a developed country that *should* be spending money on reducing greenhouse gases."

For developing countries such as China, this is a win-win situation. The Kyoto Protocol has created several clean development mechanisms that allow developed countries, within limits, to invest in emissions-reduction projects in other countries such as China. (Under the Protocol, it doesn't matter—from a global perspective—whether pollution emissions are reduced in China or in France.) China had nothing to lose by signing the Protocol, which allows Western countries and investors to fund landfills and the restructuring of coalmines, chemical plants and other polluting heavy industry in China, in exchange for carbon emissions in their own country. This system is aimed at creating a cleaner environment in China and other developing countries without them having to pay for the clean-up themselves.

Developed countries such as Japan, which finances Carbon Capital, are creating a carbon fund that will underwrite pollution-reducing projects in nations such as China, Cambodia and Vietnam. Such efforts are progressive. But more often than not, the countries' interests are misaligned. For instance, the U.S. will want to buy carbon credits from China or another developing nation as cheaply as possible, while the developing country will wish to sell its carbon credits for as high a price as possible.

The United States says it has no intention of signing the Kyoto Protocol as long as China and India don't have caps limiting their emissions. In turn, China and India don't see why they should have caps if the Americans don't sign. Traveling across the Himalayan plateau I had become acutely aware of the dangers of global warming. If the ozone layer continues to crack, our glaciers will melt. The Brahmaputra, Ganges, Mekong, Yellow and Yangtze rivers all have their origins in the Himalayan glaciers. If they melt, two-thirds of humanity will have no water to drink. Yes, we can save and give our children money. But in the future, will we be able to give them drinking water?

Compromising Agreements

How might the standoff be resolved? "Enforcement of international agreements on the level of trade and investment depends on each nation-state involved, because local enforcement may not be consistent across jurisdictions," says Walden Bello. "We should make a distinction between trade and finance issues, and the enforcement of other more pressing matters, such as the environment. Given the emergency character of our global environmental crisis and the impending threat of global warming, you need some strong agreements between nations accompanied by an even stronger global enforcement mechanism."

"The United States only adheres to agreements that suit its needs at any particular time. As China's economic and political might grow, might it do the same?" I asked Bello. "If so, what kind of consensus can we have on our environment and future security?"

"In the areas of trade and finance, we need international agree-ments, but we don't need centralized disciplinary mechanisms," he replied. "However, in the case of both the environment and global security, we *do* need these enforcement mechanisms at the international level."

Carbon-credit certifications are being regulated by the United Nations, the international organ entrusted to manage the creation of Clean Development Mechanisms (CDMs), also known as Carbon Emissions Reduction (CER) credits—effectively, a permit. According to Mark Dembitz, "The process of establishing these credits is a mature one. However, the mechanism for trading them is not yet mature."

At present, market trading of CER credits is being pioneered by the European Union Emission Trading Scheme (EUETS). In this area, Europe has clearly taken a concerted lead. While the United States has not yet established a national CER credit trading market, a number of environmentally conscious individual states have created their own localized trading systems. Hence, given disparate approaches, it is unlikely that the world will have a unified carbon-credit trading system in the foreseeable future. Instead, we may expect to see 50 or more local trading systems evolving in the years ahead. In the future, carbon-credit trading may therefore evolve like a currency market with, say, one European credit being worth two American credits.

Thus, carbon credits are mature as a concept, but the mechanism for trading them remains immature. Moreover, their purchase remains unregulated and largely voluntary, depending on the level of consciousness of their social and environmental responsibilities of the corporations involved. For instance, every time an HSBC executive takes a flight, the bank buys carbon offsets from various sources. Such an approach involves corporations and businesses taking responsibility for their environment upon themselves.

A different system of trading credits will be required for the voluntary carbon-credit market to be regulated, and this has yet to evolve. Whether global regulatory mechanisms can require corporations to purchase carbon offsets for the environmental costs they incur, such as air travel or industrial development, remains to be seen and will be hotly debated in coming years as a global political issue. Possibly a redefining of the "shareholders' value" concept, or method of evaluating a corporation's share value, will incorporate environmental impact offsets and could facilitate the voluntary carbon-credit market by effectively making participation a regulatory requirement.

But is carbon-credit trading really going to cut carbon dioxide emissions, or is it just another way to put off facing the problem head on? "Ultimately, carbon trading *will* reduce carbon dioxide emissions," Mark Dembitz believes. "But it is not the ultimate solution. The ultimate solution is to create a world that doesn't rely on hydrocarbons to fuel its energy."

Global Warming a Global Priority

In summer 2008 Beijing hosted the Olympics with the slogan, "One World, One Dream." It almost certainly meant something different to the world than what Beijing's leaders were dreaming about, which was a spectacular fanfare glorifying excess. Hyper-growth in the steel, cement and aluminum industries to create the Olympic infrastructure in turn transformed China into a mass importer of resources and an exporter of inflation. But now that the party is over, Beijing's self-congratulating municipal leaders have found themselves in the worst-polluted environment in history. China's cities are not just miserable places for their citizens to live in, they are threatening humanity's existence.

In 2008, when China debuted on the world stage as a major consumer society, its achievement was characterized by highways clogged by gas-guzzling, pollution-emitting vehicles, and the massive infrastructure construction boom attributed to the Olympics. China's construction is inefficient and wasteful. Its numerous new golf courses, reflecting the country's newfound vulgarity, are an inexcusable luxury in a nation where water is precious and clean water scarce.

Chinese officials would be well advised to visit neighboring Bangladesh, rather than Las Vegas, to glimpse where the country is headed. This is precisely what I did. In Bangladesh, global warming causes incessant flooding of the lowlands, where poverty is a daily reality. In Dhaka, I met with Nobel Peace Prize winner Muhammad Yunus, of Grameen Bank. "Global warming is now at a serious stage, and greenhouse-gas emissions are growing," he said. "Europe itself is producing more emissions. The United States accounts for over 25% of the world's greenhouse-gas emissions. Europe is concerned, but the U.S. does nothing and refuses to sign the Kyoto Protocol. This has now become a less effective instrument. And China has become the biggest polluter itself. So it is now not just America's contribution, but China's! All its power is based on dirty fuel. China will get worse. Next to follow is India. So, now three nations have joined the club."

China and India's refusal to cut their carbon emissions unless wealthy countries such as the United States take the lead is understandable. Indeed, former U.S. President Bill Clinton recently supported this position in an article published in the *Financial Times.* "I think unless we take the lead in the United States, we'll never get the Indians and Chinese to do it... ," Clinton wrote. "But we will never be able to persuade them of that until we put our money where our mouth is."[1]

Yunus offers another explanation. "The real problem is lifestyle. We can agree about having non-smoking areas in public places, because one's smoking may destroy another's health. What about wastefulness of lifestyle? How can some nations retain lifestyles that destroy other people's—for instance, by buying gas-guzzlers? This lifestyle is not consistent with our planet. How can you enjoy life on this planet if your lifestyle is destroying the planet? It is like partying on a boat while lighting a bonfire on that same boat."

What needs to be done is clear, Yunus believes. "The Kyoto Protocol is a non-binding agreement. What we need is a binding agreement. It must be done through the United Nations, and done now. There is not enough time left before 2012. By the year 2050, we must reduce our greenhouse gases by 50%. But the United States doesn't want to sign the Kyoto Protocol. So, we must get the U.S. to join. Many people in the United States are for the Kyoto Protocol, but the government continues to block it.

"We should start to color-label products. Red-coded products destroy the environment. Yellow-coded ones may destroy it. And green-coded products do not destroy our environment and their consumption should be encouraged. These ideas must be passed on to our children, who must live on the planet after we are gone."

"American values include the right to bear arms and to drive big, energy-wasteful cars," I said. "What must we consider or reconsider in establishing our own values?"

"We should not talk about the United States and Bangladesh," Yunus replied. "Instead, we should talk about the next generation. It is they who will suffer from what we do!"

Bangladesh is already feeling the effects of our global irresponsibility. I recall driving across rural Bangladesh with an employee of Muhammad Yunus and seeing many houses—sometimes whole villages—surrounded by floodwaters. Bangladesh is an agricultural, rice-growing nation, with very little pollution created through its industry. But the country, which is less than a meter above sea level, is nowadays a victim of rising sea levels caused by global warming.

Yunus is seeing the unfolding global tragedy on the front lines. Sitting in a Starbucks in Beijing, New York or London, we cannot see the effects of our greenhouse gases. We're in fish bowls isolated from a vast tragedy which is coming round the corner, and which will hit us like a train. The starkness of what our planet is about to face is made clear to me every time I return to Lhasa. Lhasa's airport stands beside the Brahmaputra River, the mother river of India. This is the source of water for South Asia. But as glaciers in Tibet are retreating, caused by the direct effect of greenhouse gases, Sahara-type sand dunes and entire deserts are forming in the bed of what was once the Brahmaputra River. We are looking at our future of sand dunes and deserts, or in the case of Bangladesh, floods and tidal waves.

Yunus explained: "The rising sea level will destroy the ecology of our country. We will have more floods at a greater cost. This is a small country with a big population. Our people will have to move inland. The poorest people in our country live in marshland. Saline [water] now rushes in from the shoreline. People become refugees. For us, this is a question of life and death. We must take this seriously. Increased greenhouse gases are already destroying our planet."

The United States, China and India—the world's present and future economic superpowers—need to take clear positions and lead the world in adhering to sincere commitments to reduce greenhouse-gas emissions. While the former Bush administration failed to assume global leadership on one of humanity's most important issues, the environment and subsequent survival of our planet, with a new administration under Barack Obama there is hope that America can take the lead, together with China and India, in pushing forward programs to cut greenhouse gases globally. This will mean a severe curtailing of our own consumption, which in turn will change the consumption-driven growth models which China and the U.S. have adopted. This will mean adjusting and recreating our whole value system. The Obama administration should aggressively push for America to join the Kyoto Protocol. Without U.S. leadership, little will get done on this front. If the world has one dream, it should be to reduce greenhouse gases. Humanity's survival will depend on it.

Endnote

1 Christie Freeland and Edward Luce, "Bill Clinton interview," *Financial Times,* September 23, 2007.

Ǝ

8

THE MICRO-CREDIT REVOLUTION WORKS
SMALL FINANCE IS BEAUTIFUL AND CAN IMPROVE LIVES

Piety lies not in turning your face East or West in prayer... but in distributing your wealth out of love for God to your needy kin; to orphans, to the vagrants, and to the mendicants; it lies in freeing the slaves, in observing your devotions, and in giving alms to the poor.

—The Quran (2:177)

An Idea Whose Time Has Come

I first met Professor Muhammad Yunus, known to the world as "banker to the poor," in the autumn of 2006, after it was announced that he had won the Nobel Peace Prize. He had just arrived in Beijing to speak at a micro-credit conference. Founder of the Grameen ("village" in Bengali) Bank in Bangladesh, which pioneered the grassroots credit model based on human trust rather than physical collateral, Yunus put a new spin on humanism, declaring that credit is a human right. His words rang in the ears of his Chinese hosts, and their echo reverberated in Washington.

At a reception welcoming him to Beijing, the humble, almost self-effacing Yunus declared, "For the first time, the Nobel Peace Prize has been awarded to poor women who must struggle for their lives."

That night, Yunus reflected on the humble beginnings of an idea that has now sparked a revolution in economic development. When Bangladesh became independent, Yunus was teaching economics in Tennessee. He returned home, where he found his country in the grip of famine. "I became involved in the poverty issue, not as a policymaker or as a researcher, but because poverty was all around me and I couldn't turn away from it. In 1974, I found it difficult to teach elegant theories of economics in the university classroom, while in the background there was a terrible famine in Bangladesh. Suddenly I felt the emptiness of those theories in the face of crushing hunger and poverty. I wanted to do something immediately to help the people around me, even if it was just one human being, to get through another day with a little more ease. That brought me face to face with poor people's struggle to find the tiniest amounts of money so they can eke out a living."

He recalled how institutional economics training taught one to think in terms of the millions and billions of dollars required to finance big infrastructure projects. But for most impoverished people living in a country with a per-capita income of US$128 per year, access to just 10 or 20 dollars can change their lives for the better. Yunus recalled: "I was shocked to discover a woman in the village near our campus who had borrowed less than a dollar from a moneylender, on the condition that he would have the exclusive right to buy all she produced at the price that he decided. This, to me, was a way of recruiting slave labor. I decided to make a list of the victims of moneylenders in the village. When my list was complete, it had the names of 42 people who had borrowed a total amount of US$27. I was shocked. I offered that sum from my own pocket to get these villagers out of the clutches of the moneylenders. The excitement that was created among the people by this small action got me further involved. If I could make so many people so happy with such a tiny amount of money, why shouldn't I do more of it?"

From this simple approach to assisting the victims of abject poverty, Yunus created the concept of micro-credit. It has since revolutionized not only the basic assumptions of macroeconomics, but also the very function that banking should play in human society.

Yunus's idea empowers individuals not just with micro-credit, but also with self-esteem and self-identity. It is literally a world removed from white-collar banking, where commercial financiers require applicants for loans to have sufficient collateral in the form of assets. This is the rich supporting the rich, where loan negotiations are conducted not in simply constructed village "banks," but on golf courses or in well-appointed offices.

Institutions such as the IMF and the World Bank send their Washington-based, black-suited consultants into underdeveloped countries often facing crises of a social or natural catastrophic nature. Armed with economic theories, but with little knowledge of the local conditions, socio-cultural undercurrents, or the life-or-death problem of finding enough to eat that is many people's daily life, they tend to lecture rather than listen. Often, their lending policies come with conditions attached that are far from the realities of life of the people who should be benefiting from the funding. The result is economic havoc, poor social self-esteem, and an emasculated ethnic identity.

Mike Moore, the former WTO director-general and prime minister of New Zealand, once said to me: "Local needs must be taken into account.

That is why I am a great admirer of Muhammad Yunus. He created a model where the amount of money involved is so small, the bureaucrats can't get their hands on it. If you're building an aircraft or an airport, there's a lot of money involved and the politicians and bureaucrats will steal it. But in the Yunus model, the funds are so small they can't steal them. They are not even there to cut the ribbons for his projects. Many Western commercial banks are looking at it as a model to come into the market."

Officials from the Poverty Relief Department of China's State Council are now developing schemes throughout China based on the Yunus model, which provides practical ways to close the gap between the urban rich and the rural poor in developing countries. "The essence of my argument here today," Yunus explained to delegates at the Beijing conference on micro-credit, "is that in order to reduce, and ultimately eliminate, poverty, we must go back to the drawing board. The concepts and institutions that created poverty cannot be used to end poverty. If we can intelligently rework those, we can eliminate poverty."

Some 58% of Grameen's borrowers have moved out of poverty, a phenomenon the bank tracks and measures carefully. Even here, Yunus provides new criteria. Instead of the mainstream institutional approach, which uses annual per-capita income to determine whether people have shifted above the poverty line, his organization asks harder, more relevant questions of its lenders. "Do you have a roof over your head, warm clothes for winter, safe drinking water and sanitation? Are your children in school?"

"We are so much influenced by orthodox economics that we forget that our forefathers didn't wait for someone else to create jobs for them," Yunus said. "They just went ahead in a routine manner to create their own jobs and income. They were lucky. They didn't have to learn economic theories and end up believing that the only way they could make a living was to find a job in the job market. In the West, if you can't get a job, you march in the streets in protest! In Third World countries, even if you marched in the streets there would be no job for you. As a result, the poor go out and create their own jobs. Since economic textbooks don't recognize them, there are no supportive institutions and policies to help them."

It is this pragmatic approach that has caught the attention of NGOs and governments worldwide and that is now inspiring officials in developing countries to confront the challenge of bringing huge numbers of people out of poverty. Where the Washington Consensus's theoretical models of free capital flows, sudden privatization and turnkey capital markets have failed, Yunus has brought to the table an alternative approach that empowers people not just with cash, but also with a newly awakened sense of pride in who they are.

The Nobel Peace Prize, normally awarded to pro-Western politicians, has now gone to an Asian humanitarian offering an alternative path to both economic betterment and self-pride using the simple tools of common sense and compassion. But has the death knell really rung for the Washington Consensus?

That seemed to be the feeling among the guests at the cocktail reception held at the Bangladesh Embassy in Beijing to welcome Yunus. Most of the attendees were ecstatic, even euphoric, that night. It felt like the beginning of a new Asian era—perhaps even of a Himalayan Consensus. As a bright red banner welcoming Yunus to the reception proclaimed, using the words of Victor Hugo, "There is nothing more powerful than an idea whose time has come."

Journey to Dhaka

The next day, I spoke by phone with Ashfaqur Rahman, Bangladesh's ambassador to China. He agreed with my view that a turning point had been reached. There was now a liable, Asian-initiated model for sustainable development that could provide an alternative to the Washington model. Such a turning point hadn't been seen since the Bandung Conference in Indonesia in 1965 or the Non-Aligned Movement summit in Algiers in 1975, both of which sought to articulate an independent, non-aligned pathway and paradigm for developing nations to follow. We then talked about the idea of an evolving Himalayan Consensus to counterbalance that of Washington. Rahman suggested that I take the notion a step further. He invited me to Bangladesh to visit himself and Professor Yunus, to see what could be done.

Nine months later, Ambassador Rahman personally hosted me in Dhaka. On my arrival, he drove me to the premises of the Bangladesh Rural Agricultural Committee (BRAC), one of Bangladesh's largest NGOs. The organization epitomizes the concept of cultural sustainable development by employing poor village women throughout Bangladesh to weave or embroider pillowcases, rugs, scarves, stuffed toys and baskets. In addition to offering employment, BRAC provides careers advice and other support for cultural identity and sustainability. "There are over 7,000 NGOs in Bangladesh," Rahman told me, noting that they were offering a host of grassroots solutions and alternatives to those espoused by the Washington Consensus.

Bangladeshis had no choice other than to come up with their own solutions for development using scarce resources. The World Bank and IMF approaches of top-down infrastructure spending only bred corruption, and little of the funding reached the masses. Moreover, the political conditions that were demanded in exchange for soft-loan funding tended to emasculate and disenfranchise the poor, compounding their frustration and locking them into cyclical poverty.

"The IMF didn't want to invest in any kind of agricultural business, which is more relevant in Bangladesh than big infrastructure. IMF policy supports infrastructure," explained Shamimur Rahman, a Grameen Bank officer who helped me during my visit. "The IMF asked the government to close down jute mills because they run at a loss. But jute is one of the most important crops in Bangladesh." I learned that people throughout the nation depend on the crop for weaving ropes, mats and certain textiles. Many of the products made by village women under the BRAC program come from jute.

The IMF even insisted on following its fixed model of cutting price subsidies for oil and gas, demanding that Bangladesh export its oil reserves in exchange for foreign exchange reserves. It failed to see that most of the population is barely subsisting. Any price hike in oil will impact the national transportation sector, sending rice and basic commodity prices out of reach for the average Bangladeshi. The result will be economic and social chaos, as occurred in Indonesia in 1997 when the IMF insisted on removing subsidies from edible oils and staples, sending prices skyrocketing. Rioting erupted in the streets and President Suharto was forced to step down. Short-lived governments and Bali bombings followed. Indonesia was never the same afterward, but the IMF got what it wanted: the fundamentalist application of its textbook theories on free markets.

Even on the critical issue of flooding, perennial in Bangladesh given its low altitude and monsoonal climate, the IMF couldn't help progressively. Funding was proposed for rural river dredging. However, after intensive preparation, the project couldn't be properly implemented because of the conditions applied by the donor organizations. The funds were diverted to central Asia instead.

Today, cyclical poverty abounds in Bangladesh, a nation that 400 years ago was one of the richest in the world. Why? Globalization in another form reached Bangladesh in 1779, in the form of the British Raj. When Britain's American colonies declared independence in 1776, London calculated its tax revenues and determined that additional resources were needed to hold the Empire together. When the colonial governor of North America, General Charles Cornwallis, lost the Battle of Yorktown, Britain was prepared to give up the low-revenue-yielding American colonies in favor of keeping its grasp on the Indian sub-continent. Cornwallis was transferred to India as viceroy in Delhi, where he instituted a land revenue system of "permanent settlements." Under this system, areas of the country were contracted and subcontracted out to local commissars, who extracted funds in the form of contractual tax payments from the land-tenured peasants. The system succeeded in systematically impoverishing the rural populations of what today are Bangladesh, India, and Pakistan.

"Was this a precursor to the Washington Consensus policy of stimulating cyclical poverty and impoverishing people?" I asked Ambassador Rahman.

"The parallel is far-fetched," Rahman laughed. "But in some ways the mentality is the same. The British tried to use the 'permanent settlement' as an alien-applied financial lever of the times. It went against local ways and in turn impoverished the people. In some ways, the IMF's insisting on the use of certain financial tools that are inappropriate for local situations creates the same result."

Bangladesh's past prosperity saw its final denouement during World War II when the British, fearing a Japanese invasion of the country's vast and sophisticated network of canals and delta rivers, burned the entire Bangladeshi fleet of rice boats. "We were a nation of rice traders," Rahman explained. "So this broke the back of our economy. Then, in 1943, famine hit, and destruction and destabilization occurred. Values changed."

The next day, Rahman invited me to speak at the Bangladesh Enterprise Institute, an investment strategy and anti-corruption "advocacy" center. The institute promotes alternative policies to Bangladesh's various government institutions and helps to highlight government priorities on particular advocacy issues. I was invited to present my ideas concerning a Himalayan Consensus.

I discussed the vision emerging behind such a consensus: three pillars consisting of a mutual and equal exchange of development experiences in place of a model; drawing upon the intrinsic local philosophies of compassion contained in the religions of the Himalayan region (Buddhism, Islam and Hinduism); and independent, locally based solutions for political evolution and self-governance.

Rahman mused to the forum: "So there is a natural logic to what you are calling for in the Himalayan Consensus. The Himalayas do not keep us apart, but bring us together. The nations of this region can feed upon the Himalayas and get nourishment from their ice, water, flora and fauna. It is the natural flow of culture."

He then ended the forum with a story. He recalled having a conversation in 1985 with the late Indian premier Rajiv Gandhi, for whom he was serving as host officer during the first plenary summit of SARC (the South Asia Regional Cooperation). Sri Lanka's "wise man," President J.R. Jayawardene, had made the comment: "Today, six small boats are tied to a big boat," referring to the South Asian countries and India. "We would like to see if we will sink or float."

"As we came out of the plenary, Gandhi asked if I had heard Jayawardene's comment," Rahman recalled. Gandhi continued: "It is unfortunate that we are all of the same cultural background but not cooperating. All the rivers of the Himalayas that come to South Asia do not flow north to south. The Indus flows to the Arabian Sea through India and Pakistan; the Ganges flows from India to Nepal to Bangladesh; the Brahamaputra flows through China and India to Bangladesh. It must be that the Almighty ordered we should all cooperate. By virtue of nature, we are already all linked up."

The Social Business Model

While in Dhaka, I shared many of my views concerning the Himalayan Consensus with Muhammad Yunus. I told him that I was disturbed by the Washington Consensus approach, and by the symbiotic relationship between conditional soft lending by financial institutions such as the IMF and the World Bank and short-term corporate interests. I asked Yunus what he thought.

"In the name of business, they destroy societies and the future," he said. "They take mines, and miserably plunder a nation. Now it is the army of companies that threatens a country that is not doing business their way. They make a show of power if you don't do things their way. Meanwhile, they forget the environment, forget people, forget culture, and destroy anything in their quest to make money."

We talked about the need to re-engineer corporate values, and about the very concept of shareholder value. In the 1980s, financial market analysts talked only of a company's profit and loss in evaluating its performance. In the 1990s, companies were valued using the new concept of "shareholder value," which seemed to be a calculation based on how much money the management could blow on luxurious living. Now, in the first decade of the new millennium, it is time we adopt a new concept of compassionate corporate values based on what a company does for the society from which it benefits.

After creating his micro-finance model, Yunus was now pioneering a new concept of "social business." I asked him to share this new vision.

"We need to popularize social business," Yunus explained. "Now the only thing people can do is to create trusts and foundations to give money as charitable donations, because the system only allows charity, not really responsible business. Charity is good, but to run a charity you must always find money. Charitable funds have only a one-time use. Once the money is given, it is gone. If you give it, you need more. But with social business, life has endless life. It keeps recycling by its own income. So, it can go on forever."

I asked him for an example.

"In 2006, we created with Danone Yogurt of France a joint Grameen-Danone joint-venture to produce fortified yogurt for malnourished children. Doing so, we include all the micro-nutrients missing from their diet and sell it cheaply. We want poor children to have rich, delicious yogurt. The more of it they ear, the more they will regain their health; and the more we can have them take, the more we can help. We want healthy children. The profit stays with the company to be reinvested for expansion to get more nutrients to more children. If we use just charity, then we can only give one yogurt per child. Then we have to find a way to pay for it."

Yunus gave another example. "We want to create solar businesses, not to make money but to help people by using bio-gas, cow dung. In this way, we can create our own natural non-polluting gas and stop cutting down trees."

"What is your long-term vision for developing the social business concept?" I asked.

"With social business we must do several things," Yunus said. "Today, there are institutional arrangements for profit businesses—for instance, the stock market. You go to buy stocks in the stock market for only one objective—profit. So, there should be a separate stock market with social businesses dedicated to health care, helping the poor, bringing forests to countries where they don't exist, bringing drug addicts in off the street and giving them self-employment. Then people can go to the stock market and look for companies that will help HIV/AIDS victims or that reach out to the poorest villages. We then need information. To know about profit-making businesses, we have the *Financial Times* and the *Asian Wall Street Journal*. We should have a *Social Times and* a *Social Wall Street Journal* to tell us about new social ideas and opportunities as well. A social enterprise needs social expertise, and so we should be training social MBAs and keeping track of their impact on our people.

"We need a parallel system," Yunus went on. "Profit maximization is one thing. But we should also develop new rating agencies to track the impact of social enterprises. For instance, the profit-makers' medicines are sold in highly priced packaging, which adds to their bottom line. But if I am a social business, I can take the same product without the fancy packaging and sell it at a reasonable price to people who couldn't otherwise afford it.

The actual product is identical, and poor people who can't afford 10 dollars to pay for fancily packaged medicine can now get it for 50 cents. Retroviro is a medicine used in the treatment of HIV/AIDS. It costs US$3,000 per dose, but it can now be produced for only US$300. Capitalism caters to the rich and by its nature supports profit-maximizing businesses, whereas social businesses will sell products that are affordable to you. This is what I want to use, to adjust globalization."

Yunus explained further how Grameen Bank works. "Everyone is interested in how much money we lend, how we get paid, how the money is returned, how accounts are kept—everything about money. But Grameen Bank is not about money: 90% is about people. The bank's only collateral is trust."

To date, Grameen Bank has provided a total of over U$$6 billion in loans. The repayment rate is 99%. It has given collateral-free, income-generating loans, housing loans, student loans and micro-enterprise loans to nearly seven million poor people in 73,000 villages in Bangladesh, 97% of them women. "We focused on women because we found that giving loans to women always brought more benefits to the family," Yunus noted. "Inside every human being is care and concern. I may be a stern moneylender, but I will want to help a sick person. We all have a soft heart. But economic theory denies this. This is why there are so many problems."

Building Community Spirit Along with Grassroots Businesses

Yunus arranged for me to visit village lending centers in impoverished rural areas about half-a-day's drive from Dhaka. Here, women could borrow U$6 to set up tiny businesses ranging from fish breeding to betel-nut harvesting and poultry raising. A loan of US$12 will allow a family to purchase a small rice paddy and begin self-sufficient farming. The small repayments are made at lending-center meetings. A village lending center consists of a pavilion with corrugated iron roof and benches. Each week borrowers congregate here in groups. Each group of five women has an elected leader who collects the interest payments and represents the group in the meeting. The branch manager will visit the village center to collect the interest. Women bring their children, and the atmosphere is more that of a social gathering, where they exchange family news and business experiences, than a visit to a bank to make a loan repayment.

If a family can build up its own business—say, opening a tiny roadside shop—Yunus will lease them a mobile phone. They can then use the phone to provide public telephone services, thus becoming a mini call center. On the back of micro-credit, Yunus offers education loans and pension funds. Thus, step by step, a family can work its way out of poverty and into a sustainable business.

"The most important step in ending poverty is to create employment and income opportunities for the poor," Yunus explained. "But orthodox economics recognizes only wage-employment. It has no room for self-employment. But self-employment is the quickest and easiest way to create employment for the poor."

While such approaches are non-conventional, defying all the textbook formulas for economic development and all the MBA courses on credit and finance, Yunus's efforts have proved that they work.

In addition to its lending centers, Grameen Bank supports the establishment of community information centers in villages. The centers already offer Internet services and provide information relevant to the community, such as job vacancies, exam results for school children and the price of rice. (Farmers have traditionally had no systematic means of pricing their rice, other than information passed by word of mouth.) This not only marks an innovative approach to finance and banking, but also encourages the building of community spirit.

During my several days spent visiting the Grameen rural bank branches and village centers, I met with many individual borrowers.

Bakul had four children but no means to support them, not even a roof to keep them dry during the rainy season. Her husband was contracted as a laborer in Saudi Arabia, but the earnings he sent back were not enough to support his family. In 1992, Bakul joined Grameen and took out a loan equivalent to around US$7.50 with which to purchase a corrugated iron roof for her home. In 2002, her husband returned to the village and they started a fledgling betel-nut business with Grameen's support. Bakul borrowed around US$15 to cover her children's school fees and to invest in land. Today, she is proud of her "strong house with electricity," and all her children are in school and even beginning high school.

Another village woman, Nur Jahan, borrowed around US$8 to start a business growing vegetables. Her husband was a farmer. Once the business stabilized, she doubled the loan to start a business selling small trees. Through these small businesses she has been able to support and educate her six children.

Tamina told me she had nothing to her name when she joined Grameen Bank. Her husband, a carpenter, was working as a contract laborer in another country. Initially, Tamina borrowed US$8 from Grameen to lease land; she then drew down a second loan of US$15, which she invested in two cows and 24 kilograms of rice. Today, she is proud of her tiny business.

She has a good house, a parcel of land to farm, and her three children are all studying.

De Ruba joined Grameen in 2000, when she borrowed the equivalent of about US$7.50 to start a betel-leaf business. For seven years she continued to reinvest everything in betel leaves. She then requested another loan of around US$4 to purchase a parcel of land and another of US$15 for building materials. Her two goals are "to have a strong house and children all in school." Her ambition is to expand her business to assure more education for her children.

Delowara, aged 35, was a fisherwoman who borrowed around US$8 to invest in a fishing pond. After repaying the loan, she borrowed a further US$15, which she invested in baby fish stock for breeding and expansion of her business.

A 36-year-old woman first borrowed US$7.50 to invest in a farming plot, seeds and fertilizer. She then borrowed US$10 to buy a calf, which she raised and sold in the market. From the proceeds, she purchased rice seedlings to expand her farming business.

Most of Grameen's borrowers share similar dreams—a solid house over their heads, children in school, and their own business through which to improve their lives. Grameen's model of providing micro-loans defies traditional institutional banking practice, because it is tailored to the needs of each individual borrower. Grameen has succeeded in shattering institutionalism and taking it out of banking practice altogether. Its managers are not just bankers, but also business advisors, social-family counselors, and macroeconomists in the sense that they consider the impact of loans upon people's lives.

The economic formulas that underpin the work of bodies such as the World Bank and the IMF don't consider factors such as transportation costs, price hikes, the affordability of education, and how any tiny shift in these factors can disrupt—even destroy—the lives of those attempting to get by on incomes at, or just above, the subsistence line. Feedback about such policies goes unheeded. "They are the economic bosses," I was told repeatedly. "Of course, they don't listen."

Not Just Money, But Trust

"The poor always repay their loans," said Muhammad Yunus. Such a statement goes against the accepted wisdom of institutional bankers, but it is the actual experience of the Grameen Bank model of micro-finance lending to the impoverished. I asked why. "Somebody receiving a micro-credit loan is being given not just money, but trust from Grameen Bank," Yunus explained. "If someone trusts her with what is for her so much money, she will work very hard to repay it." If borrowers don't repay their first loan, then there is no second one. Borrowers therefore feel not only a duty to pay back the money, but a new confidence in their ability to make their business succeed when they have done so. In developing the Grameen model for providing credit without collateral, Yunus incorporated an understanding of local social and human psychology, and knowledge of the village network culture. Social linkages are critically important in Bangladeshi village society. Several factors are at work simultaneously:

1. Poor people repay while saving, and when they finally have an asset to their name and some savings, they become more secure and confident.

2. With an education loan for their children, village borrowers have hope that their children will rise out of poverty.

3. Grameen "members" (as the bank refers to its borrowers) actually purchase a share in the Grameen Bank, making them part of a prestigious organization that has won the Nobel Peace Prize.

4. Borrowers are grateful to the institution that has helped them to rise out of poverty, and are aware that by repaying a loan, they can get another.

5. Most borrowers are Muslim, for whom it is a sin to die without repaying a loan.

Borrowers fear losing social prestige if they fail to repay their loans on time. Because the repayment amounts are so small, the weekly installments are affordable. Moreover, a poor person sees what the rich have and fail to use. For that reason, they are more determined to make the most of each opportunity given to them.

I asked one Grameen area manager what was his greatest challenge working at the bank. "To alleviate an entire area from poverty," was his immediate answer.

I then asked what he found most satisfying about his job. "My greatest frustration is if we give a borrower tools but she doesn't use them. We will try to work with people and to empower them by removing obstacles. My greatest joy is if they can do it all themselves—it is heavenly joy."

Grameen Bank's success lies in its ability to go against the grain of institutional banking, which is characterized by an extensive bureaucracy, inflexible credit criteria, and an inhuman approach to customer relations. Grameen adopts flexible policies, has only a small bureaucracy, and keeps its operational costs low. The result: Muhammad Yunus has turned around the very concept of credit for seeding start-ups.

Moreover, Yunus has even extended his idea to help beggars stop begging and become entrepreneurs. According to Grameen's Struggling (Beggars) Members Program, "members are not required to give up begging, but are encouraged to take up an additional income-generating activity such as selling popular consumer items door-to-door, or at the place of begging." This approach weans beggars away from begging and conditions them to begin small-scale, self-sufficient businesses. Between the launch of the program in July 2002 and May 2007, some 10% of the 90,000-plus strugglers to whom funds were disbursed had quit begging altogether. They were able to support themselves with their own micro-business ventures.

In one village, I met a beggar who was benefiting from the program. Shorola, an ancient woman, was crouched beside her cane with a basket of packaged snacks for sale. I asked her age. She claimed to be 102. Her husband had died in 1965, she said, and she had lived alone ever since, having no children to support her. Shorola's only means of survival was to beg door-to-door. For 20 years she scraped together a living as a beggar. Then one day, as she lay in front of a Grameen Bank branch begging, the manager offered her a tiny loan and encouraged her to buy snacks to sell in the market. Within 31 weeks she had repaid half of the loan.

"Is your snack-selling business profitable?" I asked Shorola.

"If I did not make profit, then how can I eat?" she replied with a hint of sarcasm.

"When you are older, will you carry on with this business?"

"If I don't carry on, then who will feed me?" she responded, even more sarcastically. Then she smiled faintly. "I have stopped begging and now have my own business. Now I feel better about myself."

Lending to Address Real Needs

Yunus's model of humanistic lending tailors credit to the needs of people, rather than tailoring people to the rules of the financial institution. Under Grameen's Struggling (Beggars) Members Program, the first rule is: "Existing rules of Grameen Bank do not apply to beggar members; they make up their own rules."

To date, the IMF has refused to consider this model of micro-finance, even after Muhammad Yunus received the Nobel Peace Prize. This baffles staff at Grameen Bank. "The IMF does not have a single program of micro-credit for poor people," notes Shamimur Rahman. "They have so-called micro-finance institutions to lend money to the middle class and the rich, but not to the poor, so as to avoid IMF risk exposure."

Locked in by its blinkered classroom theories, the IMF still refuses to acknowledge the power of bottom-up, grassroots economics. Instead, it insists on engaging in heavy, top-down infrastructure projects, from which its self-appointed advisors and favored contractors reap profits from soft loans bound in conditionality. The IMF sends its "experts" to advise a country on economics, and to ensure that the conditions it has imposed are adhered to. "But we don't need foreign expertise," said Rahman. "Poor Bengali people have no shortage of ideas. How can the IMF send advisors to a rural village region and advise on the economics of business in a village, when that advisor has never been to a village in his entire life?"

"Right" vs. "Wrong" Globalization

One evening during my visit to Dhaka, I asked Muhammad Yunus how he felt about globalization.

"The issue of globalization comes to me every day," he said. "Those who take an anti-globalization position are confusing the issue. Globalization has been here for centuries. The ancient trading routes of Central Asia, the sea routes from Europe to India, these were all expressions of globalization; and so was colonization, for that matter. Only these things are now happening at a greater speed and with more business products."

"So, in your view, globalization isn't new?"

"Globalization is the urge of human beings to go out," Yunus laughed. "We cannot isolate ourselves, or we will just become tribes."

"So, globalization has both advantages and disadvantages?"

"Our garment industry flourishes because of globalization, and we will grow as a result," he replied. "China is growing because of globalization. Taiwan and Korea are growing because of globalization. But it takes a lot of hard work to prevent the strength of big capital from controlling your economy. As the first principle, you need a win for both sides."

He had hit on the core issue in the globalization debate.

"How can this be achieved?" I asked.

"The issue isn't globalization—yes or no?" he responded. "The question is: right globalization or wrong globalization?"

"But how can I define what is right or wrong with globalization?"

"If we don't do anything about globalization and let it just happen—

laissez-faire globalization—it will mean that the most powerful will take it all and the meek will lose everything."

"Can you describe what you mean?" I asked. "How do you see *laissez-faire* globalization?"

"Globalization is like a multi-lane highway across our world and the U.S. has the big trucks," explained Yunus. "So a small country like Bangladesh cannot find a lane because the bigger businesses from the U.S. and Japan will take all the business from the little players like Bangladesh. So, imagine a 100-lane highway. There should be traffic rules. There are lanes for trucks, for vehicles, for buses. So at least I know my rickshaw has a lane and won't be run over by the trucks! We need traffic police, too, and a traffic authority.

"So, if big businesses from the United States and Japan take over the little businesses, such as the small, family-run grocery shops, if we say this is globalization, it is the wrong kind of globalization. For instance, if I am a potter who makes pots by hand, and Western business comes in with machines, I will lose my job and the craft will disappear."

"But then how do we protect the small from being bulldozed by Wall Street capital?" It seemed to me an impossible task, but Yunus's response encouraged me to hold on to my idealism.

"Anybody who makes anything by hand must be protected and honored. Anything made by human hand, with materials from the land, must have a special price reflecting this," he suggested. "We need places in every shopping mall for these products to reflect how people use their individual time and talent. The U.N. should be the only global authority and it should have an agency for this. If a multinational food chain comes into a neighborhood, it should not push out the local family-run grocery stores. Instead, *they* should be brought in. Textile makers must be brought in and not destroyed. Each nation should decree human rules governing business going abroad."

"So, we need to understand the sources and power of globalization, but rearrange the rules, making them fairer and setting the order right?" I asked.

"Today, globalization doesn't have traffic police," Yunus replied. "All the problems arise from this. As a first principle, we need rules. We need a body to govern the rules. We need to have penalties and fines. Otherwise, free-for-all globalization will become the new business colonization. Moreover, it will become colonization of the poor, because jobs will be taken over by big machines and capital."

"Why do the models imposed by the Washington Consensus end up creating more misery in the world than happiness?"

"With all of our economic theories, we forget the environment, forget people, forget culture, and destroy anything to make money," Yunus said sadly. "This is the inherent fault in economic theory, which creates an artificial human being who knows how to make money because maximizing profit is the sole basis of business. But human beings are bigger than just money. A caring human being is somebody who jumps in to help others. The compassionate, caring human being is left out, so in economic theory, the only ones left are the people making money. Economic assumptions forget the compassionate people."

Ǝ

9

BEGIN BY RESHAPING VALUES
THE GROSS NATIONAL HAPPINESS ALTERNATIVE

Gross National Happiness is more important than Gross National Product.

—**Jigme Singye Wangchuck**

Re-defining Wealth

In November 2007, I visited the Himalayan Kingdom of Bhutan in search of the inspiration behind a new measure of wealth, the concept of Gross National Happiness (GNH). GNH turns on its head the traditional Gross National Product formula for measuring economic success. It shatters assumptions that more wealth and consumer-driven marketing cycles create better social development. Indeed, it holds that the "invisible hand" of Western economics shatters traditional society and culture, leading to social disorder, unhappiness, dysfunctional lives and political instability.

The concept of GNH came to public attention in 1986 when Jigme Singye Wangchuck, the fourth King of Bhutan, used the term in an interview with the *Financial Times* of London. Deflecting criticism of the isolation of the closed Himalayan kingdom and Bhutan's low GDP rate, the monarch made his famous statement: "Gross National Happiness is more important than Gross National Product."

The concept shattered traditional Washington Consensus assumptions and touched a chord with people worldwide who were calling for a measure of national success other than the conventional one of GNP. It questions all the economic assumptions that underlie the post-Bretton Woods global order, and presents a potential paradigm for re-evaluating the way we measure economic achievement and corporate values. Moreover, it has implications for how we measure the way we spend our lives.

At Bhutan's international airport in Paro, the kingdom's cultural power was clearly evident. The road from Paro to the capital, Thimphu, wound through some of the most pristine and well-protected natural environment on earth, testimony to the efficacy of careful, sustainable growth that places the indigenous cultural identity ahead of the global melting pot.

At the carefully preserved timber-and-stone guest house, I was greeted by Datong Tuku Rinpoche, a Bhutanese lama and guru to one of the royal princesses. The richness of Bhutan's culture and the pride of the Bhutanese in having preserved it against the onslaughts of Western commercialism was evident everywhere.

We were joined by Dr. Karma Phuntsho of the Loden Foundation, a lecturer on Bhutanese history, religion, philosophy and socio-anthropology at Cambridge University.

"Everyone in government has taken up the idea of GNH. It has become a slogan," he said. "It helps the government find a balance between tradition and modernity. It encapsulates the middle path. It is a conceptual guiding principle. You can keep in sight what you want."

Nevertheless, Bhutan faces many practical problems and realities of development, he said. The "Land of the Thunder Dragon" is landlocked and isolated. Some 30% of the population remains below the poverty line. "People are lacking in material comfort. We need schools and medical facilities," he explained. "We need roads, electricity, and outside exposure, both for grassroots development as well as our internal spiritual development." As almost an afterthought, he added that the current (fifth) King of Bhutan has shifted his own focus to economic development.

Measuring Gross National Happiness

I recall Arundhati Roy expressing her own concerns over the blind application of GDP as a measure of national economic success and, in turn, good governance. In India, she said, "economists cheering from the pages of corporate newspapers inform us that the GDP growth rate is phenomenal, unprecedented. Shops are overflowing with consumer goods. Government storehouses are overflowing with food grains. Outside this circle of light, farmers steeped in debt are committing suicide in their hundreds. Reports of starvation and malnutrition come in from across the country. So, dangerous levels of malnutrition and permanent hunger are the preferred model these days: 47% of India's children below three suffer from malnutrition; 46% are stunted. Utsa Patnaik's study reveals that about 40% of the rural population in India has the same food grain absorption level as Sub-Saharan Africa. Today, an average rural family eats about 100 kg less food in a year than it did in the early 1990s. The last five years have seen the most violent increase in rural-urban income inequalities since Independence."

Instead, GNH calls for a "middle way" between the extremes of eco-liberal fundamentalism and socialist excesses. It brings right into the economic equation the question of humanity, feelings and compassion which, as Muhammad Yunus pointed out, Western invisible-hand economists simply ignore or factor out of their greed-oriented assumptions. Bhutan's concept of GNH calls for a more humane approach to growth, emphasizing ethnic identity as opposed to global consumer cloning. This tiny Himalayan kingdom shuts the door right in the face of melting-pot approaches to economic and social development.

According to Bhutanese scholars and political leaders, there are four recognized pillars of GNH:

- economic development
- environmental preservation
- cultural preservation
- good governance.

While such concepts should already be recognized as universal values, there are some critics of GNH within Western economic institutions. Mainstream Western economists argue that happiness is subjective and so cannot be measured. The GNH indicator should therefore, in their view, be declared irrelevant.

In response to such arguments, the Bhutan Studies Center is now developing an index for GNH, by documenting beliefs from all parts of the world about what constitutes happiness. But Bhutanese scholars also express some concerns. "While happiness indicators [across the globe] may be similar, they may not fit into our own cultural context," said Thsheing Phuntsho, a researcher at the Center, whom I visited soon after my arrival in Thimphu.

So far, nine indicators of GNH, known as the Bhutan Development Index (BDI), have been developed by the Bhutan Studies Center:

- psychological well-being
- time use—amount of time devoted to work/leisure/religion
- health
- education
- cultural aspects—diversity and resilience
- governance
- community vitality
- ecological diversity and resilience
- economic living standards.

In 2006, the Bhutan Studies Center undertook a field survey of nine districts in Bhutan, but the survey covered only 350 respondents. A second nationwide survey commenced in December 2007. "Whatever test we run, it does not come up to our expectations," explained Thsheing Phuntsho. "There are 19 different dialects in Bhutan."

The danger is that by seeking to measure GNH, it will become empirical and thus negate the entire concept. By trying to fit GNH into Western modules of economic theory, it may become open to arguments from more mainstream Western economic institutions. This could undermine its very ephemeral nature, which puts spiritual needs on a par with material needs, thus offering a new, alternative paradigm to traditional measurements of economic and, in turn, national success. In a way, Thsheing Phuntsho summarized everything when he nodded toward the cremation ground on the other side of the river from the Bhutan Studies Center and exclaimed: "It reminds us during our study of the impermanence of all things."

Thinking Outside of the Economic Box

For those at the core of this concept, developing an index for GNH seems less important. "To talk about GNH, you must look from different contexts," explained Lungtaen Gyatso, director of the Institute of Language and Culture Studies at the Royal University of Bhutan and a practicing monk.

"You cannot say that what is agreed in Bhutan cannot be accepted in the U.S.," he continued. "While talking about GNH in a Bhutanese context, we must understand factors such as our geographic location. We are a tiny kingdom located between China and India. Our survival between giants is a great thing. India was under British rule, and Tibet was taken by China, but Bhutan survived and this is a miracle for us. In international forums, people criticize Bhutan for holding on to our culture so strongly. We are a small country of half a million. We may be small, but we are recognized around the world not for our economic status but because of our traditions. And our traditions talk a lot about happiness."

"Do you feel the threat of globalization?" I asked.

"Because of the tiny size of our population, we fear cultural erosion. So the government, in the name of GNH, is trying to educate our people in cultural survival. Globalization is moving toward a mono-culture. We want to stick to what we are. When we talk about GNH, we are talking about our values. Preservation of our culture is important to Bhutanese. It is important to look at our values and our local cultural system. The global economy is at a crisis point because of the degeneration of our environment. And this is a concern for the whole world. By serving as an example of environmental protection and slowing down its environmental degradation, Bhutan can contribute to the world at large. The natural environment plays an important role as part of GNH."

Lungtaen Gyatso then explained how Bhutan's government applies GNH in its administration of the country.

"There are several levels. At the state level, sound policies must be applied that will give our people a better place to live. At the individual level, we must ask how individuals can play a role in this process and in implementing these policies."

"How does this work in the government administration?" I asked.

"At the government level, we are talking about creating conditions that will localize happiness—that is, the spiritual well-being of people—through good governance and good leadership. Then you must go to the grassroots where people live to see how it really works. So, for Bhutanese, happiness is possible."

He gave me an example. "Plans are on the rise for our ore industry; consumerism is also becoming more and more prominent; and people want to establish power plants. While this will bring in billions of dollars in material and economic benefits, we must ask two commonsense questions. First, what will be the environmental impact—will it degrade or compromise the environment? Second, how will it affect our traditional cultural system? If this industry makes people's living conditions more difficult, or causes dislocation, or has a negative impact upon their homes and lifestyles, then we will hold back the project!"

I was impressed with this wholesome approach to development, and thought about how China frequently dislocates entire villages, destroying forever their traditional way of life for the sake of an industrial or infrastructure project. This was China's approach to state capitalism. I asked Lungtaen Gyatso what would be the Bhutanese approach.

"We are not interested in the state giving everything to people," he replied. "Rather, we can create conditions for everyone to play a public role and participate." He then went on to explain the role of Buddhist philosophy in the Bhutanese approach to democratic participation. "Buddhism, whether you call it a religion or a philosophy, is unique. It believes in equality. Buddha talked about 'all sentient beings,' so forget about human beings alone—even reptiles and insects are intimately interconnected. That teaches us to respect each other and the environment. So, stop thinking about *yourself [as in laissez-faire* capitalism]. Buddhism says not to look at finding happiness for yourself, but at making others happy. There are two kinds of happiness: material happiness, and happiness in your mind. Both are dictated by external factors. You should look to provide happiness to others through a good, pure heart and tolerance of others. This fits our GNH model."

When I asked Lungtaen Gyatso what he foresaw for the future development of GNH as a concept, he smiled. "This is just the beginning," he said, "and Buddhism says there is no end to anything."

Giving Ancient Wisdom a Modern Twist

I made my way to the UNESCO office in Thimphu to meet Dasho Meghraj Gurung, a board member of the Bhutan Studies Center. A Bhutanese of Nepalese descent, Dasho Meghraj Gurung had been instrumental throughout his career in articulating the concept of Gross National Happiness.

"To understand the genesis of GNH," he said, "we must go back to the essence of our traditional culture. Our own cultural construct was greatly influenced by Buddhism. Within this context, people have already internalized the notion of everlasting happiness. My own understanding of everlasting happiness was an abstract notion of how to free our life of suffering. Basically, we suffer because we need wisdom, which is normally looked at from the intellectual perspective. But in Buddhism, it requires esoteric training to acquire wisdom. Most traditional people internalize these notions."

Central to the exposition of GNH was Bhutan's unique history. The great tantric master Padmasambhava, known among Tibetans as "Guru Rinpoche," or the "second Buddha," traveled to Bhutan several times to teach Buddhism. The pre-Buddhist religion of Tibet and Bhutan was Bon, in its root form essentially a sophisticated form of nature worship.

"Before Buddhism came to Bhutan, because of environmental resource constraints, we had a symbiotic relationship between man and nature. Because people lived their lives close to the environment, Guru Rinpoche's ideas clicked. Bon was already here and so Guru Rinpoche wasn't moving into a vacuum. He in turn spread Buddhism, but he didn't change the local cultural context. Buddhist saints accepted local cultural input. Guru Rinpoche declared all Bon deities protectors of Buddhism, so there was cultural continuity. Many local saints then became viewed as the living Buddha."

I found in this explanation many lessons on developmental economics. One cannot bring outside ideas and theories into a local context without absorbing or being absorbed by that context. Only in this way can there be a merger and, in turn, positive evolution of ideas and approaches, rather than self-defeating conflict. There is no reason for conflict. To some extent, the Washington Consensus intolerance of localism may come from roots implanted in the religious ethos of Washington—the Judeo-Christian tradition of right versus wrong, good versus bad, us versus them—which cannot translate into Asian cultures, which seek a broader consensus rather than schism.

Dasho Meghraj Gurung continued: "In 1960, we ended years of isolation when a route to India was built. The first five-year plan was conceived by the third King, who was mindful of the need for cultural sustainability to be a part of the process of change, and this ensured that our development process would be a continuity of our culture. This was the indigenous approach to development.

"The fourth King came along and declared, 'GNH is more important than GNP,' shaking the assumptions underlying economic policy worldwide. One view is that GNH is rooted in Buddhism and is individual, but we can create the environment or conditions that will enable us to be happy. GNH creates a new paradigm driven by a different perspective concerning the meaning of life. It seeks to remove all sources leading to conflict."

"That runs straight against the grain of Washington Consensus thinking," I suggested. "At the same time, isn't the World Bank trying to understand the concept?"

The World Bank approach is grounded in classic neo-liberal economics, which Dasho Meghraj Gurung explained comes down to the "whole issue of need."

"All of us are needs-driven—the need for security, sustenance, love—an economic constant since the beginnings of humankind," he said. "So, how to satisfy needs? Happiness can transcend this."

He then shrugged. "We [Bhutan] are not all that Shangri-la, after all. In 1971, my cousin went to Japan and came back with dollars, which I had never seen before. So, I went neo-liberal. But we cannot sustain that. The U.S. wants China and India to cut down on carbon dioxide emissions, and India and China want the U.S. to cut down. But meanwhile, the world is being destroyed. We are heading toward a day of reckoning."

"So, you gave up on being neo-liberal in the end?"

"Never approach this issue with 'I have all the answers,' because you never do," Dasho Meghraj Gurung replied. "This is the problem with neo-liberalists. They believe they have all the answers. They do research, but in the end they create their own reality, because what they believe in becomes their reality.

"We need a new development paradigm to regenerate values. Relations now are all being defined by dollars. Somehow, the human being is lost in the process. A new ideological base gives bigger meaning to life. Let's make life more comfortable with less conflict; let's bring health care back to the people. Remember, development is like this: the individual must find his own path. That is what Buddha said. But we can create these conditions and give his meaning a modern twist."

Maybe that is what the Himalayan Consensus is all about.

The Prime Minister Who Dared to Push GNH

GNH is now threatening to turn upside down the assumptions of conventional economists and is thus attracting widespread attention. Lyonpo Jigmi Y. Thinley, who served several terms as prime minister of Bhutan, was elected to serve again in Bhutan's first democratic elections, held in March 2008. He has been credited with being the key instrumental voice in promoting Gross National Happiness as a new benchmark for measuring national success. He clearly enjoys widespread popularity—something to be said for GNH.

He took the time to meet with me before the elections, to talk about Bhutanese politics, GNH and globalization. While Bhutan held vociferously to its cultural traditions, the introduction of U.S-style bicameral elections seemed somewhat incongruous; so I began by asking: "Why has Bhutan, a traditional monarchy where the king is so popular among his subjects, suddenly embarked on adopting Western-style democracy?"

"Adopting democracy is a decision by the leadership, not by a restless public," he explained. (Bhutan's former King, Jigme Singye Wangchuck, chose not to try and hold on to his royal authority, being mindful of the internal conflicts that plagued Nepal for over a decade as a result of misrule by that country's recently deposed king.)

"Why did you decide to establish the Druk Phuensum Tshogpa party and re-enter politics?"

"My decision to go back into politics was driven by fear that there may be a derailing of the GNH policy," he said. "We need to continue to breathe life into our goals of social justice and human rights."

"When last serving as Bhutan's prime minister, were these the issues you considered most in governance?"

"Bhutan is located between the two most contentious countries in the world, and there are compelling forces of globalization that have created new fears," he replied.

Certainly, in the 1960s and 1970s, India was paranoid about visitors entering Bhutan, so the country was pretty much closed. During the 1980s and 1990s, Bhutan pushed increasingly to assert control over its external affairs. In 2006, a formal treaty with India gave Bhutan its own foreign relations functions. In reality, however, its government still consults India on foreign policy.

An underlying sensitive consideration is that Bhutan's border with Tibet lacks clear demarcation. Given the nomadic Tibetan population of the area, this impacts ethnic grazing and migration rights. Meanwhile, China's government is now undertaking road infrastructure projects in the disputed border areas.

"My role was greatly influenced by my own understanding of the world. We wanted to develop a government that was a democracy, and to establish a positive outlook-based civil service, which would guide the development of our education system. While advancing the role of development, we needed to design a foreign policy that could negotiate us through multilateral and international issues and project Bhutan as being balanced. Of these priorities, GNH was a guiding light. I was honored to spread the idea!"

"It is true that you were the main beacon spreading this concept across the globe. Even the World Bank has been forced to reevaluate its policies and to try and understand the role of GNH and recognize its potential. How did the concept arise, and where did it begin?"

"The concept of GNH emerged with the fourth King of Bhutan, His Majesty Jigme Singye Wangchuck, who took over stewardship of the kingdom in 1962. The young visionary understood the people and was willing to break with convention. He sought a new paradigm of development. He was more interested in the end, rather than the means. He began talking about the concept of Gross National Happiness, so by the time of his coronation, it was natural and obvious. But it came to public view in 1986 when he was interviewed by the *Financial Times*.

"He was dissatisfied with the progress of developing countries; by their inability to choose their own path of development, by the environmental destruction that ensued when they followed another's path, and by the resulting cultural damage. The King was willing to make sacrifices in the interests of people's happiness, and that is why the GNH concept is here to stay in the hearts and minds of Bhutanese people.

"When he looked at the development models of industrialized countries that depicted relentless growth, he felt that material goods didn't necessarily produce happiness. Happiness is defined by the mind and body, and moreover by the right to choose a sustainable form of development.

"GNH is a policy of equitable and balanced distribution of the benefits of development for all spectrums of society, such as the promotion and preservation of culture, low-density development of towns, and vast tracts of environmentally protected land. Look at our country's foreign policy!

Bhutan has no relations with the G5 nations that comprise the U.N. Security Council!"

"That is most admirable," I said. "It seems, though, that many economists are now trying to quantify GNH, even to create an index for it. Aren't you afraid that by quantifying it in material terms, something which by its nature is determined by emotional rather than purely physical factors, this concept, which makes economists think outside of the box, will be put in a box?"

He replied: "I have never supported moves to develop the GNH concept in a quantitative manner, as you cannot quantify the causes of happiness. Living with happiness is the most important element to be measured. To quantify is to adopt the same economic-approaches that we are seeking an alternative to."

GNH Activism

In November 2007, an eclectic gathering of Asian politicians, Buddhist, Hindu and Taoist leaders, NGO activists, and scholars met in Bangkok to challenge the conventional values of the Bretton Woods mainstream economic order and to advocate gross national happiness as a new economic paradigm.

Ironically, Thailand, which had followed the import substitu- tion/export promotion economic model and enjoyed rapid growth rates throughout the 1980s and 1990s, was facing its own dilemma. Looking to its Buddhist roots for a more sustainable and harmonious growth model than the self-serving, greed-driven neo-liberal/neo-conservative model it had adopted in recent decades, the Thai government turned for advice to—of all places—Bhutan. The youthful fifth King of Bhutan visited Thailand, where he was greeted by thousands of young people almost as if he were a rock star. The Thai people saw in the tiny Himalayan kingdom a possible model to regenerate Thailand's own once-pacifist, environmentally sensitive Buddhist values, now smothered in exhaust fumes.

Political and economic introspection in both countries had led to the Gross National Happiness Conference in Bangkok. It was preceded by weeks of preparatory meditation retreats and visitations along the Mekong River, from Laos to Bangkok. When speaking about the Himalayan Consensus, I was surprised by how quickly delegates from Thailand stressed the need for Laos, Thailand, Cambodia and Vietnam to be included in the equation, in the same way as the Mekong flows through all those countries on its journey from Tibet to the sea. This reflects the view of Rajiv Gandhi that this greater

Himalayan region is interlinked by geography, sociology, economics and the powerful philosophies of Hindu, Islam, Buddhism and Taoism that traverse this region and bring it together as Asia. It is time for Asians to take pride in their own ethnic values and realize that the power of their economies and social philosophies can serve as both new epicenter and source of universal values for the new era.

One of the most outspoken activist speakers at the conference was Sulak Sivaraksa, president of the Sathinkoses Nagapradipa Foundation. Born in 1933, he has witnessed both turbulence and stability in Thailand's ever-evolving political arena, and as a social activist he has contributed to guiding that process. In many ways, Sulak, a devout Buddhist, has become a political and social institution in Thailand, having personally fought for justice, peace, democracy and sustainable livelihoods for many decades.

Sulak Sivaraksa is known foremost as an activist, and then as teacher, scholar, NGO founder and author of more than 100 books and monographs. More than anything, he is a philosopher at heart. Ever spritely and interested in new ideas, Sulak took a break from the conference to share his views on unilateral materialist globalization and the need for a worldwide revolution based on Buddhist values.

"Our values are fixed by globalization, which means they are fixed by American multinational corporations," said Sulak. "This is Americanization. They have the best guns. So if you don't like it, they will invade you. Look at the examples: Afghanistan, Iraq and, of course, Vietnam before. Their values are driven by greed—what is best for *me*! For that matter, India and Thailand are now also under the U.S. sphere of control."

From his perspective, the promotion of global neo-liberalism with its facade of a free market following an "invisible hand" is, in itself, flawed. Greed alone cannot be the fundamental basis for sustained economic growth when factoring fabrics of social community into the picture.

"In Buddhism, there are three root causes of suffering: greed, ignorance and anger." He pointed out that most of the world's catastrophes—political, economic, environmental and military—were rooted in these three pursuits, the very values underlying the globalization of American capitalism.

"We need a new world view," he said. "We need someone to translate into wisdom and understanding, and in Buddhist teachings, how to be natural. We need social change and social equality to be put into a modern context. Killing isn't enough. We need a new model of peace. The Buddhist concept of *samadhi* isn't just about being a goody-goody, but about actually helping others to step out from suffering."

I asked him how, in practical terms, this might be achieved in the context of the current global dynamics.

"Check globalization!" he responded immediately. "How to save the world from globalization? Determine how to keep the world happy for the next generation, and care for the environment. Globalization needs to be rooted in local culture. Change the world, but honor Mother Earth."

"As a first step, many NGO activists are calling for the dismantling of institutions such as the World Bank and the IMF. Do you think this will really check globalization?" I asked.

Sulak Sivaraksa chuckled. "It is easy to say 'Overthrow the World Bank,' but we need dialogue with the World Bank, and its economists need to be humble. Every World Bank representative lives in a big house and its visiting economists stay in five-star hotels. They should live with the poor. According to their recommendations, the poor all need motorcycles. No, they need dignity and their own culture!"

"You have often spoken of an 'Asian challenge' to the globalization of Westernization—or Americanization." I said. "Can you explain what you mean by an 'Asian challenge'?"

"In Buddhism, we challenge the traditional hierarchy. If we want to be serious, we must challenge our own culture and not blame all things on the West. Cultural integrity means diversity. The West has gone wrong by advocating only one acceptable way—Western democracy. If we want an Asian challenge, we must bring all religions together. Look, even Buddhist temples in Sri Lanka have Hindu gods within. We must have cultural integrity, but be aware of globalization. Indonesia is a good example of cultural integrity. It was first Hindu, then Buddhist, then Muslim. Their former president once said, 'In order to be an Indonesian Muslim, you must have cultural roots in Buddhism and Hinduism.'

"Religions cannot come together—partly because we are tribal, and religion is tribal, so the less educated one is, the more fundamentalist one becomes. But religion is also universal. Everyone needs to be less selfish and more compassionate, to be more progressive for each religion. Make religion more meaningful to the young. We must be more skillful. We are losing our nature. Buddha is not Buddhist and Jesus is not Christian. People put labels on them."

He was right: of course the problem is labels. The anti-globalization movement isn't really anti-globalization when it comes to universally needed technologies and health care, but it *is* opposed to globalization of a single value system and political framework, including the economic fundamentalism that goes with it. But, at the same time, the Western media often criticize Asia's economic growth at the cost of political reform.

Sulak Sivaraksa concurred: "Lee Kuan Yew talks about Asian values with no human rights. Fine, but nobody wants to be tortured."

"What about the rise of China as an economic and, increasingly, political power? Does China's approach—which broke from the World Bank's and the IMF's approach—serve as an alternative model, an economic middle way?" I asked.

"Mainland China has switched from Maoism to consumerism," Sulak replied. "Remember, they came from feudalism. China is rooted in Confucianism and Buddhism. Then it became labeled an economic superstar. Now they are rich, and the Chinese are mimicking the West. Buddhism has only been revived there in the past two decades."

"Can Tibet become China's source for reviving spirituality?" I ventured. "At least a set of values that isn't about blind consumerism, money and brand worship still exists there."

"His Holiness [the Dalai Lama] says we must not hate them [the Chinese], but help them. China, with wisdom, will be able to see that the West is hypocritical. They [the West] claim to support Tibet and freedom, but what they really want is more money from China!"

"So, what is the economic middle way?" I asked. "Can Bhutan's concept of gross national happiness—the subject of this conference—really offer an answer?"

Sulak Sivaraksa laughed. "The king's GNH goes smack up against GDP."

On leaving the Gross National Happiness Conference, I mused less on GNH as an economic measurement and more on the values underlying it.

Defining the Alternative and Defying the Mainstream

China has long adopted the standard: GNP growth will satisfy the people as long as they can be persuaded to keep consuming and do so by upscale spending lured by branding—essentially, the American consumer cycle model. Western and Chinese economists argue that without material growth, the spiritual factor cannot be considered. I asked Bhutan's Prime Minister, Lyonpo Jigmi Y. Thinley, what he thought.

"When the market ethics move in, who is to deny that a better standard of living can arise?" he replied. Agreeing only partially, he challenged the view, asking: "But is that how we define quality of life, by 'you are not buying enough of this and that, so you need to buy more?', GNH suggests that maybe there are different kinds of markets."

"This is a huge proposition to make," I said. "Maybe we should be re-evaluating what qualifies as 'lifestyle,' so that it's not how many cars or Louis Vuitton bags one owns. Likewise, companies need to be evaluated by a different measure than the 1990s one of shareholders' value; one that measures how much a company is doing to save energy, restore the environment, and take social responsibility. In this regard, is global warming topping Bhutan's global agenda?"

"In the Himalayan region, we are so vulnerable to global warming," Lyonpo Jigmi Y. Thinley said. "Imagine if the Mekong River dries up? What will happen? This is not farfetched. We are much more vulnerable and at the forefront of change. We have no physical security against climate change in Bhutan. There are banana trees growing in the Thimphu Valley where I live. Imagine! This was unprecedented not long ago. And the diminishing flow of our rivers will impact on our revenues, as we depend on exporting hydropower. Moreover, we are now threatened by a new phenomenon, melting ice from glaciers affected by global warming is causing lakes to overflow, which leads to flooding. We are very worried about these aspects of global warming in Bhutan."

"Some have questioned the relevance of GNH to other societies, as it is a concept that has evolved in a Buddhist country. Do you think it is more appropriate for Buddhist countries?" I asked.

"I try to avoid linking GNH to Buddhism," he replied. "The religious sentiments embodied in the GNH concept apply in all cultures. It needs to be cross-cultural. If it is linked to Buddhism, people of other religions may reject it. If it is a Buddhist idea, then of course it is easier for Buddhists to understand, accept and internalize it. But at the same time, we don't want to say it is Buddhist and then exclude others."

"Many people in Asia are now calling for something called 'Buddhist economics.' How would you describe this idea?" I probed.

"Ringu Tulku Rinpoche said that 'happiness is the absence of suffering.' Buddhism has everything to do with avoiding the causes of suffering, and one cause of suffering is greed, which is the basis of the globalization of consumerism.

"We need a clearer world view—one that increasingly supports a holistic approach. Even as we speak, America's role is diminishing. We need to redefine globalization and bring in some new dimensions that relate to the finite world in which we live. We need to live, produce and consume more consciously, and bring world responsibility back into the globalization process.

"Globalization has to have a new set of dimensions. At the moment it is only economic and, frankly, to do with security in terms of hardware. We need new social dimensions too. We need to redefine wealth. Is it a goal, a target of competition to continue to pursue wealth? What really constitutes wealth? Material accumulation? Or is it greater spirituality within the concept of what is sustainable material development?"

"How do you feel about the emerging concept of a Himalayan Consensus as an alternative to the established Washington Consensus?" I asked.

"Why not?" said Lyonpo Jigmi Y. Thinley. "In fact, it is already happening. There have been a series of activities between the Mekong delta and Bhutan, which region is linked by a strong Buddhist culture. Yes, the compulsion is powerful in this region. All great rivers start from a trickling creek."

"So, in the end, where does GNH stand in the anti-globalization/ globalization debate?"

"GNH is not anti-globalization," Lyonpo Jigmi Y. Thinley smiled. "Globalization is a reality, but *how* it happens is the question. It should happen in the GNH way, which is a holistic, sustainable way!"

3

10

EMPOWERING THE MARGINALIZED
TO STOP TERRORISM, FOCUS ON ITS ROOTS

The fundamental duel, which seemed to be that between colonialism and anti-colonialism, and indeed between capitalism and socialism, is already losing some of its importance. What counts today, the question which is looming on the horizon, is the need for a redistribution of wealth. Humanity must reply to this question, or be shaken to pieces by it.

—**Frantz Fanon,** *The Wretched of the Earth*

The Root of Terrorism

On January 26, 2007, I was sitting in the coffee shop of Islamabad's Marriott Hotel when the lobby was rocked by a large explosion that sent people diving under the tables. Within minutes, the place was swarming with media and military men. It was the first suicide bombing to hit Pakistan's capital in five years. I had been sitting smack in the center of the targeted zone, and survived thanks to a thick wall and a security guard, who tragically lost his life. I later learned that a young suicide bomber had tried to enter the hotel lobby through the parking lot, but that he was stopped by a suspicious security guard. That brief delay saved my life because the bomb was timed.

The attack made me think a lot about what caused people to become suicide bombers. Such incidents are fodder for the Western media, who perpetuate the idea of instability in the region. However, finding a solution to the problem of suicide bombers means digging deeper than is possible with a sound bite.

I asked myself why the suicide bomber had attacked my hotel at that moment. Apparently, I was the only American within the targeted zone at the time of the explosion. Was his martyrdom in response to something I, as a symbolic American, had done, I wondered? Searching for an answer, I recalled an event that had taken place earlier in the week.

An American drone plane flying into Pakistan air space from across the Afghan border had bombed an Islamic *madrasa* school. Its mission had been to kill suspected members of the Taliban. Eighty children lost their lives in the attack. There were no Taliban anywhere nearby.

Arundhati Roy, later reflecting on this analyzed how terrorism arises when peaceful dissidence fails. "Perhaps they [the marginalized] wonder how they can go on a hunger strike when they're already starving. How they can boycott foreign goods when they have no money to buy any goods. How they can refuse to pay taxes when they have no earnings. People who have taken arms have done so with full knowledge of what the consequences of that decision will be. They have done so knowing they are on their own. They know that the new laws of the land criminalize the poor and conflate resistance with terrorism."

I wondered how Washington's vow to bomb the Taliban back into the Stone Age[1] was going to win the war against terrorism. It certainly wasn't winning hearts and minds. If anything, it would guarantee that the war on terrorism would wot end. Relatives of the young victims of such an inhumane attack might be expected to use whatever tools were available to try and avenge their deaths.

By undertaking such bombings of Islamic schools, the U.S. military, acting on policy from Washington, is almost certain to guarantee an increase in the number of suicide bombers. Why would a young man, with his whole life ahead of him, wish to end it so abruptly? I could think only that he, and others like him, had no hope at all for the future.

Re-empower the Madrasas

Kamrin Lashari, the mayor of Islamabad, had invited me to visit Pakistan to exchange views on a new approach to development. Lashari was undertaking programs to restore the ancient quarters of Pakistan's cities and to re-empower rural villages with cottage industries and sustainable-tourism development. He took me to visit a village tucked away in an idyllic valley on the outskirts of Islamabad, where an ancient mosque was under restoration beneath a cliff face dotted with Sufi meditation caves, and where the local crafts industry was blossoming.

Lashari asked me to address the city council at the headquarters of the Capital Development Fund, the organization responsible for Islamabad's infrastructure and urban development. I spoke about ethnicity as a core aspect of re-empowering marginalized people and about the role of micro-equity and cultural-preservation tourism in contributing to sustainable development. It was during this speech that I first attempted to define the ideals of a Himalayan Consensus; that by drawing on the philosophies of compassion found in Buddhism, Hinduism and Islam as they meet and interconnect on the Himalayan slopes, a new, more compassionate and sensitive approach to development can achieve much more than traditional economic models that are often imposed on developing countries. I was pleasantly surprised by the positive reception my ideas received from my all-Muslim audience.

I talked about our Buddhist monastery restoration work in Tibet, how we were building clinics in monasteries, and the re-empowering of monks by training them as paramedics. I explained that our program had provided modern medical skills that could be used in conjunction with traditional herbal medicines. The clinics had provided the monks with a sustainable livelihood and expanded the role of monasteries as community centers providing social outreach services.

The city council of Islamabad saw the connection I was making with Pakistan's own *madrasas,* or religious schools. Seen by Washington as hotbeds of fundamentalism, they could be turned into incubators of social harmony through vocational training, community cottage-industry development and the re-empowerment of ethnic pride through economic self-sustainability.

I learned that many children sent to study in the *madrasas* are street kids who are often difficult for their parents to discipline. The *madrasas* provide social structure through religious studies. When these children emerge from the *madrasas,* they are enriched with Islamic religious knowledge, but are lacking in the skills necessary to support themselves. Without a sustainable livelihood, they either have to open their own *madrasa* or work for a religious organization or cause. Disenfranchised from their own heritage by the American-dominated mainstream media—from the news industry to Hollywood—that often belittle and lampoon their beliefs and ethnicity, they turn back to the mosque for psychological security and assurance of identity.

A fraction of the funds spent by American taxpayers under the Bush administration for its "War on Terror"—which sometimes included bombing *madrasas*—could be used, through appropriate local foundations, to support religious work. This extensive social network of religious schools could be used to create community outreach through vocational skills programs and support for cottage industries. Think of the sense of security it would bring if people had a life to look forward to, and a means of making it happen, I suggested to Islamabad's city council. The response was immediately positive, and I was soon offered an opportunity to establish a branch of Shambhala Foundation in Islamabad.

That afternoon, following my speech, Lashari whisked me off by jeep caravan to Lahore, where he had served as mayor, to witness the meticulous work he had undertaken in restoring the old quarter of this heritage-rich

Moghul city. Through revitalizing the ancient markets by turning them into modern, open-air pedestrian boulevards with hygienic food stalls and diverse crafts, Lashari had brought back to life historic neighborhoods left behind by the values of globalization. His vision in action presented an ethnic-based development model arising from a rich heritage, empowerment through pride in one's ethnicity, projected on to a program of sustainable economic development for the future.

Changing Globalization

Lahore's labyrinthine streets are filled with the mixed smells of spices and exhaust fumes, and the noise of motorcycle rickshaws. In a way, Pakistan is confident of its own comparative advantages: a progressive and creative popular media industry that is already exporting rock groups to India and launching dozens of new television networks; and a hotel and food-beverage service industry that could potentially outclass even Europe's most snobbish hoteliers.

However, Pakistan is troubled by the ongoing conflict in Afghanistan and tensions in Iran, countries with which it shares long and porous borders. Such perceived instability has severely affected Pakistan's growth, though its potential shouldn't be underestimated. In some ways, Pakistan's economy could be prepared to grow in leaps and bounds, but the ongoing violence in Afghanistan, aggravated by the American presence, destabilizes the region and stunts growth. Arguably, the only economic growth area since the U.S. invasion of Afghanistan has been in the cultivation and export of opium.

Calling for New Values to Uproot Problems

Regardless of their differences and similarities in development, experiences are being shared across South Asia. This is what the Himalayan Consensus is all about. The emerging development model for these countries is one based on their experiences of coping with harsh conditions and realities *as they exist,* not as theorized in the laboratories of America's East Coast think-tanks or universities. So, unlike the theoretical approaches, these practical solutions may just work.

"A new value system is required, calling for closer international economic cooperation and more balanced trading relationships, involving a shared-help developmental model," Riza Mohammad Khan, Pakistan's foreign secretary, explained to me at the Foreign Ministry in Islamabad. "We need better management of the globe. We will destroy it, if we are not careful. We are now a global village."

Clearly, the economic relationships among South Asian countries are symbiotic. They could serve as an important piece in the jigsaw puzzle, as the pieces continue to fall into place for an emerging consensual model of economic growth and shared prosperity across the Himalayan plateau.

For Khan, the question of development begins with economic sustainability, from which political development can naturally occur, and not with making economic development dictate political systems and, in turn, ethnic, social and religious values.

"Isn't it more important to get rid of poverty?" Khan asks. "In Pakistan, we are struggling with poverty and looking at alternatives. Trade is more important than aid because it builds value for the population. Overriding are economic interests driven by our mutual needs to eliminate poverty through growth. A new focus on economic and social development will characterize this new phase."

Khan calls for a fresh approach in this new epoch of regionalized world conflict against a backdrop of growing American-style globalization. "It is time to herald a modern era for South Asia, a new direction with efforts placed on reducing poverty," he says, as opposed to perpetuating the old era of feeding regional conflicts through the post-colonial, divide-and-rule approach dictated by Wall Street capital, Washington aid, and military adventurism.

In fact, new paradigms for economic development are emerging from across the Himalayan area. Nepal has offered its own set of solutions for peaceful convergence by bringing the Maoists, with their social alternatives to the IMF's political agenda, into a coalition government. Bhutan has proposed that GNH be used as a new measure of growth. Success derived from application of the micro-finance model pioneered by Muhammad Yunus of Bangladesh is spreading throughout the region.

Where external interference can be minimized, we are seeing some surprising and creative solutions coming out of the Himalayan plateau. Nepal's Maoists came in from the cold and joined a coalition government as a mainstream party, in the process unraveling a problem as seemingly intractable as Kashmir. "Such a solution [to the similar Kashmir imbroglio] will create a new phase in Pakistan-India relations," predicts Khan.

It seems that all the parties are aware that stability is essential for trans-Himalayan economic development. This is the only formula that can alleviate problems among the world's more impoverished regions. Such concern now overrides narrower interests, which have obstructed progress in the past. With peace and stability, energy and Rinds can be redirected toward better things, such as alleviating poverty in the region and integrating the economies of South Asia so that each country can draw upon its relevant comparative advantages and—alongside China—help create a new Himalayan triangle of growth and prosperity.

The Tashkent Forum

The first international conference to be held in Uzbekistan in five years opened on October 28, 2006 under tight surveillance and security. The Tashkent Forum of Silk Road Cities, which was attended by the mayors of places such as Xining, Lanzhou, Islamabad and Tashkent, and with representatives from the United Nations Development Program (UNDP), the United Nations Conference on Trade and Development (UNCTAD) and the WTO, sought to lay foundations to integrate the economic interests of China, Kazakhstan, Kyrgyzstan, Pakistan and Uzbekistan under the U.N. umbrella. It was hoped the forum would revive and give new substance to an ancient spirit of regional connectivity. For two days, it seemed as if the cities along the Silk Road in some of the most isolated, disregarded and misunderstood parts of the world were anticipating a renaissance.

"We are confident that peace and development are closely interwoven," stated the Tashkent Declaration, "and that challenges related to improving living standards, development and equity always remain relevant to the global community." Khalid Malik, the United Nations' chief representative to China, who chaired the convocation, had invited me to speak at the forum and to read the declaration.

"To address such challenges related to improving living standards, development and equity always remains relevant to the global community," said the declaration. As I read these words aloud in a somber conference room in Tashkent's cavernous meeting center, the logic of the declaration seemed to strike at the core of the security and globalization conundrum facing this region.

I continued to read: "To address such challenges, it is necessary to continue working on the development and realization of a strategy and programs that would allow the well-being of the population to improve and lead to harmonious regional development."

I was fully in agreement that sustainable economic development and respect for the diverse ethnicity of each culture are key pillars in assuring social harmony. Indeed, they are the basis of peaceful living and the global integration of positive forces involving trade, technology and health care.

That means *not* "bombing you back to the Stone Age," as the U.S. State Department had threatened Pakistan's President Pervez Musharraf if he didn't align himself with Washington's program to eliminate the Taliban. Such an approach has since proven to be a formula for incubating, rather than containing, terrorism. If terrorism is to be reduced and eventually eliminated, a new formula is needed. Terrorism is rooted in discontent. Programs aimed both at alleviating poverty through sustainable development and at re-empowering people through increased self-esteem should be the logical first step.

"This [Silk Road Forum] is designed to create a platform from which the people of this region can move ahead," explained Khalid Malik during a break in the forum. "Fundamentally, the ninth to the thirteenth centuries were the golden era of the Silk Road, characterized by a free exchange of ideas and religious philosophies, together with commodities. It was a time of great prosperity. For the renewed prosperity of the people along the Silk Road, openness is needed."

An advocate of ethnic diversity, he added: "Their cultural diversity should be seen as a strength, not a weakness. Through this Silk Road initiative, we are creating a new community based on this diversity."

There is no one more qualified to speak on this subject than Malik. When he walks through the labyrinthine bazaars of cities such as Bukhara and Samarqand, craftsmen look up from their work, recognize him, and step forward to embrace him. A blacksmith shows Malik how his shop has expanded. A spice merchant offers him cardamom-flavored coffee from his home-cum-teahouse.

In each small household-shop hangs a UNDP certificate recognizing the craftsman's contribution to Uzbekistan's national heritage, personally signed by Malik when he served as U.N. representative to the country nearly a decade before. With this umbrella of international protection, Uzbekistan's craftsmen were able to revive their traditional crafts using private enterprise to sustain their livelihood and growth, remarkable in an environment (a former Soviet Republic) where the state sought to retain control over all aspects of life out of security fears.

"You cannot have sustainable peace without sustainable development," Malik says. "People need jobs, better education, careers. History has taught that you need development efforts for that to happen."

In the bazaar, Malik studies the knot weave on a restored antique tribal carpet and suggests to the weaver-retailer how he might better appeal to the tourist market that is anticipated, but yet to materialize. Malik explains his philosophy succinctly: "Demonstrate to people that they can invest in their own future. Give them a new sense of hope. Provide goals they can reach." There could be no more appropriate mantra for the anti-globalization movement that is seeking a new platform of consensus.

This more realistic approach, sensitive to local conditions and cultures, stands in stark contrast to regional re-engineering experiments—Afghanistan is a case in point—where model systems have been imposed upon countries inappropriately, leading to their rejection. Violence and social breakdown follow. There is little room to talk core economics, the foundation necessary to begin developing social structures upon which practical political progress can rest.

This first regional forum of Silk Road cities sought to address hard-core issues that remained as obstacles to cooperation. For instance, a proposal was put forward for multi-country visa recognition (along the lines of Europe's Schengen visa arrangement, which did away with border controls for Europeans) to case frontier difficulties. Another was for the region's collective re-branding as "The Silk Road," in an attempt to overturn the maligned image perpetuated by mainstream international media, with input sought from advisors from Hong Kong. The need to bring together private- and public-sector interests was argued as being a key to progress. A softer, more holistic development model was proposed, with cooperation—not confrontation—as its core principle, to assure long-term security through coordinated economic development instead of violent repression.

"So, is the Washington Consensus dead?" I asked Malik. "Is it time, do you think, for a new Silk Road Consensus?"

Malik shrugged. "I think it is time for an East-West Consensus instead."

Kabul's Aid Conundrum

In late May 2006, a huge riot erupted in Kabul, Afghanistan. It began when a U.S. convoy of humvees sped through the city, smashing into several local cars and killing civilians. The convoy was immediately surrounded by angry Kabul citizens. Panicking, the American soldiers opened fire. President Hamid Karzai made no public attempt to quell the exploding tensions, and chaos ensued. As the rioting spun out of control, the guesthouses of foreign aid experts and executing agencies were pillaged.

Why, one might ask, would Afghans attack the foreign aid agencies and experts who, in theory at least, are present in their country to help them?

In truth, most Afghans cannot differentiate between NGO aid workers and military personnel. This is understandable, as the distinction between them has been severely blurred in Kabul. A lot of aid for Afghanistan has been funded in cooperation with the U.S. military, either directly or through side arms of the U.S. government. One way or another, it could be seen to be connected, if just by association, to the U.S. military or American intelligence community. Much of the aid is being pushed toward the sensitive border areas, where U.S. forces are facing the most resistance.

At least that is how the Afghans may see it.

Less covertly, American military personnel have been reportedly overseeing and even directing aid work in Afghanistan. It is little wonder, then, that Afghans cannot differentiate between aid programs that might be intended to help improve their lives and what many Afghans interpret as their own colonization, or at least administration, by a president backed by foreign armed forces.

The aid donors are those same countries comprising the military coalition, mainly the United States and Britain, with token presences from Germany, France, Japan and Italy. Because these donors control the purse strings, they set the agendas. Not surprisingly, the NGOs and implementing agencies are from these countries as well. So, the NGOs are there because of the donors. "Foreign aid is a business, an industry like anything else. Should we assume that people working under U.N. contracts are any different from those working under GE [General Electric]?" said Jiang Xueqin, a public information officer with the United Nations Assistance Mission in Afghanistan (UNAMA) in Kabul.

There are many layers in the aid food chain and it is not surprising that funds are siphoned off at each level. The result is that very little money actually gets to the local people. With excessive overheads, too many mouths to feed, and minimal supervision of aid agencies on the assumption that aid is about humanitarianism and not about business, there are many opportunities and temptations to loot the aid cash that is in circulation.

USAID regulatory practice requires funding only to U.S. contractors. Companies such as Halliburton—formerly run by Vice President Dick Cheney—and construction conglomerates, such as Louis Berger, get the turnkey contracts. Locals cannot benefit directly, except at the bottom of the food chain. The commercial practice side of humanitarian aid permits the main contractor to take 40% off the top before subcontracting down the chain to designated "experts," typically other foreigners with little or no knowledge of the local problems, culture or language. There are thousands of such foreigners present in Afghanistan, earning average salaries of around US$200,000 a year. Along with their "expertise," they have brought with them an economic model. It is called inflation. The trickle-down effect of inflation hurts the local people the worst, heightening their resentment toward the perceived aid-supported foreign shadow government. Rather than combating inflation, the government becomes the very cause of it. Those at the bottom don't benefit from the aid.

"I feel very strongly that we, the international community, are not helping the Afghans," said Jiang, a Canadian. "We are making the country a lot worse. We are making it more likely that genocide will occur in a short time frame after we leave and the four major ethnic groups [Pashtuns (Pathans), Uzbeks, Tajiks, and Hazaras] begin to really fight each other. In the long run, this will come back and haunt us."

UNAMA serves as a coordinating body for all the U.N.'s operations in Afghanistan, which to date have been guided by the U.S. military, giving Jiang an eye-opening course on Washington Consensus developmental economics and its role in dismantling, rather than building, nations.

In 2006, shortly after starting as a U.N. press officer, Jiang attended a UNDP seminar. Some 20 "experts" with Ph.D. degrees had been brought into Afghanistan in order to brainstorm programs on how to build a government more suited to the country than the present federal model. They proposed a model with highly centralized powers in the executive office. Jiang raised his hand and questioned their approach. "President Karzai is Pashtun, and you have three other ethnic groups that all hate each other. So, how can you impose the authority of one ethnic group on all the others?"

The experts knew that Afghanistan has ethnic and religious divisions and religious extremists. But if they were to factor in all these problems, there would be no solution. The only way forward, they agreed, was to adopt an artificial model based on presumed assumptions that required all the problems to be factored out.

Jiang said of this approach: "To work in development, the first thing one must understand is local people and local problems, and give local people ownership over the problems. If you just go in and build schools, they don't know what to do with them. If you just go in and override people's cultural prejudices, they will turn them against you."

The Ethnicity Factor

"The Americans will have trouble succeeding in this country," says Jiang Xueqin, "because they are blind to these ethnic rivalries. Many advisors sent to make policy come from Washington with preconceived, blinkered perspectives. They are not in tune with the realities of life in Afghanistan. But, sooner or later, they will figure this out and start to back one ethnic group, which will probably then 'cleanse' another. This danger could arise in Afghanistan over the coming years, thereby creating a new Darfur. And this is what I fear the most for the Afghan people."

As an example, Jiang points to incidents of local Afghans burning USAID-constructed schools. Shaking their heads in dismay, foreign experts ask: "Why would anyone want to burn down a school in their own community?" and demand that the practice cease. Jiang decided that he would try to find out what the local people thought.

He learned that most Afghans were hostile about schools being built in their communities in the name of President Karzai's government, which was established after the U.S.-led invasion of the country in 2001. While the invasion had succeeded in toppling the Taliban, most Afghans see Karzai as a puppet of foreign interests. Therefore, they view foreign-funded schools as symbolic of imposing an American brand on their local culture. Burning the schools is considered by the local people as an acceptable way for their communities to defend themselves. The same thing had occurred when the Soviets invaded Afghanistan and built Russian-style schools.

"To blindly blame school burnings on the Taliban and 'reactionaries' is wrong," says Jiang. "Such accusations don't bother to understand the roots of the issue. Lack of sensitivity to local cultural differences plays a part, by alienating popular trust. In the USAID-built schools, the curriculum requirements don't account for local sensibilities. Boys and girls go to school together, but this is alien to their culture. It is an imposition of cultural values that are foreign and intrusive. You cannot destroy a people's sense of identity and continuity. If you try, of course they will fight against that."

The People Don 7 Buy It!

My thoughts turned to what author and activist Arundhati Roy had said about the subject during our meeting in New Delhi. "Since the United States is the richest and most powerful country in the world, it has assumed the privilege of being the world's number one denier of genocide," she said. "It continues to celebrate Columbus Day, the day Christopher Columbus arrived in the Americas, which marks the beginning of a holocaust that wiped out millions of native Indians, about 90% of the original population. (Lord Amherst, whose idea it was to distribute blankets infected with the smallpox virus to Indians, has a university town in Massachusetts and a prestigious liberal arts college named after him.)

"In America's second holocaust, almost 30 million Africans were kidnapped and sold into slavery. Nearly half of them died in transit. But in 2002, the U.S. delegation could still walk out of the World Conference Against Racism in Durban, refusing to acknowledge that slavery and the slave trade were crimes. Slavery, they insisted, was *legal* at the time. The U.S. has also refused to accept that the bombing of Tokyo, Hiroshima, Nagasaki, Dresden and Hamburg—which killed hundreds of thousands of civilians—were crimes, let alone acts of genocide. (The argument here is that the government didn't *intend* to kill civilians. This was the first stage in the development of 'collateral damage.') Since the end of World War II, Washington has intervened overtly, militarily, more than 400 times in 100 countries, and covertly more than 6,000 times. This includes the invasion of Vietnam and the extermination—with excellent intentions, of course—of three million Vietnamese, or some 10% of the population.

"None of these has been acknowledged as war crimes or genocidal acts," Roy emphasized. "Robert MacNamara—whose career took him from the bombing of Tokyo in 1945 (1 million dead overnight) to being the architect of the Vietnam War, to President of the World Bank—now sitting in his comfortable chair in his comfortable home in his comfortable country, said that the question is, 'How much evil do you have to do in order to do good?'"

As explained earlier, Western models for development that might appear sound in theory don't necessarily fit the local contours when imposed on different cultures, religions and tribal boundaries. "We have internalized the entire Washington Consensus," Jiang observes. "We cannot debate in our media anymore. People are not thinking. They don't ask questions, and they accept things at face value. But in the meantime, local people's way of life is threatened. So they will fight back."

Marginalizing Poverty and Terrorism

"When my tyre was flat in Pakistan's countryside, many villagers came to help," recalls Donglin Li when I spoke to him at the UNILO offices in Islamabad in January 2007. "Touched by their kindness, I offered money but they all refused. In Islamabad, I have a papaya tree in my garden, but nobody steals the fruit. I think it has something to do with Muslim inter-community support." Li is acutely tuned into the problems of a developing transitional economy, and is aware of the need for solutions to be sympathetic to local conditions and cultures.

Pakistan is a case in point, he said. "GDP growth should create employment, but often it expands the income gap. Because of globalization, the rich become richer; but the poor should not become poorer."

UNILO numbers indicate that economic growth has been reflected more in rising levels of productivity and less in growing employment. While world productivity has increased by 26% over the past decade, the global number of those enjoying employment rose by only 16.6%. This means that income gaps are continuing to widen, even at accelerated rates.

UNILO numbers reveal that during this past decade of unprecedented prosperity, unemployment hit young people the hardest, marginalizing 86.3 million youth, representing 44% of the world's total unemployed, in 2006. Most are between the ages of 15 and 24, the prime age range of suicide bombers.

As an example, UNILO has adopted its own two-pronged micro-finance program in Pakistan. An anti-child-labor fund of US$15 million is boosting parental incomes and getting children out of work and into schools. TREE (Training for Rural Economic Employment) provides training to accompany micro-finance, which is key for self-employment. The programs empower the poor not only by providing financing but, equally important, by supplying a support system that helps build self-confidence. "Our scheme involves a village community of 20-30 people to create 'collective collateral,' which is a social rather than a financial guarantee," says Donglin Li. "Through this grassroots networking, our lending-return program enjoys a 95% success rate."

Could such models also serve to cure terrorism at its roots? As mentioned earlier, for a fraction of the amount the Bush administration spends on bombing diverse ethnic tribal groups, and Muslims in general, vocational training and micro-enterprises could be organized based around Islamic schools, whose existing and vast popular network could change the direction of people's lives by changing their outlook.

As one official in Islamabad explained: "Terrorism happens not because people have a political agenda, but because they have no hope. They have been marginalized from society. When the international media demonize their only beliefs, they have no choice left but to become radicalized."

Endnote

1 Former U.S. deputy secretary of state, Richard Armitage, following the 9-11 terrorist attacks told then Pakistan president Pervez Musharraf, "we had to decide whether we were with America or with the terrorists, but that if we chose the terrorists, then we should be prepared to be bombed back to the stone age." *In the Line of Fire,* by Pervez Musharraf, p. 201, Free Press, New York.

∃

11

"HIGH TIME TO SHUT UP"
MOVING TOWARDS MULTILATERALISM

This is an assembly of embattled peoples, and the battle is being developed on two equally important fronts which require all our efforts. The struggle against imperialism for liberation from colonial or neocolonial shackles, imposed by political arms or firearms or a combination of the two, is inseparable from the struggle against backwardness and poverty; both are steps on the same road leading toward the creation of a new society of justice and plenty.

—Che Guevara[1]

Africa Unite!

In November 2006, the African Forum was held in Beijing and was attended by 48 African heads of state. Over 500,000 police were on duty along the Chinese capital's wide boulevards, which were plastered for the occasion with billboards displaying African fauna. This prestigious event had the tightest security China had seen since the fiftieth anniversary celebrations of the founding of the People's Republic in 1999. Roads and enterprises were shut for the occasion, and for the first time in years, Beijing had traffic-free streets and blue skies.

Meanwhile, Africa bears the scars of tailed international aid lending programs in the post-colonial era. Its economies have been sidelined by Western developed countries, and the living conditions of its human populations are largely ignored. American aid floods instead into Israel, most of which is used to purchase military and hardware technology from America, while only peanuts are thrown to Africa.

I was fascinated to observe the events in Beijing. By hosting arguably the largest assembly of African heads of state and ministers ever gathered outside of a U.N. General Assembly session, the Africa Forum was an attempt to re-engineer China's diplomatic image as a donor country concerned about the dilemmas of the developing world.

By playing the trade-and-resource card, China stepped into a void where it can have a positive impact. Africa is a continent forgotten and ignored by the West. So, in hosting a Bandung-style conference, China could be repositioning itself as a central player in a new kind of non-aligned movement.

"When will China stand up to America and speak out for us to the rest of the world?" asked Dr. Farouq Abou Zaid, dean of the Mass Communications Faculty at Cairo's MISR University for Science and Technology. His plea reflected the hopes of many young African intellectuals on this new relationship with China. However, China will probably adopt a more economically tactical and less ideological approach to its own and Africa's development problems than Zhou Enlai sought at Bandung.

Zaid and other geo-political idealists in Africa's educational institutions may be disappointed. China will manage its foreign affairs by doing business with everyone simultaneously. So, while it may use Africa for U.N. voting on certain key issues that are in its immediate mercantile interests, it will also cuddle up to the G7 for their lucrative upscale markets. There is no ideology at play. Money is China's driving force, not some love of humanitarian idealism. Its geopolitical strategy is based on economic considerations. At the Africa Forum, multilateralism for China means expanding trade (predicted to be worth US$50 billion in 2008) and securing resources to ensure that trade remains sustainable.

This matter-of-fact business approach may be helping Africa to crawl out of poverty by spreading China's new wealth through resource investments, and by creating the infrastructure needed as a catalyst for development and to create lower-end markets for Chinese-made goods. In other words, is the China development model being applied to Africa?

For Africa, fed up with failed Western aid programs and its own indebtedness, China's write-off of its debts in autumn 2006 was welcome news and a badly needed break. Nevertheless, Western critics pointed out China's failure to follow international lending standards, or to protect human rights or fight corruption and nepotism in Africa.

Reza Aslan is one of America's most renowned Islamic scholars, a professor at Santa Barbara, and author of an illuminating book on the history of Islam, *No god but God*. I sought him out to ask him whether he thought China was creating a new kind of colonial relationship with Africa.

"Presidents George Bush and Hu Jintao are the same, only one uses military means and the other economics," he said. "China is creating a post-colonial relationship with the rest of the world, and it is almost as insidious as the European colonialists as it involves ravaging of natural resources for economic benefit for the elite of that land. China creates economic relationships with companies in these agricultural lands, and manages to withdraw all the resources it needs without forcing any kind of restrictions or conditionality. They [the nations] don't have to change their behavior. They don't have to do anything to continue this economic business with China, as long as the business relationship is in place. The obvious example is Sudan. It is hard for the rest of the world to press Sudan for a solution without the cooperation of China, who will not do anything to disrupt the flow of oil. That type of relationship is as insidious and disruptive as colonizing people. In the post-colonial world, you can colonize other people without leaving your home or office. You simply empower an elite in the colonized country to do the work for you. As long as resources flow, everybody is okay."

Meanwhile, the Africans blamed the institutional lending criteria applied by the World Bank and the IMF, which they saw as attaching burdensome and often impractical conditions that were the cause of their cyclical poverty. In fact, more aid money is spent on consultants' expense accounts, or on missions to evaluate and re-evaluate what other missions have already assessed, than finds its way to hard-core aid and poverty-relief programs.

Out of Stagnation

"But why China?" asked Dr. Farouq Abou Zaid, dean of the Faculty of Mass Communications at the MISR University for Science and Technology. "China progressed, so why not Egypt?" He points to the IMF policies of privatization and elimination of subsidies as tools for benefiting the rich social elite who end up with capitalist monopolies, at the expense of the broader population which once benefited. "In the end, when these [IMF-World Bank] programs are finished, who runs the country—local people or foreigners?" he asked.

I traveled to Egypt in 2006 to speak with academics and NGOs in order to better understand how China and Africa might form a partnership, political as well as economic, with the aim of achieving a new era of global consensus.

Cairo's architecture resembles Shanghai's. This city of magnificent art deco buildings is experiencing a construction boom that is reminiscent of the massive infrastructure developments that accompanied the opening of the Suez Canal in 1869 and the completion of the landmark Aswan Dam in 1933. Today, the suburbs are filled with unplanned red-brick tenement buildings, monuments to economic policy gone awry. During the 1960s, Egypt adopted import substitution/export promotion policies similar to those adopted by Japan, South Korea, Taiwan and Singapore, and with equal success. Then, in the 1970s, the IMF stepped in, demanding that President Anwar Sadat lift subsidies and privatize the state sector. In January 1977, riots broke out. Egyptians were angry and frustrated that the government's neo-liberal, pro-IMF policies were derailing the country's economy. Many of them turned inwards and the mosque became a psychological sanctuary.

"Ten years ago, this place was like Istanbul or Beirut," explained one foreign diplomat. "Egyptian women wore tight jeans, fashionable clothes and jewelry. Now you see this less and less. More are behind the veil, or wear only black. During Ramadan, many people now fast very strictly. Some won't even use eye drops!"

Economic stagnation brings social frustration, fueling the rise of a more fundamentalist brand of Islam. New social pressures have arisen. More and more people are rejecting American-style globalization and its inherent values, and turning back to their own traditions. In Egypt, this is often expressed by wearing the veil and practicing polygamy, leading to higher birth rates. Egypt has a population of just under 80 million, with Cairo being home to 17 million. The city is bigger, more densely populated, and more clogged with traffic than even Beijing. Egypt's population is growing by 1.2 million annually, straining its infrastructure and resources. A comprehensive birth-control program has been adopted, albeit with Egyptian characteristics. While for two decades China penalized families for having more than one child, Egypt only imposes penalties after the fifth child.

The bureaucracy is inflated and corrupt. Gamal Abdel Nasser, the late president, guaranteed university graduates government jobs, a socialist measure that was popular with young people. But like China, which also once guaranteed employment for its university graduates, Egypt has found itself with a stifling government bureaucracy that cannot function due to the oversupply of officials and undersupply of things for them to do. Lethargy breeds incompetence and petty corruption, making civil servants an unpopular irritant. Such problems cause society to turn inward, to seek other sources of consolation and more legitimate forms of authority, such as religious guidance.

Many fear rising religious extremism. If there was a truly free election in Egypt tomorrow, ballots would all go to the Islamic Brotherhood, an unofficial political party or shadow force now prominent throughout society and capable of mobilizing big numbers. The concern of many is that a declining economy will stimulate introverted emotions and fan religious fundamentalism. Zaid shrugs, "How can you be an active member of society when you cannot even make ends meet?"

The Post-Colonial Arrangement

In my conversation with Reza Aslan, I recalled my university days of studying Third World politics and development. I had kept a quote above my desk from the book *The Wretched of the Earth,* by Frantz Fanon. The guru on Third World revolution had argued that when a people are confronted and oppressed by Western culture, they turn inwards and back to the symbols of their own culture, such as seeking refuge in the mosque. I asked Aslan whether he thought Fanon's words still hold true. "Do they explain the global Islamic revolt against the globalization of the kind of Americanization that we have witnessed under the Bush administration?" I asked.

"It's a true statement," said Aslan, "but more complicated than that. It goes back to the colonial experiment in Egypt and North Africa, when colonialism was understood by locals as an attack on Islam and Islamic culture. In the Middle East and most parts of the world, religion provides a sense of culture and, moreover, of identity. So this exploitation had as its ultimate purpose—unapologetically—the replacement of local culture with European culture. This was what was seen as 'progress.' The view of most Egyptians and people in other colonized lands is that their sense of civilization is taken for granted until it is challenged by European colonialists, when the question becomes, 'Who are we?' And, as you know, the easiest sense of collective identity that most people have is either their cultural or religious identity. So, as a response to colonialism, they looked to Islam for a sense of identity. At the time, it wasn't a religious or mosque-based movement."

"Did the mosque serve as a center or base for an Islamic response to the colonial setup, as it is now in the case of the neo-colonial setup?" I asked.

"The first attempt to create a collective response to colonialism was from those outside the mosque," Aslan explained. "Although people like Mohamed Abdul Said Acmenan, in India, used metaphors and images of Islam to mobilize collective action against colonialism, they were clearly outside the mosque structure. When colonialism ended, these places were placed in the hands of secular regimes, either monarchies based on accommodation with the West or, when these failed, some nationalist, military dictatorship—nevertheless, secularist post-colonial regimes. In this regard, when that sense of identity was going to form and become a nationalist identity, regardless of whether the opposition was democratic, that opposition to society became mosque-based. And so it isn't true that the primary opposition to colonial rule was mosque-based. It was only at the end of colonialism, and with the emergence of the state as a secular regime, that the opposition became mosque-based, and this is the case today."

"Did the shift occur as a result of seeking to articulate an identity?

Or was the reason political—to avoid suppression through religious-based protection?" I asked.

"If you look at modern Egypt, if you are a socialist-based opposition, you are in prison; but if you are a mosque-based opposition, you will have at your disposal the only free space in society—the mosque. A regime that docs away with all opposition except that which is mosque-based scores points with the population, because it is seen to be pious and as not suppressing religious expression while yet being on the verge of being taken over by fundamentalists held in check by the regime's 'democratic' dictatorial policy. A U.N. Arab development report calls this 'legitimacy of blackmail'."

"Is this the prevailing pattern?" I asked.

"This is what we are seeing in Musharraf's Pakistan," Aslan replied. "He has convinced the Western world that if it wasn't for his military rule, the fundamentalists would take over. But we know in Pakistan that even when the fundamentalists muster their forces, they cannot take more than 3% of the vote. So there is no way that there can be a fundamentalist takeover. We provided him with US$11 billion and the thing we thought could be prevented has become a reality."

The Islamic Response to Globalization

"Egypt is a dictatorship, and we give the government US$2.3 billion a year in aid, much of which is used to buy weapons," said Reza Aslan. "Jordon received US$1.2 billion, Pakistan and Saudi Arabia about the same amount. I don't think it is a coincidence that the vast majority of our allies in the Arab world are dictatorships. We have never done much to truly try to change that relationship. There was an attempt by the Bush administration to push for democratic change, such as in Iraq. But top-down democratization never works. If democracy is to take hold in any part of the world, it must be indigenous and have its root in the culture. It cannot be American-style democracy plopped on to these countries without being translated into a language that will be familiar to them."

"So, you don't think that America can succeed in globalizing its form of democracy through top-down approaches enforced by unilateral military ventures?" I asked.

"This notion of removing the government and replacing it with an elected government, even when at the grassroots level there is no democratic infrastructure, and expecting it to develop naturally, is flawed and won't function in any society," Aslan replied.

"Likewise, the economic approach of the Washington Consensus?" I asked.

"It is very much about cultural policy. The notion that the cultural artifacts that have created the Western world as a conglomeration of wealthy, capitalist, industrial nation-states can be imposed on other countries without any attempt to adapt them to different cultures just doesn't make sense. Let me give you an example.

"Kanan Makiya is the Iraqi exile who was so vocal in talking the Bush administration into declaring war on Iraq. He tells the story of watching the Super Bowl with President Bush in the first week of February 2003, before the war on Iraq began in March. He found himself explaining to the U.S. president that there is a difference between the Sunni and Shiite sects. He wasn't explaining *what* the difference is, but just that there *is* a difference. One month before the invasion, President Bush didn't know who he was about to start fighting against."

Aslan frowned. "This is a rejection of the need to know. This administration has the idea that knowledge or intelligence about the enemy and others is a secondary concern, and that force of arms will always bring about the desired outcome. Force of arms will ultimately lead to any knowledge you want about your enemy. If you can crush your enemy, then you can take your time to learn about them. Now you can see the result of this notion in Iraq and Afghanistan. But in this broad war of ideals that we are supposed to be fighting against terror, it is a 'might-before-mind' mentality."

"Is this outlook driven by America's belief in its own cultural superiority?" I asked. "Is the globalization experiment an attempt to have the whole world embrace—and therefore validate—America's culture, politics and economic system?"

"I believe that we are dealing with a new kind of 'Orientalism,' in terms of how the U.S. is dealing with the Middle East," Aslan said. "Edward Said [a Palestinian activist, literary critic, writer, and musician (1935-2003)] said that with knowledge comes power. If you know the other, you gain power over them. So much of the work done by 'Orientalists' in the Middle East during the nineteenth and twentieth centuries was aimed at understanding it in order to gain power over it. Recently, America has engaged the Middle East in a kind of reversal of this: by gaining power over the other, you will gain knowledge of them. The American administration made no real attempt to understand the situation in Afghanistan and Iraq. It effectively disregarded the need to know anything about them and instead focused on imposing its will on them by force. Regardless of whether this is economic or military power, it is a reversal of 'Orientalism'."

"So, economic and military might precludes even having to bother to understand the people you plan to conquer and whose culture you plan to obliterate?"

"In a globalized world, there is no difference between military might and economic might," Aslan said. "America's view is that if there is something it needs to know about Sunnis and Shiites, it will learn it by means of military occupation."

"Do you think the Washington Consensus approach toward globalization is partially a neo-colonial experiment?" I asked.

"The colonial experiment is continuing in a neo-colonial way, with multinational corporations taking on the role of colonizers of the colonial era. The East India Company was the eighteenth-century version of a multinational corporation, and the same thing is happening now. You may not see British and Dutch administrators, but their companies still have enormous influence over their former colonies' economies, governments and, of course, culture."

"So, does the export of American culture actually facilitate U.S. multinational corporations gaining economic control? Do you see political arrangements as collaborations with the elite decision-makers in each country to facilitate the process?" I asked.

"When we talk about Western hegemony over culture, that almost entails a voluntary acceptance on the part of the colonized, as it is an advantage for the decision-makers and elite in that country," explained Aslan. "The elite want McDonald's and the IMF, because their presence provides an advantage to the upper echelons of society. The lower levels don't make the decision. So, hegemony involves voluntary acceptance by the colonized community."

"What happens if there is resistance from within a country to that colonization?" I asked.

"Al Qaeda is a separate matter, because it is a transnational organization that believes the idea of the nation-state is anathema to Islam," explained Aslan. "However, when it comes to nationalist groups such as Hamas, Hezbollah and the Egyptian Islamic Jihad, they absolutely get their recruitment and ideology from opposition to Western hegemony. It helps them draw the clear-cut lines between the 'in' and 'out' group."

"How do they draw the line?" I asked.

"The 'in' group benefits from hegemony, so the 'out' group doesn't. It's easy, therefore, to decide who is 'us' and who is 'them.' It is easy to decide who are these nationalist resistance organizations. So, they see their primary target as the near enemy, which is their own government, political religious leaders, and those in their society who have in one sense or another sold out to the enemy and are benefiting from globalization and hegemony. There is no question that this is where they draw their fire from."

Islam and the Himalayan Consensus

Aslan and I moved on to discuss the concept of a Himalayan Consensus, one of the pillars of which is the alleviation of poverty and reduction of income gaps in order to create a more equitable world. I was particularly struck during my first trip to India, when visiting a Hindu temple, to find dozens of volunteers providing free meals to hundreds of street people. Such giving is a pillar of Hindu philosophy. Likewise, compassion and alleviating the suffering of others is a central tenet of Buddhism, so we constantly reach out and donate to medical and educational projects, and give alms to the poor. Alms-giving is also one of the Five Pillars of Islam.

Reza Aslan explained: "An amount of 2.5% of one's income is *zakat*. It's not the same as 'charity,' which you can and should give. The idea of *zakat* focuses not on the person who is receiving the alms, but on the person giving them. It is not charity, but virtue. In Islam, which is very community-based, everyone is responsible for everyone else. *Zakat* isn't about distributing funds, but rather about the strongest in a community taking care of the weakest."

"Does the principle apply to all Muslims?"

"This was the case when the community of Muslims numbered a few hundred, but now it is in the billions," Aslan explained. "How *zakat* develops in each community is different. In Saudi Arabia, you will be taxed and the taxes will be distributed to the poor. In other places, you give to the imam at your local mosque and he gives it out to whoever needs help. *Zakat* isn't voluntary. If you don't pay *zakat,* you are not a member of your local Muslim community."

I said, "Our Buddhist belief is that you benefit more by giving than taking, which is the opposite of the Judeo-Christian capitalist view that there is no free lunch and that only the strongest will survive, because it is their imperative right—due to God, or something like manifest destiny. What is the Islamic view?"

"The Western notion that the weakest are in that position because they are not working hard enough or are not determined enough to succeed is not the case for Islam," Aslan replied. "The weakest are the responsibility of the strongest. There is a sense of obligation; the strong in the community are obligated to take care of the weak in that community. It is an anti-Calvinist notion."

He explained that much of the American/Western view that there is "no free lunch," and that the world can be seen in black-and-white terms, is actually Calvinist in origin. "Calvinists say that if you are strong, then God wanted you to be strong; if you are poor, it's because God wanted you to be poor."

"Of concern to me is the global outlook of the Washington Consensus," I said. "Its economic and political views are fundamentalist—it judges the world through a prism of right versus wrong, black versus white. These are essentially Judeo-Christian values, which have become the basis of economic and political fundamentalism."

"When we say Judeo-Christian values, particularly within the U.S., we are talking about Calvinist values and the notion that prosperity—your economic status—is an indicator of your salvation," Aslan said. "This notion is the basis of the Protestant ethic, even though there aren't so many Calvinists. So, I am loath to criticize the U.S. for not following values that it claims its society is based on, because that won't happen. You are right that the Judeo-Christian-Calvinist principle is very much a part of the way we approach the world—if you don't do things the way we do it, you won't be successful, and if you are not successful, it means there is something wrong with your culture that does not let you have this economic development. That's the Calvinist view. Because the U.S. is success-fill, it must be blessed by God. So, that is why it is successful."

The other similarity that struck me was how both Buddhism and Islam are less religious orders than community-based ideals; or, rather, communities linked and inspired by higher sets of ideals for a better social order.

"One thing that doesn't get enough attention," Aslan said, "is how *all* religions have played a role in creating the globalization order. At the heart of Islam is *Ulma,* a notion of community spirit transcending individual wealth or status. Regardless of your caste, nationality or ethnicity, you are part of a greater community. Salvation for the Muslim comes through his membership in this globalized community. Religions create world empires and transnational identities, which, when it comes to Islam and Al Qaeda, offer the most pervasive challenges to globalization."

This is one aspect of the Himalayan Consensus idea that I have been advocating. Buddhism and Islam have another commonality, in that each speaks more about followers being part of a powerful transnational community rather than simply a localized religion. In Buddhism, it is called *Sangha;* in Islam, *Ulma.* It is the global identity within these transnational communities, whose world-view is based on economic principles of compassion, not greed, that offers potential for worldwide resistance to America's politically motivated globalization agenda. I asked Reza Aslan to explain the Islamic perspective.

"Four of the Five Pillars of Islam are rituals and not beliefs," he said. "The first is profession of faith and initiation into *Ulma.* The other four keep you in the *Ulma*. How do you recognize that you are a part of this community? By the way you pray and give alms. So, if you can, you meet once a year in Mecca to remind you that you are part of a single community. This is *real* globalization. Jihadism is anti-nationalist in the sense that all Islamic organizations—of which Al Qaeda is only one, though it is highly visible— aim to create a collective identity beyond borders, beyond boundaries, and to reunite the *Ulma* under their leadership into a global caliphate."

Toward Himalayan Consensus

During my time spent living in Tibet and traveling through Nepal and Bhutan, I learned that the Buddha had been a revolutionary who sought to overthrow the caste system and called for equality. After reading Reza Aslan's book *No god but God,* I realized that Mohammed also was a revolutionary calling for egalitarianism in the society of his era. I have always been impressed by this shared aspect of Buddhism, Islam and many other religions: their call for equality. I see a visible manifestation of this every morning when hundreds of Tibetans prostrate themselves outside Jokhang Monastery in Lhasa, just as Muslim congregations bow down in unison while facing towards Mecca. Rich man and poor man are united in their devotions and humility.

In both the Buddhist and Islamic world-views, we are all equal in our impermanence on this earth. *That* is reality, not the illusion of material gain or one's social status. Perhaps it is this call for equality that the West finds most threatening, causing its media to demonize both Islam and Buddhism and to give them the status of cults, rather than religions. It is perhaps this globalization of equality, which both philosophies call for, that most threatens U.S.-style globalization.

"How do you interpret this?" I asked Aslan.

"The very foundation of Islam is social egalitarianism and the elimination of differences based on ethnicity, caste or wealth. This notion is threatening to societies like the West, where values are based on concepts of merit and the Protestant work ethic, and Calvinist concepts of determination. It is this that makes the West so paranoid about Islam and leads it to engage in identity politics."

"What do you mean by 'identity politics'?"

"The simplest way to form identity is in opposition to another," Aslan explained. "In the past, Americans were opposed to communism. If you were *not* opposed to communism, you were literally considered by the authorities— such as Senator McCarthy and other Americans—to be un-American. Now, it is the same with Islam. In the eyes of Americans, there is a clash between geographic regions, but religion has nothing to do with geography. There has been an enormous interaction over the centuries between Islam and 'Western civilization,' for want of a better term. Their effect on each other has been profound. There would not *be* Western civilization without Islam; it simply would not exist. People like President Bush are creating phony categories for no other reason than to create political identity."

"Is this globalization of a new identity that transcends borders the ultimate way to defeat the Washington-centric global order?" I asked.

"This idea is so attractive for the young, integrated, politically active Muslims in places like London," explained Aslan, "because it recognizes that the nation-states we all live in have failed; secular nationalism has failed to ward off great wars. It has failed because it has left behind the poor, and because it is under the thumb of a handful of powerful nation-states who exert their will over everyone else. So you hear this argument from most anti-globalization movements. Jihadism's answer to a failed world is a new globalization, which anti-globalization religious-globalizationists refer to as a 'caliphate'—a world where all cultures will be united by religious identification."

"Can people be mobilized globally in the interest of this response?" I asked.

Aslan considered my question for a moment. "They have become so enormously successful because they have a global vision, and because there is no center of the Islamic world as there is with, say, Catholicism. There is no single spokesperson. It is a wide-open, globalized identity defined only by its individual members. No one can deny membership of this world to a person who says they belong to it. There is no Muslim pope in charge of Islamic doctrine, no censor of the *Ulma*. It is only in the past century or so that a sense of nationalism has been imposed on this transnational religion. The vast majority of Muslims are comfortable with this, as in a sense it is a reversion to our transnational identity."

I asked Reza Aslan whether he thought Buddhists and Muslims might unite globally with those identified as the anti-globalization movement to form a pan-national constituency calling for new values of environmental protection, poverty alleviation and world peace.

"*Why* don't these movements come together?" Aslan repeated my question. "Because they have separate identities—not ideologies. Their ideologies may be similar, but their identities are different. Many people ask why four British-born Muslims—totally assimilated, from comfortable middle-class families, and literate—could plan and execute the London underground bombings in July 2005, having decided that their identity lay more with a small group of cave-dwelling Jihadi in Afghanistan than with their own state. The answer is that the Jihad movement has used symbols to create new identities that are not limited by national borders. They then use that identity to mobilize collective action. That is how the social movement of Jihadism—and that is what it truly is—survives."

"Is it conceivable, then, that we could mix-and-match Buddhist, Islamic and secular symbols to create a collective identity?" I asked.

"One of the great ironies of all of these transnational and anti-globalization movements is that they thrive by using the tools that globalization has provided, such as the Internet and satellite television. By these means, British-born Muslims and Muslims everywhere can find out about and identify with cave-dwelling cultists in Afghanistan, instead of defining themselves in the terms of their own society. Those of us who are actively involved in trying to find an ideological counterweight to transnational ideologies of violence and bigotry must use the same tools that allow globalization to function. It is a battle that is taking place on the Internet and on satellite television. That's why we jokingly call the opponents of globalization 'anti-globalization globalists,' because they require the tools of globalization to spread their anti-globalization message.

"Muslim and Christian clerics need to come together and ask the leaders of the two religious movements to join together in a globalized way to defuse the rising animosity between Christians and Muslims. One way of doing this is by finding symbols that are meaningful to both, in order to create a common identity' that is opposed to the rise of fundamentalism in both religions."

"What about the Himalayan Consensus approach?" I asked, ending our conversation almost as we began it, reminding myself that the word "revolution" means the completion of a cycle. "Could a Himalayan Consensus—pulling together the philosophic pillars of Buddhism, Islam and Hinduism into a new global, non-Western consensus on social values, economics, and politics—lead us into a new era of global cooperation that will alleviate poverty, close income gaps, preserve our environment, and stop this endless cycle of economically-based, self-serving warfare?"

"A Himalayan Consensus, and other transnational global con-glomerations—whether economic, political, or religious—essentially are what we are going to be seeing for the rest of the century," Aslan replied. "Globalization is not a linear phenomenon, as we see this convergence of common sets of ideas. We will never see one global ideology, but a connection of consensuses, conglomerations and gatherings around common ideas. What you envisage in regards to a Himalayan Consensus is what we will be seeing from here on out. We saw it with NATO, and we saw it with the European Union, which is a good example of economic consensus. And this is the future of the planet. I think it is a movement that will accelerate as we move into the post-nation-state world, where nationalism becomes less and less a primary means of collective identity. As people begin to revert to more primal forms of self-identity—based on their culture, religion, tribe— these kinds of consensuses will become the primary mode through which international relations are experienced. I cannot imagine that in the next century international relations will be taking place among nation-states; they will be taking place instead among global consensuses."

The Globally Discontented Unite

"It is high time to shut up," declared Sha Zukang, China's ambassador to the United Nations, in Geneva in August 2006. He was referring to American politicians who were complaining about Beijing's growing military expenditures. China's total arms budget is a mere fraction of that of the United States, while China's population is five times larger, he pointed out. In his view, this type of political pressure applied by a foreign power is unfair and unnecessary, doing little to promote world peace and perhaps stimulating more violence as a result.

Within a month of Sha's comment, a chain of similar events unfolded. In late August, Iranian President Mahmoud Ahmadinejad addressed the 60th Session of the United Nations General Assembly. "If some, relying on their superior military and economic might," he said, "attempt to expand their rights and privileges, they will be performing a great disservice to the cause of peace and in fact will fuel the arms race and spread insecurity, fear and deception. If global trends continue to serve the interests of small, influential groups, even the interests of the citizens of powerful countries will be jeopardized."

Ahmadinejad warned that "the prevalence of military domination, increasing poverty, the growing gap between rich and poor countries, violence as a means to solve crises, the spread of terrorism, especially state terrorism, the existence and proliferation of weapons of mass destruction, the pervasive lack of honesty in interstate relations, and disregard for the equal rights of peoples and nations in international relations constitute some of the challenges and threats [currently faced by the world]." The U.S. ambassador walked out of the session, not bothering even to listen.

To a great extent, for the past several decades America's failure to listen to what many nations are saying is a big part of the problem. Many foreign capitals will be watching to see if this attitude will change under the new Obama administration.

In September 2006, 118 nations representing the Non-Aligned Movement of states convened in Havana, Cuba. Their joint statement reaffirmed their view that democracy is a universal value based on the freely expressed will of people to determine their own political, economic, social and cultural systems. They also denounced the brutalization of people under occupation as a grave form of terrorism. They seemed to represent a new world consensus. As Ambassador Sha had demonstrated, unlike in the past, many leaders are now willing to express their concerns openly.

Raul Castro, the younger brother and successor to Cuban leader Fidel Castro, presided over the Havana forum, which was attended by delegates from more than two-thirds of the world's nations. Castro echoed Sha's words, pointing out that the U.S. annual military budget accounts for half of all global arms spending. "To think that a social and economic order that has proven unsustainable could be maintained by force is simply an absurd idea," Castro told the delegates.

Add up the bill for all that killing and destruction and it's not surprising that people the world over are angry. Many non-aligned nations have called for reform of the U.N. to be extended to include expansion of Security Council membership and curtailment of the veto powers of its five permanent members in order to break their monopoly. Former U.N. secretary-general Kofi Annan seemed to agree that such reform is necessary if the organization is to retain its neutrality and independence. He too warned: "The perception of a narrow power base risks eroding the U.N.'s authority and legitimacy." In fact, to a great extent, this has already happened.

Nations, like the people who comprise them, are entitled to govern themselves, without another nation telling them what to think, what to believe in, or what constitutes acceptable or unacceptable behavior. "It is the U.S.'s sovereign right to do whatever they deem good for themselves," Ambassador Sha had snapped in Geneva. "But don't tell us what is good for China." His view exactly reflects what many countries feel.

The people of each nation will always want to be the ones to determine the nature of their country's future evolution and the necessity for any reforms. According to the principles of the U.N. Charter and international human-rights covenants, that is each nation's right.

In 2006, these ideas sounded outright radical to many in Washington and the major capitals of Europe. However, after the disastrous military occupation of Iraq, indenting America and bringing down the entire global financial system in its wake, suddenly in 2008 these voices finally seemed to make sense. Our entire approach to development and, moreover the social values which form the basis of assumptions concerning how the global economic order should work, need to be changed. In turn, the dynamics of international relations must be adjusted to shifting global realities. A new multilateral order must be heralded. Mutuality and equality should become the fundamental principles underlying new global economic and financial structures.

Endnote

1 Afro-Asian Conference, Algiers, February 24, 1965.

12

THE REVOLT AGAINST CYCLICAL POVERTY
NEPALESE MAOISTS COME IN FROM THE COLD

In reality, the soldier who is engaged in armed combat in a national war deliberately measures from day to day the sum of all the degradation inflicted upon man by colonial oppression. The man of action has sometimes the exhausting impression that he must restore the whole of his people, that he must bring every one of them up out of the pit and out of the shadows. He very often sees that his task is not only to hunt down the enemy forces but also to overcome the kernel of despair which has hardened in the native's being. The period of oppression is painful; but the conflict, by reinstating the downtrodden, sets on foot a process of reintegration which is fertile and decisive. A people's victorious light not only consecrates the triumph of its rights; it also gives to that people consistence, coherence, and homogeneity.

—Frantz Fanon, The Wretched of the Earth

Nepal in Transition

In early 2007, I was invited by Communist Party of Nepal Maoists to provide advice on a strategic economic policy. It was a time of transition. The Maoists had already committed themselves to a peace process, and had agreed to place their arms in U.N.-supervised cantonments and to disband their guerrilla forces. To facilitate peace in Nepal, the Maoists were prepared to enter the new coalition government as a legitimate party and to participate in establishing a constitutional assembly.

I worked one-on-one with their economic advisory board, which included people from all walks of Kathmandu life, including academics, bankers and some of the most brilliant economists I have ever met. We had intensive briefing sessions with the quiet but astute Dev Gurung, the Maoists' highest-ranking Central Committee member, who was overseeing economic policy at the time. As a political force finally coming in from the cold, they were struggling against diverse political and economic interests to find an indigenous, socially conscious market-economy model suited to the people and conditions of Nepal.

The Maoists had done their homework before inviting me to meet with them in Kathmandu. They knew about my earlier work as a financial-reform advisor to Laos and Vietnam, and were also aware of my work in China throughout the 1990s within the economic think-tank team of former Premier Zhu Rongji. Nepal's Maoist economists were intensely interested in China's model of economic development, not necessarily because it could be applied to Nepal (I don't believe such a model is appropriate) but rather because it offers an alternative to the IMF and World Bank models, which many in Nepal feel created the conditions of abject poverty and elitist corruption that led to the rise of the Maoist movement in the first place.

I found the thought processes of the movement's leaders far from radical, which is how they had been characterized by the Western media. Clearly, they sought a middle path for forging a new society that combined market forces with social responsibility. The Maoists sought to integrate sustainable, positive economic growth with the alleviation of poverty and the systematic reduction of income gaps, while encouraging Nepal to remain ethnically diverse and to thrive on the richness of its own heritage and identity, not one imported from the West.

The Maoists viewed China's experience as an example of what could be achieved by seeking an independent economic course based on local conditions and circumstances.

So, while the China model was considered worth studying, it may require different considerations for practical application in Nepal, a nation where spirituality and local tradition are evident in nearly every aspect of life. The Maoists felt that the Nepalese heritage and diverse ethnicity should not be compromised. While they sought to resolve issues arising from the need to upgrade the kingdom's communications and health-care technology, they were adamant that they did not wish to adopt America's global materialism as the Chinese had. For these reasons, one could easily comprehend Washington's knee-jerk reaction to Nepal's Maoists and its desire to suppress this popular grassroots movement.

Populist People Power

My advisory work with economic strategists inside Nepal's Maoist organization gave me unprecedented access to their leadership.

Throughout March 2007, Pushpakamal Dahal, known as "Prachanda" (meaning "the very sharp one") and Baburam Bhattarai, respectively the Mao Zedong and Zhou Enlai of Nepal's Maoists, made appearances at massive political rallies held throughout the Nepalese countryside that culminated in intoxicating day-long demonstrations of revolutionary dance, songs and speeches. I felt privileged to witness this mass outpouring of people power. I came to know Prachanda quite well and called him "Chairman"; he called me "comrade."

These mass rallies were a testament to the degree of political force that could be generated by networking at the grassroots level in an organized fashion. Village girls tossed flowers and danced in a way that combined traditional movements with revolutionary gestures, while guerrilla fighters demonstrated martial arts moves to the beat of Nepalese drums amidst a sea of red flags and hundreds of thousands of demonstrators. As a first-hand observer of the demonstrations, one message was overwhelmingly clear to me. The Maoists had an organized network of cells throughout Nepalese society that addressed people's needs at the village level, and they had the support of most people living in the countryside. Some parallels with circumstances in China during the 1940s were clear.

I learned that the Maoist forces consisted of nine "liberation fronts," each organized tightly around either a caste or ethnic group. This organizational structure makes Nepal's Maoist movement representative of these once-marginalized social and economic interests, which it has empowered politically through its own party body and collective strength. The movement had developed such a degree of organizational capability and social support that, by spring 2007, it was already poised to take power by popular election, thus underscoring their reasons for discarding force as a means of achieving their aims.

Some 40% of the Maoists are women. Encumbered and subservient in traditional Nepalese society, they have been empowered politically and now share in the struggle for social equality that women and ethnic minorities have experienced in the United States over the past century.

It was clear that Prachanda can inspire the crowds, speaking to their aspirations. "People respect Prachanda," said one Central Committee member I spoke with at a rally, as village dancers paraded past the Maoist supreme commander. "When they see Prachanda, they feel he is our leader."

During my weeks spent working with the Maoist Central Committee, I exchanged views with the party's elusive leader on a number of occasions. He expressed interest in the idea of building a Himalayan Consensus based on a combined Buddhist-Hindu-Islamic social consciousness with market forces and technological advances. He explained his own vision for Nepal, which would see it adopting an alternative model of economic and political development to the Washington Consensus through a very Nepalese "middle way," he called the "Prachanda Path."

Pragmatism Meets Idealism

Each time I met with Prachanda, it was in a nondescript safe house somewhere in the slums of Kathmandu. A motorcycle would pick me up from where I was staying, deposit me on a crowded street corner, from where I would be told to take a taxi to another busy street corner. Someone would then appear and guide me to a house where a window scout would send a signal; someone else would then appear from the driveway and direct me into an alleyway leading to another house. This process continued until, lost in the labyrinthine slums of the city, I would finally arrive at a house, empty except for the armed guerrilla guards in position on the balconies and stairwell.

I would be led to a room empty except for a single table and two chairs. A single cup of spiced tea would be placed on the table. Minutes later, with a flourish of activity and walkie-talkie static, Prachanda would enter the dimly lit room. He had the warm ebullience of a fatherly philosopher and the confidence of a revolutionary on the cusp of assuming political power.

"Nepal is rich in resources but lacking in political vision," he declared at our first meeting, when he shook my hand and called me "comrade." "Our people are poor, so we want to use the resources to build a new Nepal for them."

While the Maoists have been fighting for just a decade, Prachanda was organizing and planning the movement at least 30 years before. His acumen and sensitivity regarding historic and cultural conditions enabled him to recognize early how similar are the conditions existing in Nepal today to those that existed in China in the 1920s and 1930s: a feudal system of debauched royalists, landlords and serfs, with uneven distribution of resources and foreign control over certain aspects of the economy. He saw in Nepal's rural mountain villages and urban slums a fertile nesting ground for the dispossessed to aspire to build a new socially conscious vision of economic development and government responsibility. Maoist imagery had been used successfully to rally the rural poor and urban intellectuals. Clearly, in adopting Maoism, Prachanda had succeeded in inspiring revolution aimed at remedying Nepal's impoverished conditions.

Prachanda impressed me by being as much pragmarist as idealist, understanding the limitations of circumstance and adjusting to ever-changing conditions. A keen scholar who recognizes the ironies of history, Prachanda had grasped how Maoist ideals and organizational techniques could unite Nepal's rural-based and largely poverty-stricken multi-ethnic society into a single movement and united political force. His party offered substance and direction to a society whose economy was in freefall after decades of misdirected IMF and World Bank policies that had fed a fattened, elitist royal class at the expense of the broader population.

Prachanda's Vision

Prachanda, despite his admiration of China's peasant revolution, he clearly understood that many conditions in China could not be applied in Nepal. "When you ascend to power," I asked Prachanda, "will you create a one-party totalitarian state as Mao did, or a democracy?"

Prachanda stroked his mustache for a moment, then replied: "Mao tried his best to build a new society, despite the many complexities that existed in China at the time. He tried to undertake a big experiment. We must learn from what happened and draw the conclusion that a multi-party democracy is necessary. We wish to take part in the interim government as a legitimate political party, and to participate in the constitutional assembly to develop an entirely new government."

I was surprised by his response. If the Maoists were in fact willing to drop their one-party platform, and forgo having ultimate power, in order to participate as a legitimate party in a coalition government, it would be the first time a Communist Party that had engaged in a long guerrilla struggle had taken such a path. If Prachanda was really choosing to adopt this "middle way," he would be evolving Marxism to a new stage in practice.

Prachanda laughed, "Even Mao was willing to form a coalition government with Chiang Kai-shek against the Japanese."

"But it seems that in Nepal the Maoists are different from other communists, in that you not only accept democracy but aspire to have a multi-party, transparent and competitive system. Is that the case?" I asked.

"We support a clear and open competition between concrete candidates," Prachanda said confidently. It was plain that he lived by his convictions and was prepared to go against the mainstream. "We feel that multi-party competition is necessary to develop within this new situation. Moreover, democracy is necessary to build both a new and vibrant society." He chuckled, folding his hands across his chest. "By the way, if Lenin had lived another two to five years he would probably have realized the need for this multi-party competition within the framework of his own socialist constitution."

Marx had coined the phrase, "Religion is the opium of the people." However, I had heard that Nepal's Maoists differed from other communists in that they supported freedom of religion. I asked Prachanda if this was the case. I felt this point was particularly important, given that Nepal is a nation where every aspect of daily life seems to be saturated with a Hindu-Buddhist approach to living. In contrast, China, because of its emphasis on atheism combined with economic growth as a panacea for all social and personal ills, had created massive social distortion with deep-bedded psychological sickness.

"All religions—Buddhism, Hinduism and Islam—are part of Nepal's unified society and unique heritage," Prachanda replied. To my surprise, he then added: "We are trying to revive Buddha [who was born in Lumbini] and portray him as a hero of Nepal, and to focus attention on social harmony and the higher values of mankind. I am keenly interested in the current efforts of China's President Hu Jintao to forge a new national ideology of 'social harmony' around Buddhist philosophical tenets, which are resurfacing in their society. We are only against the adverse influences of superstition and any attempt to use religion as a means to gain state power." (I assumed that Prachanda was referring to either the Taliban or the Bush administration.)

Clearly, Prachanda is a social pragmatist who understands the national unifying power of Maoism as a revolutionary ideal, or vehicle for an uprising. At the same time, he appears acutely aware of the need to depart from Mao's original line in order to build and administer a new nation where substantive changes will stick and a sustainable economy can be developed.

I asked Prachanda if he was aware that the Western media were presenting his leadership, and Nepal's Maoist movement, to the outside world in negative tones, and whether he had thought about re-labeling his party after coming to power.

"Mao was great, because he unified his country," Prachanda replied. "But we want to develop Maoism with a new label. We share his original vision of the need to change society for the better, but in this century we must do so by being integrated with the entire world. We are trying to undertake a new experiment in political construction, to reorganize Nepal's state system through the parliamentary process. We want a mixed economy. We wish to build a new Nepal."

Breaking the Poverty Cycle

In spring 2007, Nepal's Maoists put down their guns and joined a coalition government as a legitimate party. All the coalition members determined that the next stage would be to elect a constitutional assembly, which should include the Maoists, in drafting and adopting a constitution to be followed by transparent open elections for a new parliament and future government. The first open elections for a constitutional assembly were postponed, following pressure by the U.S. government, which feared the rise of a socialist government through the democratic process.

Washington's fears were premised on the obvious. Without question, no leader from among Nepal's seven other recognized political parties could stage such massive demonstrations or bring the same numbers to Kathmandu's streets as Prachanda. The scale of the Maoists' political momentum and broad-based support conveyed the clear sense that their rise to power wasn't in question. The only question was when, and by what path. In seemed incredible to me that the Western media were not presenting these facts.

The overwhelming observation of many on the ground was that Nepal's Maoists would take power through a popular election, or if the elections were derailed by royalists or external interference, then by force. Either way, they seemed intricately organized, creatively resourceful, and extremely determined.

"Feudalism can do away with the monarchy without changing the social structure," observed Baburam Bhattarai. "For instance, India is an example of feudal capitalism; while China is a different form of capitalism altogether, a mixed economy, which did succeed in doing away with feudalism." It is the Maoists' intention to modernize Nepal by breaking down its feudal social and economic structure.

Many long-term foreign resident observers in Nepal believe that past policies of the IMF and the World Bank have created conditions of cyclical poverty in Nepal, giving rise to the Maoist movement there.

"It is totally inevitable for a cause like the Maoists to arise in Nepal," observed Ian Baker, a *National Geographic* explorer, author of numerous books on the Himalayas and Buddhism, and a longtime resident of Kathmandu. "Apart from its name, it is largely a rural-based revolution of people who have been marginalized from Nepal's development and evolution. They have chosen a model out of their lack of international suaveness—a model discredited as a red flag among Western nations promoting Americanization under the glove of globalization." He noted that, over recent decades, "Western donor countries [by channeling aid money through Nepal's royal family] have created an entire culture of corruption against which the Maoists have risen up."

Baburam Bhattarai explained: "U.S. aid-funded projects that lasted only for periods of five years created distorted development, which fueled conditions for revolution in the countryside."

World Bank representatives have met with Maoist economists in order to pressure them to accept conditional packages of economic aid. According to top economists within the Maoist organization, World Bank representatives have insisted that if Nepal wants to attract foreign investment it must have rules assuring that labor can be fired at any time without compensation.

"How can we do this?" asked Maheshworman Shrestha, an economics professor who heads the Maoist economic think-thank. "We have labor unions and workers' rights! The IMF-World Bank proposal is a pre-capitalist ideology that is in the interests only of capitalists. Both labor and capital are necessary for development. We accept this and don't want class struggle; we want to strive to bring the stakeholders together. How can capitalists get only more profit, and the lower levels not receive benefits such as health care, training and education? Surely, we can all increase our profits together?"

So, for Nepal's Maoists, the conditions proposed by the IMF and the World Bank seem exploitative and destined to fuel the same conditions that once gave rise to their own revolution. While the Maoists are open to policies that can encourage direct foreign investment, they wish to reserve certain sectors—such as Nepal's cottage industries—for the Nepalese alone.

I asked Prachanda if the U.S.-led media barrage against his movement had created many misunderstandings, particularly concerning the future economic policies of Nepal's Maoist party. "I understand it is not your intention to adopt communism or socialism per se, but rather a mixed economy—maybe along the lines of China incorporating market policies with social welfare concerns. Is this your vision for Nepal's future economy?"

"The economic policy of China has become a great success," Prachanda replied. I don't want to follow blindly the IMF and World Bank, either. China went from socialism to capitalism, and we want to go from capitalism to socialism. For both, it is a matter of finding an economic middle way. In Nepal, we call it the 'Prachanda Path'."

"It is clear that, like so many developing and transitional countries, Nepal will have to reject the IMF-World Bank standard formulas. But can you really find an alternative to the Washington Consensus mainstream model?"

"We cannot ignore globalization and capitalism. We want a mixed economy that combines socialism and market economics," Prachanda said. "This combination is necessary. We cannot copy any single method of either old socialism or old capitalism. We need a new model for this society."

Prachanda Wins!

When Prachanda's Maoists had walked out of the coalition government in September 2007, he had placed two demands on the table: abolish the monarchy, and declare a republic immediately, heralding free democratic elections. Nepal's unpopular and dictatorial king finally abdicated in December 2007 and Nepal was declared a republic, heralding a new era of potentially popular democratic participation. The king's abdication represented a great political victory for Prachanda.

But how will the Maoists weather the transition from organizing mass street protests to lobbying in the halls of parliamentary power? Before these historic events, Prachanda had met with me in a Kathmandu ghetto to discuss the challenges facing the new Nepal.

"We are doing something new," explained Prachanda. "According to our assessment, we are fighting for peace."

That peace was almost derailed in 2007. Fearing a surge in votes for the populist Maoists, the U.S. initially sought to keep them out of the coalition government. Other parties knew that they needed Maoist participation— given their massive following among villagers and the urban poor—to make any coalition government legitimate in the eyes of the Nepalese people. Washington then applied pressure to delay the constitutional-reform assembly elections, further deferring democracy. Ironically, the Maoists support a democratic agenda that is not unlike what many people are struggling for elsewhere, but they remain mislabeled as terrorists by Washington. Where democratic experiments have failed in Afghanistan, Iraq and now Pakistan, a legitimate one that remains unrecognized is still under way in Nepal.

Despite U.S. attempts to keep the Maoists out of politics by blocking the democratic constitutional process, Prachanda's political daring in evolving his movement into a parliamentary political party has been lauded across South Asia. It is even seen in Sri Lanka as a possible solution for its own Tamil Tiger imbroglio.

"After ten years of civil war we must create a new Nepal through peaceful means," said Prachanda. "Dozens of comrades have sacrificed their lives for peace. We are telling the world that these sacrifices have been for peace and democracy. We are interested in peace and in being a legitimate party in government.

"What do you mean?" I asked.

"Like Pakistan and Afghanistan," Prachanda replied. "A dictatorship dressed up as democracy."

"What do *you* want?"

"We are interested in peace and in being a legitimate party in government," Prachanda replied.

"What is your key concern now?" I asked.

"Disturbances and civil unrest in the Tharai [region] could have a disastrous effect in Nepal and surroundings. If Nepal disintegrates, the whole South Asia and trans-Himalayan region are affected."

"Are you willing to be a mainstream political party in the end?" I asked.

"We are for real democracy, not just dressing up as a democracy. We are for real peace and real change. We want social and economic change. Our struggle is against feudalism in society, the economy and politics," Prachanda explained. "We want a real democracy representing the entire population, not just a privileged segment of it. We are in favor of elections. We wanted to have elections in June. But the Nepalese Congress Party conspired to postpone the elections. We are in favor of elections, but Western politicians have blamed us in the media, in order to postpone the elections."

"What will you do if the government doesn't hold the elections?" It was already late in the autumn. Prachanda had withdrawn his Maoists from the coalition government, demanding immediate elections, the declaration of a republic, and the complete abdication of the monarchy.

"Mobilize the masses," he declared. "Before, we were considered a minority in parliament, but we are the majority in the street. The masses support our agenda, which the Western media certainly cannot see. It is necessary to make a new interface and to clear up misunderstandings."

"What does your party want politically?"

"We want democracy for poor people and suppressed groups, and we want real change in the whole society—economic and agricultural— and to create democracy in mountainous areas in order to rebuild rural infrastructure and roads. And we want to establish an infrastructure that is consistent with an independent country."

The events in Nepal during 2007 have essentially redefined the nature of revolution not as a violent struggle, but as a movement for peace. It was one of Nepal's most tumultuous political years. It began with a peace settlement in March, when the Maoists laid down their arms and agreed to enter politics as a legitimate party. However, the monarchy and the dominant Congress Party continued to delay elections for a constitutional assembly, allegedly at the behest of the U.S. and Indian governments (according to a spectrum of sources from across the competing political parties). Frustrated by the delays, the Maoists withdrew from the seven-party coalition government, demanding the abolition of Nepal's 800-year-old monarchy, the declaration of a republic, and direct democratic elections without constituencies.

"Don't be afraid of the Maoist leadership," Prachanda advised America, with a smile. But does U.S. foreign policy ever learn from its mistakes? By isolating those whom it doesn't understand, Washington perpetually fuels its own fears.

"We are fighting for democracy and the masses," said Prachanda. "We are fighting for democracy and peace. Democracy and peace not only in our own country, but in this region—all of South Asia!"

"In doing so, are you calling for a regional consensus?"

"After the last time we met, I talked with my comrades in the Central Committee about the Himalayan Consensus," Prachanda replied. "This is a new ideal that should be developed and crystallized. This Himalayan Consensus is special, given the unique physical and spiritual dimension of this region. The political and economic institutions developing here should encompass these ideas."

∃

13

STARTING FROM THE VILLAGES
IN SRI LANKA'S COUNTRYSIDE, A MIDDLE ROAD

Hope cannot be said to exist, nor can it be said not to exist. It is just like roads across the earth. For actually the earth had no roads to begin with, but when many people pass one way, a road is made.

—Lu Xun, *My Old Home*

Diplomacy with Compassion

One cool morning late in the winter of 2007, just after the Chinese Lunar New Year, hundreds of Buddhist monks from various sects throughout China congregated at the Lingguan Temple nestled at the base of the Badachu hills in western Beijing. They had gathered to honor an unusual visit by Sri Lanka's liberal-minded president, Mahinda Rajapaksa, who had made the journey to Lingguan to present to Chinese officials a replica of the famous third-century BC Samadhi Buddha from Sri Lanka's ancient Buddhist center, Anuradhapura. The gift commemorated 50 years of diplomatic relations between Sri Lanka and China.

It is said that when the historical Buddha was cremated more than 2,500 years ago, one of his teeth was embedded in the pagoda at Lingguan Temple and another was taken to Sri Lanka, where it remains enshrined near the last king's palace in the old royal capital of Kandy. President Rajapaksa's gift symbolized the building of a new consensus between China and South Asia, based on coherent and shared values.

This event was the second visible use of "Buddhist diplomacy"—involving pacifist images—between China and a South Asian country within the space of a month. A few weeks earlier, China's then foreign minister Li Zhaoxing had visited India, where he commemorated a memorial to the monk Xuan Zang, whose fictional counterpart is the protagonist of the classic novel *Journey to the West*. It was Xuan Zang who had brought Buddhist scriptures and teachings from India to China during the Tang dynasty. Arguably, real globalization began then. Ironically, construction of the memorial had commenced during the 1950s, when the ideals of non-alignment, multilateral equality, pacifism and respect for others' ethnicity had reached a heady fever among the developing nations, freshly decolonized and still seeking economic independence. Finally, in 2007, construction was completed.

President Rajapaksa's statement to the gathering of monks outside Beijing reflected similar ideals of multilateralism and mutual respect for ethnic identity. "We have never sent troops to another country to intervene. As Buddhist nations, this is unthinkable. In the past, we sent monks to study from each other. This tradition should be revived." He immediately invited a delegation of Chinese Buddhist monks to visit Sri Lanka.

A New Asian Consensus

Later that afternoon, I met with President Rajapaksa at Diaoyutai State Guest House, the residence of foreign state leaders when visiting the Chinese capital. He had invited me to the meeting to discuss the Sri Lankan experience as an alternative to the Washington Consensus model and to explain his views on Buddhist diplomacy, globalization and the newly emerging consensus of values between China and South Asia.

"Buddhism in the region has common factors," he said. "We can share. We understand each other's inner thinking, habits and mind. We have no castes. The big-brother political attitude of a superpower must be changed. Then we will have a society where we can respect each other."

Clearly, the materialist approach is unacceptable in such a Buddhism-permeated society as Sri Lanka. Rajapaksa has built his reputation on opposing many of the IMF and World Bank approaches to materialistic development that have robbed other societies of their spirituality and fostered social ills and rising crime rates.

"They [those caught in the cycle of exported American material-ism] live with personal uncertainty," Rajapaksa said. "They have no respect for life! This can be changed. People of our region understand each other regardless of which country they are from, because in Buddhism, we are all equal regardless of our country, income or status." It is this notion of equality that overturns the Washington Consensus that might equals right and the idea that people are poor because they do not work hard enough. Among many NGOs and grassroots interest groups working throughout South Asia, the focus of efforts is on closing gaps between rich and poor as a foundation for sustainable social stability'.

Sri Lanka has many NGOs working effectively to address poverty and support sustainable enterprise at the grassroots level. Actually, they are so active they are often labeled as "anti-globalization" by Western aid agencies in an attempt to discredit their efforts. But, in fact, the NGO experience has been different from that of the industrial top-down theoretical models of the Washington Consensus. What it achieves at the village level is small-scale, but sustainable, economic growth that docs not dislocate the fabric of indigenous ethnicity and identity. This can be one of the most important ingredients in maintaining social stability if it can be combined with poverty relief in the form of practical, operational businesses, which can empower local people to become stakeholders in their own future. The effort would involve combining the material and spiritual factors as discussed in earlier chapters.

With our Western reliance on entirely empirical formulas, institutions such as the IMF and the World Bank employ primarily a material clement and ignore the spiritual, which is equally important. In the end, the results of economic formulas depend on psychology. So we cannot neglect factors relating to spirituality, ethnicity or individual identity. For all the Washington Consensus theories cooked up in institutional think-tanks, the human element is the most important and the one most often forgotten. To a great extent, it is this element that the so-called anti-globalization move-ment is asking to be put back into the formulas.

To put this into perspective, I asked Rajapaksa what he thought of the anti-globalization movement.

"We are not anti-anything," he replied, smiling. "There are simply different international approaches. The people need to retain their values. Without their values, development is useless."

Empowering the Villages

President Rajapaksa supports sustainable growth through micro-initiatives at the village level. His approach is aimed at reviving the village as a source of people's economic livelihood and psychological comfort. It should be a place where traditions are maintained and to which people can return at any time and feel at home. Rajapaksa cited the dangers of applying the Washington Consensus model to traditional societies such as Sri Lanka. They include disruptive influences, such as drug, alcohol and tobacco abuse. He has launched a widespread campaign against the use of these products in Sri Lanka and the results have been positive.

"Here, religion can keep people calm and provide the right thinking," said Rajapaksa. "When people lose their direction, they have no goals, no purpose; they then turn to drugs and alcohol." It was obvious that he saw local ethnic values as providing a counterpoint to American-style materialism, which undermines ethnic values and spirituality. "We had a street party. I saw 20,000 to 30,000 people dancing at the festival, and not a single one of them was under the influence of drugs or liquor."

President Rajapaksa has challenged and even confronted the World Bank model for development through his village-based, grassroots approach. "The World Bank said that our old buildings were underutilized, and that the people should be moved to the urban areas and their land given to multinational corporations, who could then take over the village and redevelop the land," he said. "They claimed it was a question of economic efficiency."

In his view, the World Bank approach has failed. It promotes rapid urbanization, which strands people raised in traditional rural villages in an urban oasis. Their sudden dislocation gives rise to a new form of social decay. Rajapaksa noted: "We had slums and, with them, many social problems, such as rising crime and drugs."

Sri Lanka and China have faced similar problems. But their approaches have been different. China's efforts to urbanize its townships have begun to backfire, with migrant workers rushing to already congested urban areas. While the government's goals of maintaining high levels of economic growth are increasing people's standard of living in Washington Consensus terms, their quality of lite is declining.

In Sri Lanka, Rajapaksa has faced some of the same challenges as Latin America. While providing infrastructure to rural areas, he also sought local solutions to development, such as consolidating the garment and textile industries in the countryside. However, he drew the line at creating artificial consolidated townships, as China has done. Sri Lanka has instead allowed villages to evolve naturally, rather than try to impose development according to a plan.

This organic approach has avoided some of the problems China has experienced in uprooting its culture and nearly obliterating its traditional values. China's rigid adherence to the top-down infrastructure approach, expressed by a mad rush to create instant cement-and-glass model townships, has helped foster an unforeseen level of greed, resulting in social discord. Alternatively, Rajapaksa argues that it is important to keep the village social structure intact so that its values can evolve from its traditions, rather than allow those traditions to be destroyed through abrupt and insensitive change.

Instead of multinational corporation development, what the villages need are good schools and hospitals. They need school meals. That is what the government now provides. Before, children did not even eat breakfast.

The Sri Lankan government now provides these meals free to village youngsters. But such initiatives serve to address a core and tangible need, while also rooting people in their villages and stimulating local growth and community. In Rajapaksa's view, it is essential for Sri Lankans to retain their traditional social values alongside a sustainable growth economy.

Rajapaksa's approach defies the Washington Consensus models, which have created massive impoverished slums on the outskirts of major cities in Central and South America. Development economists have dubbed this phenomenon "Latin-Americanization." Rajapaksa foresaw this danger, and by using grassroots approaches combined with government support in the right areas, he has steered his nation away from the cyclical poverty programs promoted by the Washington Consensus. "We have to provide for the practical needs of the people, not what some theorist thinks," he says.

The World Bank has finally, albeit reluctantly, been forced to recognize the success of President Rajapaksa's approach, which has seen Sri Lanka's garment industry consolidated at the grassroots level, allowing villages to absorb production. His approach has assured the livelihoods of people while preserving their village life.

Sri Lanka has achieved successes through judicious investment by the state. It refused the offers of infrastructure aid, which came with economic strings attached, that often have political implications, and which would typically lead to dislocation of social structures and thus exacerbate the process of urban Latin Americanization. I asked President Rajapaksa to explain his successful experiment with village development.

"Government infrastructure in rural areas reaches the villages where no previous infrastructure existed," he said. "At the village level, people need better roads and then they will start to move back toward the village rather than crowding into the cities. How people choose to live is something they have to decide for themselves. It shouldn't be decided by politicians, the World Bank or the IMF."

3

14

THE BUDDHIST REVOLUTION
WHY COMPASSION SHOULD BE COMBINED
WITH CAPITALISM

I will go to the jungle for justice, and the rain will be my drink.

—Traditional Chinese ballad

Politics for a New Era

At the entrance to a Buddhist monastery in Sri Lanka, my five-year-old son stared at a monkey that had descended from the trees to look for fruit among the offerings. When the monkey saw him, it fled.

"Why is the monkey afraid of me?" my son asked a monk standing nearby.

"Because you are different from him," responded the monk with a smile. "Don't you realize that? That is the problem with everything."

We made our way to the monastery's reception room, where the revered monk Athuraliya Rathana received us.

Athuraliya Rathana is no ordinary monk. He is an activist who heads Sri Lanka's influential opposition Buddhist political party, Jaikahelo Urumiya. Under his leadership the party has gained wide support, claiming 5% of the nation's population as its members. He has gone against the trend, politicizing Buddhism. While some traditionalists criticize his approach, Rathana feels it is a natural evolution. Buddhism is more an expansive, unrestrictive philosophy than a religion, he says.

"All religions practice as religions," notes Rathana. "Buddhism, however, is a philosophy. Buddhist practices all over the world are characterized first by religious practices and many rituals; second, by academic practices—for instance, many European scholars study Buddhism. The third characteristic is meditation. But in Buddhism there are many rituals; some are fixed, and in the end they are often practiced without meaning. No awareness of what you are doing means there is no meaning. It becomes blind tradition, even meditation. Some monks retreat to the forest and practice there without a social life. Europeans try to achieve personal goals of spirituality, attaining these goals by creating a self-enclosing cage. Meditation is good for spirituality, but without a physical phenomenon or the use of common sense, it cannot achieve anything."

Athuraliya Rathana is calling for a new-era political philosophy that combines social responsibility with rational economic development, and environmental protection with sustainable development. Social consciousness needs pragmatism; likewise, pragmatism needs social consciousness. Neither can stand alone. "Kindness needs wisdom," he says. "We need common sense. Without common sense, we cannot impact society. We need both the academic and the spiritual aspects. Without practice, academic exercise is not enough. Without kindness, there is no wisdom."

His comments reflect an emotion that is taking hold not only in his country, but also right across South Asia. It reflects a broader vision.

Within Buddhism today, there is another view that is calling for less reliance on ritual; rather, it advocates drawing out the compassionate philosophical elements of Buddhism and putting them into social action, which in some cases actually involves politicizing it. While there are many traditionalists who are adamantly against the notion, arguing that Buddhism should never be politicized, there is a younger movement that sees politicization as necessary to achieve meaningful social change in line with the principles of a more caring society and compassionate global economic and financial order. This seamless youth-oriented Buddhist wave can be seen emerging across national borders, in Sri Lanka, India, Bhutan, Thailand, Burma, Tibet and even in communities in Vermont and Colorado. This is really what the Buddhist revolution is all about—it's not a militant revolution, but rather a Gandhian-type movement involving pacifist politics and compassionate capitalism.

This trend could become a consensus if the momentum builds to critical mass. Could such a consensus offer an alternative to Washington's? Can China play a role?

"A year ago, I went to China," Athuraliya Rathana said. "I visited the markets there and met some people. I noticed there are no ethics and the people are not happy. They are rather like machines. They have huge, marvelous cities in China, even bigger than New York. But I think nobody there is happy. China has no ideology. The changes have brought only material gains.

"China is obtaining international power through capital and investment, but not through its cultural authority. If the Chinese try to embrace a Buddhist way of life, they will become a real giant."

Athuraliya Rathana sees such new-era Buddhist values and their economic and social applications as presenting fresh opportunities: "The modern age needs a new set of aesthetics, values and morals to replace the old." As for the idea of taking a successful small grassroots experience and turning it into a model, he says: "It is a great opportunity for the small wheel to activate the big wheel," referring respectively to the Theravada and Mahayana branches of Buddhism. The former, called the small wheel, involves meditation to enlighten yourself; the latter, the big wheel, calls for meditation combined with ritual and altruistic action to benefit and enlighten all beings. On another, more political level, Rathana says: "We as a small mechanism can activate the big mechanism."

Buddhist Revolution

"Buddha renounced politics to go sit under a tree," Ian Baker, the Kathmandu-based explorer, once told me. "Now, it is time for Buddha to walk back into politics, not sit under a tree—because the trees are all being cut down."

That is exactly what happened on September 22, 2007, when the previously unknown All Burma Monks Alliance incited a popular mass revolt against Myanmar's dreaded junta regime. A gathering of saffron-robed monks with shaved heads drew worldwide media attention when they protested peacefully for five days, before a bloody crackdown ended the protests.

Is this another spark of a new, potentially international, Buddhist political movement, I asked Athuraliya Rathana.

"Buddhism can replace Marxism," he replied. "Many Buddhist students turn to Marxism in order to change society, in the belief that Buddhism is a religion and cannot be used to change materialistic ways of life. Our party is the first one to openly use Buddhist ideals. Therefore, we can change society!"

To some in Sri Lanka, Rathana's agenda sounds radical; to others it's rational. Although his party is considered the "opposition party," he maintains direct contact with the country's president, Mahinda Rajapaksa. He reminded me that today's peripheral views may one day evolve into, and lead to, mainstream thinking. The question is, can these ancient philosophical ideas be merged across borders to form a new consensus of economic, political and social values? These ideas have already been building a seamless momentum from Sri Lanka, through Burma, Thailand, India, Nepal, Bhutan, and into China itself via Tibet.

Thai activist Sulak Sirvaraksa once explained to me: "In the English language, the word 'revolution' is always related to violence. But it does not need to be. Revolution calls for change, but its application needs to change drastically. We can have a Buddhist revolution by resorting to means of non-violence. Buddha was a great revolutionary, a *real* revolutionary, because he called for equality and liberty. As a member of the *Sangha* (Buddhist community), you can pursue liberty. India's flag adopts the wheel of Buddhism. Remember that in India's history the symbol of Buddhist emperor Ashoka was a lion—the Lion of Ashoka. He was once a lion and violent, but when converted to Buddhism he became non-violent. Buddha was a true revolutionary because he could not accept the caste system, so he became Buddhist. We need equality and liberty—globally.

"Buddha's way was to rebel and fight against the existing system as it was during his time in India. Small is beautiful for Buddhists. But Buddhism has lost its revolutionary momentum. Look at Sri Lanka—Buddhists are fighting with each other. In Thailand, consumerism has taken over. Buddhists should first come back to our roots. We need to redirect our minds from the current consumer values of caring too much for ourselves and too little for others. Society is full of oppression."

"But what are the next steps?" I asked.

"The Buddhist approach is not black and white," Sulak replied. "Whatever you do, do it to your limits and link with good friends, build up trust. Remember that the power of grassroots movements is tremendous. Take money from the business world and give it to the poor!"

Calling for a Fresh Approach

Such a new approach is badly needed, especially in the wake of the global financial meltdown in 2008, which discredited the Washington Consensus models of top-down development. South Asia—after decades of cyclical poverty now being blamed on World Bank and IMF policies—is calling for independent economic models. China's planned market growth, driven in part by infrastructure investment, is one option. It has proven able to provide a fast track for poverty alleviation. But too-rapid growth often leaves societies fractured by divisions among ethnic and income groups, especially when rising social and income expectations cannot be met. Other options—such as Bhutan's concept of Gross National Happiness and Muhammad Yunus's micro-credit initiatives—are emerging from South Asia. Nepal's Prime Minister Prachanda envisages merging capitalism with social responsibility.

"How do we eradicate poverty?" asks Athuraliya Rathana, getting to the main point. "What is the cause of poverty? Globalization is important, but we need balance. We need a common agenda to protect our environment and defeat the materialist dictatorship of the World Bank and the IMF."

I suggest that we may be witnessing the emergence of a region-wide movement that could coalesce from many disparate and not-yet coordinated NGOs and grassroots initiatives, to bring order and balanced growth, especially to societies that are trying to adhere to their traditions while bracing against globalization in the midst of discordant change. What does my monk friend think?

"We need Buddhism in order to safeguard the environment," Rathana says. "There is no happiness in material gain alone. Western people around the world are not satisfied with all of their material gains, so they are now coming to Asia for spiritual gain. Today is an era of material imperialism. Meditation is not enough. Academic practice is not enough. Ritual is not enough. We need political force using spiritual force to create a new world."

I understood what he meant. Many have criticized Rathana for politicizing Buddhism. However, in a world of discord and social inequity, he believes that egalitarianism and environmentalism must be put into action rather than remain mere words. In his view, without politicizing these ideals, nothing concrete will happen.

In the wake of the October 2008 worldwide financial crash, the idea of creating a global economic and social revolution may just be an idea whose time has come. Rethinking our values is the explosive force that can overturn the Washington Consensus, which was built on an entirely separate set of economic assumptions: that greed prevails in guiding the "invisible hand" of Adam Smith, which underlies the post-Bretton Woods, neo-liberal model of capitalism as we know it today.

My mind returned to my earlier conversation with Dr. Karma Phuntsho of the Lodecn Foundation in Bhutan. "Buddha led a movement—I don't know if you want to call it a revolution," he said. "The egalitarian principles of Buddhism assert that all people are equal. Buddha was the first advocate of equality among races and classes. We are only an assembly of physical agents and feelings.

We are only physical constituents and, without ideology and personality, we are all equal. In Mahayana [Chinese Buddhism], we are all potential Buddhas, while in Vajrayana [Tibetan Buddhism] we are all connected to the universality. Remember, Buddha's emphasis is on egalitarianism— tremendous equality."

I thought about the power of this ideal—tremendous global equality. Wasn't that exactly what the protestors of the anti-globalization (global justice) movement call for at every WTO, World Bank, IMF, World Economic Forum and G8 meeting? The ideals embedded in the vast pan-Himalayan region are integral to the philosophies underlying both Buddhism and

Islam. Isn't it time to join the two in struggling for a more equitable world? What a powerful combination this would be in re-adjusting the world economic order and calling for a more humane and compassionate vision for global development. So perhaps it is time to redefine and refocus the global social-justice movement, and bring its diverse demands into a set of focused objectives. And maybe this is exactly what the Washington Consensus fears the most.

I thought too about what Arunduthi Roy had repeatedly told me about people going into the streets and using violence only when all other options have been denied to them. I realized that to avert more social decay and violence, we need alternatives to the existing economic and financial order. Moreover, we need these options now.

I reminded Athuraliya Rathana of some lines from an old Chinese song: "I will go to the forest for justice, and the rain will be my drink." Didn't Nepal's Maoists "go to the forest for justice"—and end up being popularly elected by the people? What about the protesting monks of Myanmar? Athuraliya Rathana, who as a traditional monk would have retreated to the forest for prolonged periods of meditation, replied: "Why go to the forest? Bodhisattvas protect the people. Hatred and desire are our common enemies. Defeat them using people's power." He spoke firmly, as if giving a mandate, but in the whisper of a Buddhist monk. "Organize all people, all the suppressed—not only the poor, but the rich as well, who also suffer. They have luxury and palaces, but they are spiritually poor.

"If you can do that," he said, "then I can go back to the forest again."

Ⅎ

CONCLUSION
ENTER THE HIMALAYAN CONSENSUS
MANIFESTO FOR A PEACEFUL REVOLUTION

Unite for the benefit of your own people… unite for the benefit of your children.

—**Bob Marley,** *"Africa Unite"*

Preamble

The Call for a Peaceful Revolution

The word "revolution" is usually related to violence. But what the word really means is the full turning of a wheel. It is a call for significant change. This manifesto is not about violence, but calls for change, to prevent violence.

The points laid out in the manifesto are neither new, nor the author's alone. Rather, they reflect a collective view that has been voiced before. In fact, it has been screamed loudly time and again before television cameras during massive protests accompanying World Trade Organization, G8 and World Bank-International Monetary Fund meetings in Seattle, Genoa, Prague, Quebec and Cancun. Its chief advocates are a transnational global movement of loosely linked or sometimes unconnected NGOs and social-action interest groups. They have come together repeatedly as a single voice to express angrily the points coolly set forth below. The problem is that few have bothered to take these voices seriously.

Finally, a year after the U.S. sub-prime crisis erupted, Wall Street collapsed in the autumn of 2008. The cataclysm took down with it the financial institutions and values that have underpinned the post-Bretton Woods financial system and the Washington Consensus for development. If the movement's case, which it had voiced over the past decade, had been heeded, the global financial earthquake of 2008 might not have happened. Now, maybe someone will listen.

Clarifying Globalization

The following manifesto is not about anti-globalization as a movement. It focuses more on redefining the movement. The terms "globalization" and "anti-globalization" are often used out of context. Actually, globalization has been with us since the opening of trading routes in ancient times; it isn't anything new. The key question revolves around the right or wrong kind of globalization. More specifically, it centers on whether developing nations—and even underdeveloped regions within developed nations—face a new form of colonization in a contemporary context. The perpetrators use abstract tools such as financial levers and brand worship inculcated through modern corporate culture and mass media.

North vs. South

Bretton Woods created the "North," which consisted of social policy states, and the "South," comprising social development states. All fell under the dominant influence of the United States, exercised through highly conditional aid dispensed by the World Bank and the IMF. The alleged goal: liberalization of trade and finance. However, from the 1980s on, the approach has promoted the expansion of global capital through shock-therapy development programs at the expense of social development and human welfare. This form of so-called globalization has favored a deregulated international system that serves corporate profitability much more than the interests of ordinary human beings. Another casualty: the environment.

Why Anti-Globalization?

Let's start by asking: What is the anti-globalization movement? Why is it called anti-globalization? Members of the movement use mobile phones, the Internet and digitized messaging to organize protests. These are the very tools of the proponents of so-called globalization. One might ask: "How can this movement be against the implements through which its members organize themselves?" Others could query: "Who can be against such a wonderful thing as 'globalization'?"

It may help to stop using the terms "globalization" and "anti-globalization" altogether. The latter, in particular, obscures the movement it seeks to define, which is a global, seamless, genuinely democratic force for social justice and the nemesis of multinational corporate culture, neo-liberal economics and neo-conservative politics. It calls for a redefinition of global values—corporate, social, environmental and governmental. In turn, it seeks to establish new economic and political paradigms.

A Movement for Global Justice

Perhaps these global grassroots social-action groups and NGOs should be more usefully called the new "global justice movement." They organize protests among the globally disenchanted because they are denied access to the mainstream international media, which prefer to dismiss these voices of discontent. In fact, we have stopped having truly meaningful debate in our corporate-controlled media, which frame politically correct discussion in the narrow terms they are comfortable with. The emergence of Al Jazeera in both Arabic and English networks is one response to such developments. We don't ask penetrating questions anymore and accept reports in the mainstream Western media as truth, and then parrot it.

The push for global justice is united in one aspect: its proponents' opposition to the expansion of a system that promotes corporate-led globalization at the expense of social goals such as fair trade, social justice, ethnic identity, community sustainability, national sovereignty, cultural diversity and ecological health. The movement has a transnational vision and spirit. So far it is organized to oppose hierarchies and keep decision-making local and focused on specific issues. Its moral vision is that international grassroots values will ultimately prove to be more powerful than the instruments of financial dominance used by the institutional, corporate and political forces arrayed against them. Rather than the globalization of brand association and a consumer class driven by materialist values, the movement calls for the spread of environmental protection, health care, availability of pharmaceuticals, and access to food, clean water and education.

Article 1:

The Washington Consensus for development has failed—it has produced a global backlash. Every nation must forge and tread its own path.

Washington Consensus formulas fail because they force economic and financial models upon societies whose different cultures and conditions render those paradigms inappropriate. Capital accumulation, conspicuous consumption and the erosion of indigenous cultural values do not assure personal happiness. Economic development should improve the overall quality of life, not undermine it.

The Washington Consensus Increases Poverty

Experience has shown that Washington Consensus schemes do not eliminate poverty, but only create more of it. The International Monetary Fund and the World Bank dispatch consultants to underdeveloped countries facing crises of social poverty or natural catastrophe. The specialists are armed with economic theories but little knowledge of local conditions, social undercurrents or the fundamental problem of finding enough to eat. World Bank and IMF formulas fail to consider such factors as transportation costs, price hikes and the affordability of education. They neglect the reality that even a tiny shift in such factors can disrupt or even destroy the lives of those getting by at, or just above, subsistence levels.

Misguided Impositions

Attempting to apply theoretical models to cultures and ethnic groups for whom they have no relevance, largely to prove a point, is without value and is often counterproductive. In many ways, the Washington Consensus's adherence to free-market theory and democracy is as deluded as the Soviet Union's communist policies of another era, which insisted that a centrally planned, top-down model was the only acceptable one. Both are ideologically driven—and misguided in trying to impose on others a fixed set of beliefs and practices whether these are locally appropriate or not.

Externally imposed, culturally alien financial levers are usually ineffective. They impoverish people, bringing economic and social disaster. Western news networks like CNN and the BBC report the calamities. People sitting comfortably in living rooms in the developed world watch the programs, comment on how terrible things are and ask how they could have happened.

Every Nation Has Its Own Appropriate Model

Each country is unique and has its own appropriate model for development. There should be no single template for economic, political or social progress. Washington Consensus economists tend to be doctrinaire in their adherence to models such as "privatization," "liberalization of currency and trade" and freeing price controls. While these models may suit one country at a certain point in time, they may have little of practical value for other nations.

Outside ideas and theories cannot be brought into a local context without absorbing or being absorbed by it. Only in this way can there be a merger—and in turn positive evolution—of ideas and approaches, rather than self-defeating conflict. The Washington Consensus, however, is notably intolerant of localism. Academics in the United States look at the world's problems from detached perches in their universities and think-tanks. Their research is often government-funded with a specific political or ideological agenda, which is reflected in the work they produce. Their models are grounded in classic neo-liberal economics, which comes down to an assumption of greed as the key driver.

The Western specialists seem to believe they have all the answers. When their theories are tested in developing countries, they prove unable to cope with prevailing realities. The result: programs that undermine social self-esteem and emasculate ethnic identity. When local people's way of life is threatened, they will fight back.

Adding Need to Greed

What we need to add to the supposition of greed is the assumption of need. All people are needs-driven, and these requirements are not exclusively of a material nature. The need for security, sustenance, community, identity and spirituality can be fulfilled through other forms and these must be factored into the economic, social and political equation.

There are universal values—equity, community solidarity, justice and democracy. But the way people construct their societies and principles of sustainable development may be different. Because there are no black-and-white answers when it comes to development, experimentation is necessary.

Re-Engineering Systems

Global economic and financial systems must be re-engineered so that they no longer enforce growing income gaps between the elite and the poor. Instead, these systems should sustain and enhance our existence on the planet. Driven by short-term material needs fueled by media promotion of consumer-brand culture and melting-pot values, we are rapidly destroying our future through environmental desecration and neglect.

Article 2:

Grassroots approaches are needed to solve real problems. Globalization must be balanced to protect ethnic diversity and indigenous cultures.

Too often, economic theory neglects actual people, culture and the environment. It appears ready to destroy anything for material gain. This is the inherent fault of a philosophy that sees the maximization of profit as the sole basis of business. Adam Smith came up with the notion and we are stuck with it because none of the big-name academic economists have bothered to challenge it. Yet human beings are much bigger than mere money. A caring person takes responsibility for society, for the next generation and for the environment. Economic theory leaves the compassionate side of human nature out of the development equation. It's time to put it back in.

Sustainable Foundations Needed

Sustainable economic foundations are essential to the survival and evolution of all cultures. Idealism itself is not enough. We need to adopt pragmatic approaches and techniques to realize our ideals. If the economic rug is pulled, the remnants of cultures will be relegated to museums or become funky artifacts for consumers. But establishing functioning and sustainable businesses can assure that cultures will preserve their identities while continuing to evolve. The aim is to establish bulwarks so that the individuality of each ethnic and cultural group isn't absorbed into the American-style melting pot of accelerating globalization.

The Right to Preserve Traditions

Every society has a fundamental right to pursue its own ethnic traditions, lifestyle, culture and beliefs. And preservation of the environment is integral to the sustenance of many traditional lifestyles. Environmental degradation assaults ethnic diversity, whereas the preservation of such diversity can help protect the environment.

Western-dominated international media and education systems subtly suggest to non-Western children that if they cherish their own culture or even skin color, they are backward and should instead connect with the hip, modern mass-consumer culture. The youngsters come to abhor their own heritage and abandon their identity. Meanwhile, in the rich Western world there is an epidemic of depression, personal debt and obesity.

Cultural eradication isn't a prerequisite for modernization. Raising living standards doesn't mean replacing one culture with another. Culture can evolve with economic development and, in turn, provide the fabric to ensure social stability.

Self-Determination is Best

Each cultural and ethnic group is the best arbiter of what is most appropriate for itself. These entities have the right to determine their own future. Instead of imposing external economic or political models, concerned outsiders should focus on providing tools that empower—or re-empower—such groups, thus contributing to their development.

Ethnic diversity is essential. Why should everyone merge into a single melting pot? Of course, if every person were to think alike, it would be easier for multinational corporations to globalize their marketing efforts and cut costs against profits. But is that positive for the survival and development of the human species? Who really wants to become just another consumer zombie? Human beings are more than statistics. The quantity of life, as measured by the conspicuous consumption of branded goods, does not equate to quality of life. Small can be beautiful, and work done at the grassroots level can change lives for the better.

We Are All Responsible

Much of the responsibility for improving things rests with the big corporations and governments. But every individual must also act consciously and responsibly toward our environment to safeguard it. Indeed, each collective action begins with an individual. While much blame can be laid on the value systems of multinational corporations and their top executives, shareholders are also a part of that system. The American dream of achieving material—as opposed to spiritual—comfort has created a global system of conspicuous consumption, feeding into a single, monolithic value order.

The Melting Pot Stops Here

The melting-pot ideology, with its commercialized "mainstream" value system, damages ethnic diversity. Many of the world's social and security problems are reactions against this politically and corporate-consumer-driven attempt to eliminate ethnic diversity through the global propagation and rigid application of melting-pot values. This erodes the defining value of humanity—its diversity of ethnic identities. The melting pot must stop here.

Article 3:

It's time to revamp the World Trade Organization—and join the Peaceful Revolution.

We must recognize that nations are not created equal. Some have abundant resources because of their geography, demography or location, while others are deprived of them. There are inequities in terms of education and health-care provision, favorable climate, efficient transport links, and various other conditions. Many developing nations are the creation of post-colonial border demarcations, juxtaposing ethnic and social groups often historically at odds with one another. Unresolved problems and economic structures set up during the colonial era have been extended into our time by Bretton Woods.

Why Oppose the WTO?

For this reason, every World Trade Organization ministerial meeting has seen mass popular protests outside the convention centers where delegates from developing countries challenge their counterparts from the G8 nations. Just ask the people and organizations demonstrating in the streets. The WTO process is exclusionary and undemocratic. The body has 130 member nations, but meetings involve only 20 to 30 key countries; the other 100 normally aren't even allowed into the room. If these nations are unable to make their points in the conference room, we have to listen to what they are saying in the street. Their voices are real. This is global democracy at work.

Go Back to GATT

Before the creation of the WTO, we had the General Agreement on Tariffs & Trade, or GATT It was a flexible system that allowed a number of countries to develop using trade policies and mechanisms of trade substitution. The United States wanted a set of rules enabling it to penetrate the world economy and obtain global leverage. Washington could then create conditions enabling it to legitimize its dumping and monopolize technological innovation with trade-related intellectual-property rights. So the U.S. pushed for the creation of the WTO under the guise of forging global rules to prevent anarchy. Yet before the WTO came into being in 1995, there had been no anarchy.

The GATT's original aim was to create a forum to facilitate free-market access, particularly for developing nations, while avoiding the emergence of regional trade blocs, which might lead to protectionism. In recent years, however, the WTO has increasingly deviated from GATT principles. It has been transformed into a leverage tool for developed nations to practice protectionism in their own markets while instituting policies that have contributed to economic meltdown in many developing nations.

The WTO is Losing its Focus and Purpose

The WTO is less and less able to offer a platform for a meeting of minds between the developed and underdeveloped worlds. Part of the problem is that the organization has been misused by some narrow interests and a few dominant nations to benefit themselves. Instead, the WTO should be functioning as the biggest NGO of all, representing a broad scope of interests. It should fight protectionism not only by the struggling developing nations, but by the developed ones as well. Instead, the WTO has been evolving in such a way as to represent an entirely different set of interests and principles from its GATT origins. Rather than being the mother of all NGOs, it has become the target of their wrath.

What role should the WTO play? Should it be a debating society for a framework of principles, a facilitator for bilateral negotiations, or a tool of U.S. foreign policy? Will the WTO pursue the original GATT values of free-trade paradigms for equitable development, or will it become a rich-nations' trading club?

Reforming the Organization

Two approaches need to be adopted. The first is for the WTO to return to the path of trying to achieve the basic GATT principles. That would be the best course, given the organization's existing foundations and resources. If it cannot be done, the WTO would need to re-engineer itself and refocus its functions in order to be effective amid present realities. Its dominant members are locked into an abstraction of academic formulas.

The WTO should not become a "United Nations of trade"—a forum where poor nations can say what they wish, but rich countries continue to dictate policies. To avoid future impasses, this modus operandi has to change. Moreover, horse-trading tariffs and subsidy formulas offer political but not economic solutions.

While the WTO does bring different parties to a single table, developing nations don't always have the resources to resolve disputes with the G8 powers. A key characteristic of the WTO is that it is the only international institution that has a binding dispute mechanism. It can limit trade wars because it uses recognized, legal means to resolve differences, and its decisions are binding.

Bilateral Free Trade Agreements Can De-Politicize Trade

Two-way FTA arrangements and networks could be used to cushion the impact of sudden changes instigated by G8 players, such as the U.S., which often politicize trade. They could be of particular benefit to developing countries that don't share Washington's political views, but are unable to withstand its trade leverage.

A return to the GATT principles of supporting bilateral and multilateral agreements would be a step in the right direction. But a distinction must be made between those based on free trade and those the U.S. wants to push, together with European Union and partnership agreements. Such multilateral and bilateral accords are for economic development of the different partners going beyond free trade. For example, the option favored by Venezuela and Bolivia is to have a development agreement, not just trade accords. This is what people in the South are looking for—South-South deals that are mutual and complementary. Many fear that U.S.- or E.U.-initiated bilateral accords would be just as discriminatory as those done under WTO auspices.

We Need Regional Integration

Organic regional integration through organizations such as ASEAN and the East Asia Summit could provide better foundations than the WTO for addressing concerns meaningfully. This is especially true as the WTO is increasingly perceived as working in the interests of the industrialized powers, and against those of the poorer nations.

Article 4:

Give priority to protecting the environment. The Big Three polluters— America, China and India—must lead the way.

Among the most urgent international issues are global warming, our environment, and the dangers presented by countries that have refused to sign the Kyoto Protocol on the Environment. If the ozone layer continues to widen, our glaciers will melt. The Brahmaputra, Ganges, Mekong, Yellow and Yangzi rivers all have their origins in the Himalayan glaciers. If they melt, two-thirds of humanity will have no water to drink. Yes, we can save and give our children money. But in the future, will we be able to give them water?

Materialism and the Environmental Crisis

The world must avoid environmental desecration. We all know the damage being caused by the shortsighted pursuit of material wealth by certain individuals and corporate interests. Without a clean environment, it does not matter how many material possessions or how much money we have in the bank. They are worthless if we step out of our homes and breathe polluted air. We need to curb this excessive and irresponsible desecration of our world. Otherwise we will not have a world to live in.

The technology exists to create a plethora of alternative energies. It just has to be commercialized. What's needed is a re-think of corporate values and an institutional financial framework to achieve greater social benefits rather than pure self-interest. Shareholder value should be linked with increased social worth. Alternative-energy development can be financed, if relevant institutions change their outlook and support the effort. It comes back to institutionalizing new values.

Environmental respect is the foundation for creating a new society, a future for subsequent generations. We must protect the environment and not sacrifice it for short-term comfort or material gain, which will only be spent tomorrow. By sacrificing our natural environment, we would be doing the same to our future. By saving it, we would be protecting our own continued existence.

Leading Nations Must Lead

How can this be done? With major powers and polluters like the U.S. refusing to sign the Kyoto Protocol, how can we begin to regulate our corporations and the interest blocs that are now driving the process of global warming?

Washington refuses to sign until China and India accept conditions classifying them as developed rather than developing nations. These are the three biggest polluters on the planet. Can their leaderships not put aside narrow concerns for the greater interests of humanity and the survival of their own children? It is time for the leading nations of the world to lead in a positive manner. They need to extend their agendas beyond military action, industrial output and consumer consumption.

Article 5:

The micro-credit revolution works. Small finance is beautiful and can improve lives by restoring the self-respect of the poor.

Citizens of rich nations can march in the streets if they cannot get a job. People in underdeveloped countries can march in the gutter, but there is still no job. Because orthodox economics recognizes only wage-employment, it has left no room for self-employment. The time has come to put aside orthodox economics. Self-employment is the quickest and easiest way to create employment in the developing world. The poor must be encouraged and stimulated to create their own jobs. But since economic textbooks don't recognize the existence of the poor or their rights, there are no institutions and policies to help them. We need to create new institutions by shunting aside the old.

Give the People Credit

Let's start with a new principle. Credit is a fundamental human right. Institutional economics trains one to think in terms of millions and billions of dollars to finance big infrastructure projects. Eventually, the trickle-down effect is supposed to reach and help the poor. But how can it? All the big corporations, consultants, contractors and sub-contractors associated with granting or financing institutions have to get their cuts first. What is left for the poor?

For most impoverished people with a per-capita income of less than US$200, access to a mere 10 or 20 dollars can change lives for the better. But how do we get them even that small amount of money—and guide them intelligently on how to use or invest it? This is where micro-finance comes in. Its value needs to be recognized, and new systems created to support it.

Creating New Institutions to End Poverty

To reduce and eliminate poverty, we must ultimately go back to the drawing board. Most people in developing countries don't really need foreign expertise. How can IMF and World Bank advisors give counsel on the economics of business in a village when they have never lived or worked in one? Rather, the peasants need opportunity. The concepts and institutions that helped create poverty in the first place cannot be used to end it. So new institutions are essential. This requires fresh concepts and values.

Empower the Poor With Trust

Try this assumption: The poor always repay their loans, while the rich often don't. Why? Somebody receiving a micro-credit loan is being given not just money by a lender but social trust. People should be re-empowered with self-respect, not funding alone. A poor borrower sees what the rich have, and have failed to use. Given a chance, he will be determined to make the most of each opportunity given to him.

Rather than tailoring people to the rules of financial institutions, isn't it time to customize lending to the needs of people? With micro-finance, amounts are so small that weekly repayments are affordable. In turn, new criteria must be adopted to evaluate the results of lending policy. Samples: do recipients have a roof over their heads, warm clothes for winter, safe drinking water and sanitation? Are their children in school?

Towards Compassionate Corporate Value

Taking the process a step further, we need to re-engineer corporate culture and the very notion of shareholder value. In the 1980s, corporate performance was all about profit and loss. In the 1990s it was evaluated with the concept of shareholder value—a calculation of how much money the management could spend on luxurious living and inflated brand advertising. By 2008 the accumulated effect had fed the collapse of both global financial institutions and markets, throwing the entire Bretton Woods system into crisis.

Profit maximization is a good thing—let's be clear about that. But to think that only greed and the invisible hand should drive our world is as simplistic as believing that socialist idealism will solve humanity's problems. A middle way is necessary. Rather than excessively emphasizing corporate shareholder value, we should adopt a new concept of compassionate corporate value. A company should be assessed in terms of what it does for the society or societies from which it benefits. In a broader context, the firm's worth should be linked to what positive impact it has on global society and its efforts to protect our environment for future generations.

Create Compassionate Social Businesses

It is commendable to create trusts and for foundations to give money as charitable donations. Yet charity can be used only once. Once it has been given, a gift is gone. So we need to develop the system and merge charity with business so that support for the needy can be sustainable. Social businesses adopting the concept of compassionate capital can recycle profits into more social-action initiatives. These might include ventures to offer affordable health care to the poor, to bring forests to countries without them, and to provide self-employment to drug addicts and take them off the streets. Such businesses can represent a new form of social shareholder value, be listed, raise capital, and benefit more people.

Isn't that what profits should be all about—to benefit people? We just need to extend the concept from personal advantage to a broader social benefit. We should popularize social businesses through media support and develop institutions to achieve sustainability. Such compassionate capital can be used to advance social stability and avert chaos.

Article 6:

Societies should redefine their ideas about success. Bhutan's goal of "Gross National Happiness" provides valuable lessons.

In economic terms, it is necessary to re-examine what constitutes national and individual success—as well as the social value of happiness underlying both. Should the success of a nation or an individual be measured in material, quantitative terms alone? Today we gauge accomplishment by how much gross domestic product a country racks up, or how many luxury goods an individual acquires. Socio-spiritual happiness has no place in the measurement statistics. Ironically, in orthodox economics it is disregarded as both an assumption and a goal. However, such well-being should be both the underlying assumption and ultimate goal. For what is the point of material quantitative growth if it does not bring happiness or an enriched spiritual life to both nations and individuals?

The Search for Balance

It is true that material pursuits have produced economies of scale, facilitated international trade and improved many people's lives. That is not being questioned. But to strive for material progress alone means to live an unbalanced life. A blind quest for consumption and material accumulation leads to excess, distorts priorities and creates frustration instead of happiness. At the same time, we are desecrating the environment, destroying our planet, and leaving future generations without drinkable water or breathable air. So is the blind pursuit of materialism really worth it—or is it time to adjust our basic values and find a middle path of balance?

Indeed, are we living meaningful lives, or merely supporting a system that bestows comfortable lives on certain elites at the expense of others? Can we find a system of balance, a new value order? That depends on whether we can come to measure national and individual success in terms of socio-spiritual well-being—and whether that can be sustained on a planet of quickly diminishing resources.

Gross National Happiness

The concept of "Gross National Happiness," or GNH, originated in the tiny Himalayan Kingdom of Bhutan. The concept ventures to offer a new value paradigm by turning orthodox economic GNP on its head. GNH has four recognized pillars: economic development, environmental preservation, cultural preservation and good governance. Bhutan questions all the economic assumptions that underlie the post-Bretton Woods order by presenting a potential paradigm for re-evaluating the way we measure economic achievement and corporate value.

For Bhutan, it is important to prioritize traditional values and local culture. Indeed, GNH rejects many of the standard Western yardsticks of achievement. These include GNP as the dominant economic measure, melting-pot theory that creates a mass consumer class, underlying assumptions that greed and the "invisible hand" are the ultimate levers for economic adjustment, and the idea that the accumulation of consumer brand items can offer people sustainable happiness.

At the same time, GNH cannot be developed in a quantitative manner, as the concept of happiness cannot be measured in numbers. This goes back to the problem of orthodox economics. Its assumptions leave out the human side—emotion, compassion, spirituality. Yet these are factors that drive people as much as material ones.

Broaden the Factors

Washington Consensus development models envisage industrialized countries enjoying relentless growth. But material goods do not necessarily produce happiness or well-being. GNH is a policy that aims at the equitable and balanced distribution of the benefits of development for all levels of society. It involves the promotion and preservation of culture, the low-density development of towns, and the maintenance of vast tracts of environmentally protected land.

The GNH model is anchored on a core assumption. It is that an individual will find it more fulfilling to live a balanced life than one devoted to the pursuit of material gain. What people should strive for above all is to live a life of compassion. Do something to help others, even if it is a single person, to get through another day with a little more ease. By giving, we receive much more. If we begin with this idea, the whole concept of corporate shareholder value begins to change.

Restoring Human Happiness

Happiness is an abstract notion of how to free ourselves from discontent and suffering. In Bhutan it is defined by having one's mind and body in balance and by the right to choose a sustainable form of development. While many developed industrial societies are awash with consumer goods and luxury brands, their denizens suffer depression and are socially dysfunctional. Why? Because we lack balance, a result of our own skewed values. Essentially, we suffer because of our greed. So we must stop thinking about ourselves selfishly in *laissez-faire* capitalism terms and begin respecting and caring for one another. In Bhutan, respecting the environment is more important than accumulating the trappings of a luxurious life. Environmental protection is a key pillar of GNH. The global economy is at a crisis point. It is connected not only to Wall Street excesses, but also to the degeneration of our environment.

Article 7:

Marginalized groups need to be empowered. That would help stop terrorism at its root.

Economic stagnation brings social frustration, which helps fuel the rise of fundamentalism in all forms. Islamic fundamentalism is just one example. New social pressures are emerging. More and more people are rejecting American-style globalization and its inherent values, and turning back to their own traditions, most obviously expressed by wearing the veil. When a people are confronted and feel oppressed by Western culture, they turn inward—to the symbols of their own culture. By doing so, they reinforce and assert their threatened sense of identity, usually of a cultural or religious nature. That explains why the rapid rise of radicalized Islamic groups has been a key response to colonialism and its contemporary forms. Declining economies resulting from instability or externally imposed embargoes stimulate introvert emotions and inflame religious extremism.

Marginalizing People Breeds Terrorism

Terrorism happens less because people have political agendas than because they have no hope. They have been marginalized from society. How can those who cannot even make ends meet be active participants in society? When the international media demonize their sole beliefs, they have no choices left. In frustration, they become radicalized. Disenfranchised from their own heritage by a critical global media, they turn back to religious sanctions for psychological assurance and security.

Groups that have been extremely marginalized become extremely radical. They are then labeled "terrorist." Yet we conveniently forget about institutionalized terrorism. One common form: officially sanctioned embargoes that starve people and deny them medical care. Another is military occupations that enforce overt colonialism when more subtle financial and media levers fail to penetrate people's lives and beliefs, bringing them in line with the standards of Washington Consensus globalization.

Invest in People's Future

Instead of undermining or browbeating communities, we should be building them. Demonstrate to the disenfranchised that they can invest in their own future. Give them a sense of hope. Help set up goals they can reach. Education, in the form of training, and micro-finance are powerful tools. Together they can lay foundations for future self-employment. Such programs can empower the poor by providing not only financing but, equally important, a support system that helps build self-confidence.

That is where community building comes in. We should create a model of local development suitable to each community. Rather than fear the power of ethnicity, we should harness it to build stable social-identity groups. Respect for each culture's diversity is critical to assure social harmony and peaceful living.

Such approaches could serve to cure terrorism at its roots. For a fraction of the money Washington spends bombing diverse ethnic tribal groups and Muslims in general, vocational training and micro-enterprises could be organized based around *madrasas.* These are-Islamic schools whose vast existing networks could change people's lives, in turn transforming their global outlook.

Turn Madrasas into Vocational Networks

Indeed, *madrasas,* widely seen in the West as hotbeds of fundamentalism, can be turned into incubators of social harmony. Through appropriate local foundations, this network of religious schools could be used to create a community outreach through vocational skills programs and support cottage industries. Think of the sense of security it would bring if people have a life to look forward to and a means of making it happen.

Article 8:

The United Nations needs to be made more representative—and democratic. In individual countries, only bottom-up—not top-down—democracy will work.

Many non-aligned countries have called for the expansion of the United Nations Security Council and curtailment of the veto powers of its five permanent members in order to break their monopoly. Perceptions of an unrepresentatively narrow power base risk eroding the world body's legitimacy and authority. Nations, like the people who comprise them, are entitled to govern themselves without other countries telling them what to think, what to believe in, or what constitutes acceptable or unacceptable behavior.

New Global Threats Require Sensitive Multilateral Brokering

The challenges and threats currently facing the world include the prevalence of military domination, increasing poverty, the growing gap between rich and poor nations, violence as a means of resolving crises, the spread of terrorism (especially of the state variety), and the existence and proliferation of weapons of mass destruction. Other problems relate to the pervasive lack of honesty, and a disregard for the equal rights of peoples and nations, in international relations.

Multilateral, interactive behind-the-scenes brokering, applied with patience and consistency, can be effective in resolving conflicts. On the other hand, unilateral force and imposed ideologies merely entrench conflict, unleashing more chaos down the road. Aid agencies come in to rebuild a war-stricken occupied nation or territory. Funds are corrupted, babbling consultants spin ineffective policies, and economic anarchy returns. Yet people watching it all on CNN and the BBC still wonder why there is terrorism.

Democracy Does Not Come From the Barrel of a Gun

Democracy is a universal value based on the freely expressed will of peoples to determine their own political, economic, social and cultural systems. Brutalizing them under military occupation is a grave and cynical form of terrorism, even when conducted as part of an exercise to force-feed "democratic" systems on those who don't have them.

Top-down democratization does not work. If democracy is to take hold in any part of the world, it must be indigenous and rooted in the local culture and its values. Western-style democracy cannot be imposed onto alien nations without being translated into a language that is familiar to them. The United States cannot succeed in globalizing its variety of democracy through top-down approaches enforced by unilateral military initiatives.

The American adventure in Iraq, for example, involves removing a foreign government, replacing it with an elected one, and expecting it to develop naturally—in the complete absence locally of a democratic culture and infrastructure. The underlying assumptions are deeply flawed, if not outright absurd.

Nations Must Determine Their Own Future

Indigenous populations will always want to determine the nature of their nation's evolution and the need for any reforms. They don't want their futures to be dictated by distant powers, or shaped by ideologies alien to their ethnicities or geographic identities. Such realities underscore the need for more regional forums to devise substantive development programs, multilateral trade agreements and policies on banking, securities and financing policies appropriate to the needs of nations within those regions.

Nations want to find their place in the world through localization or regionalization, not globalization. Global ideals must be examined in terms of their compatibility with local conditions and customs. Where such compatibility does not exist, alternative paradigms and solutions must be found. Forums should be encouraged to generate new approaches and ideas, not least to prevent nations and peoples from being marginalized and, in turn, radicalized.

Article 9:

Why has China succeeded where Africa failed? The key to overcoming cyclical poverty lies in devising and applying locally rooted solutions.

Africa is a screaming example of the foregoing failures. The continent bears the scars of ineffective international aid programs in the post-colonial era. Its economies have been sidelined by Western countries, and the living conditions of its populations are largely ignored. American assistance floods instead into Israel, propping up its military state apparatus, while only peanuts are tossed to Africa.

Africans blame the institutional lending criteria applied by the World Bank and IMF, which they see as attaching burdensome and often impractical conditions that become the cause of their own cyclical poverty. In fact, more aid money is spent on consultant expense accounts, or on missions to evaluate and re-evaluate what other missions have already assessed, than on real poverty relief. G8 member states may debate a project for years without reaching consensus on the conditions to be attached to their aid. Such approaches have left Africa without infrastructure and far behind in development terms.

Keys to Beijing's Success

China progressed, but not Africa. Why? One key reason is that Beijing spurned the World Bank and IMF policies of privatization and elimination of subsidies. It saw them as tools to benefit the rich social elite, who end up with capitalist monopolies at the cost of the broader population. When these programs are finished, foreigners, not locals, essentially run the country. That creates broad resentment—and instability.

Successful development requires understanding of local people and problems. Indigenous populations need to be given ownership of their problems. Aid providers who ignore or override people's cultural preferences and prejudices will quickly run into resistance. Applied insensitively, international assistance may actually backfire. It often brings inflation, whose trickle-down effect hurts people. Covert U.S. military support behind aid carries overt political conditions, turning intended beneficiaries into opponents. Peace becomes improbable, if not impossible.

Political and Economic Stability Is Essential for Development

Without peace, money cannot be channeled into the alleviation of poverty in stricken regions, followed by the economic integration of these regions to give them comparative advantages. So stability is essential. Development begins with economic stability, from which political development can naturally occur. It does not begin with making economic development conditional upon political systems that may bring prevailing ethnic, social and religious values into conflict.

Trade is more important than aid because it builds value for the population. Grassroots programs can foster social stability through pro-riding vocational-skills training, developing industry, and re-instilling ethnic pride through economic self-sustainability.

Forms of Government Are Less Important Than Actual Accomplishments

Forcing models of government by attaching conditions to lending is counterproductive. Never underestimate the power of bottom-up grassroots economics. It can effectively displace heavy, top-down infrastructure growth models where self-appointed advisors and contractors reap profits from soft loans bound in conditionality.

The role of government should be to alleviate poverty, close large income gaps, protect the environment to ensure the survival of future generations, and give people hope for a better future. The form that a government takes, or the political model that it adopts, is less relevant than what it is able to accomplish. Aid organizations should be guided by these notions.

Article 10:

The Himalayan revolution is under way. A development paradigm based on the timeless values of great Asian civilizations can bring new hope to the world.

Throughout the developing world, NGOs and ethnic or local interest groups are rejecting Washington Consensus views. But they have yet to agree on an alternative. China's experience could be a key catalyst for a new consensus. But does Beijing realize this—and might it wish to assume such a role? Can it? For the international community waiting to see how China will rise, the ideological vacuum needs to be filled. For the moment at least, the idea of a "Beijing Consensus" being applicable anywhere other than China is an open question. What we need is a new epicenter, a new consensus that can offer a viable alternative to Washington's.

So let us get far away from Washington to come up with a fresh agenda. We will draw upon values rooted in the historical and spiritual philosophies of the Himalayan region, fusing and integrating them into a new platform that incorporates social, political and economic paradigms. It is time for the diverse peoples of Asia to take pride in their indigenous values. They should realize that the power of their economies and social philosophies can serve as both the new epicenter and a source of universal values for our era.

In an age of accelerated global warming, we should remember that the Himalayan mountain range is the water source for all of Asia—east, southeast and south. So let it be a font of inspiration as well. We should recall the reflection of Rajiv Gandhi, the late Indian premier, that this greater Himalayan region is interlinked by geography, sociology, economics and the timeless philosophies of Hinduism, Islam, Buddhism and Taoism. In contemporary terms, we can dub the product of this sweeping multicultural confluence the Himalayan Consensus.

Introducing the Himalayan Consensus

The **first pillar** of the Consensus urges an end to the blind application of Washington Consensus economic fundamentalism, which bears virtually no relation to local realities. Instead, adopt indigenous solutions or pathways to economic development. In the case of China, an unabashed combination of planning and market functions have been deployed as needed. And as India has proved, economic models stemming from the grassroots can be as valuable as top-down stimulus programs driven by fixed-asset investment.

Each country in the region faces a similar challenge: to reduce poverty in relatively densely populated rural areas. Needless to say, the experience of each nation differs according to local conditions and cultures. For instance, while China's emphasis is on GNP growth, Bhutan calls for growth to be measured by GNH. Bangladesh adopts micro-finance. Nepal and Sri Lanka empower people through NGO initiatives. Each approach must be respected in its own right, applied and adopted as suited to the unique circumstances prevailing in each country.

Reject Global Models, Seek Local Solutions

Each nation or region should adopt economic solutions according to its own conditions, without enforced adherence to any single model. Countries should share their development experiences, with positive results achieved through an emphasis on grassroots imperatives, micro-finance, and combined market and planning approaches. To facilitate such exchanges, new forums need to be created.

None of this dismisses top-down infrastructure fixed-asset spending as economic stimulus, as different approaches can be adopted simultaneously. Remember that the power of grassroots movements is vast. Money should be channeled from the business world to the poor. During such economic transition or reform, excesses of all kinds need to be avoided as much as possible. Flexibility and open-mindedness should become watchwords. What the Himalayan Consensus does reject outright is the dogmatic application of Washington Consensus-style "shock therapy" through such measures as the sudden liberalization of foreign exchange and capital markets, or premature privatization without the necessary infrastructure and social apparatus.

Drawing on the Values of Buddhism, Hinduism, Islam and Taoism

The **second pillar** calls for engaged social interaction without violence, and broad egalitarianism and equality. These are goals common to Buddhism, Hinduism, Islam and Taoism, indigenous creeds from which the Himalayan Consensus draws its underlying values. The philosophies have similar aspirations for equality among peoples, closure of the gaps between rich and poor, a universal right to medical treatment, and respect for the environment as the basis of humanity's own sustainable development, including finding peaceful solutions to global conflicts.

The Himalayan Consensus prioritizes the alleviation of poverty and the reduction of income gaps in order to create a more equitable world. Visit any Hindu temple in the evening and one will find food being provided to the poor. Likewise, compassion and the alleviation of others' suffering is a core tenet of Buddhism, a form of gaining merit. Buddhists constantly reach out and donate to medical and educational projects, and give alms to the poor. Alms-giving is also one of the Five Pillars of Islam. Muslims consider it not charity but virtue, which is community based. Each person is responsible for everyone else. The strongest in the community takes care of the weakest.

Himalayan Consensus values hold that one benefits more from giving than taking. This is the opposite of prevalent Western credos such as "no free lunch" and "only the strongest survive," or the notion that the weakest are in their position because they do not work hard enough or are insufficiently determined to succeed.

To Every Country its Own Politics

The **third pillar** is that every country should have the right to develop its own political system. The right to self-determination, independent of any other country's dictates, should be a universal value. Just because one country's political system works well for it, that is no reason to assume it will work well elsewhere. In fact, cultural, historical, social, economic and political differences put the odds against it. Attempts to force one system onto other nations that are not interested should always be condemned.

The Himalayan Consensus Has Far-Reaching Relevance

The Himalayan experience gains broader relevance because of the sheer number of ethnic and tribal groups in each country bordering the world's mightiest mountain range. Most of the constituent nations have dozens of different linguistic groups in the region. The situation is readily shared with many African countries, large parts of central Asia, the Middle East and also Central and South America. None of these regions adopts the melting-pot culture and each defends the ethnicity of its own people strongly, albeit often in different ways, with sharp, sometimes deadly, confrontations erupting. But that is the reality many countries face—and effective development must take it into account. In these nations, good, responsive government will naturally mean something different from what it is in America or Europe. The Himalayan experience can offer valuable, practical lessons—on the positive as well as the negative aspects.

To be responsive to popular needs, each body politic should effectively represent its own ethnic, religious and social groups. Indigenous models of participatory government should be created based on the foundations of each nation's cultural, tribal, historic, political and economic structures, as relevant. The emphasis should be on evolution, rather than reform. Such ideas may be anathema to Washington, but the repeatedly proven reality is that forcing an American model of government on countries with few historical, social or cultural ties to the U.S. leads almost invariably to ineffective rule, political instability and socio-humanitarian disasters. We must continue to resist this modus operandi.

In the decades ahead, we will see transnational, regional and global conglomerations—economic, political and religious—becoming actively involved in bilateral or multi-lateral trade, aid, finance or conflict mediation. New institutions will arise organically as the U.N. and WTO repeatedly fail us. These organizations too will globalize, for globalization is not a linear phenomenon but constant conversions of common sets of ideas. We will never have a single global ideology, but rather a connection of consensuses, conglomerations and gatherings around common notions. The Himalayan Consensus is one path toward the future. There are many others, including different kinds of regional consensus—the Andes Consensus, or the Islamic Consensus, for example. The successful ones will become new institutions and those that fail may merge.

Guerrilla Television and Bloggers of the World Unite!

The formation of such movements will accelerate as we move into the post-nation-state world, where nationalism becomes less and less a primary means of collective identity. As people revert to forms of self-identity based on culture, religion and ethnicity, these kinds of consensus will become the primary mode through which international relations are expressed and experienced.

International relations will go beyond dialogue among the nation-states. They will be conducted in the context of global transnational consensuses, and the revolution will be in the changing values of our system and our social conscience. The battles will continue to be fought with the tools that have enabled globalization—the Internet and satellite television. Guerrilla networks working through interactive websites and bloggers will arise and unite. So tune in!

ョ

INDEX

Discovery Publisher is a multimedia publisher
whose mission is to inspire and support personal
transformation, spiritual growth and awakening.
We strive with every title to preserve the essential
wisdom of the author, spiritual teacher, thinker,
healer, and visionary artist.

www.ingramcontent.com/pod-product-compliance
Lightning Source LLC
Chambersburg PA
CBHW031152270326
41931CB00006B/244